SUCCESSFUL

Home Gardening

E. Gordon Wells, Jr.

Cover photo:

The author and his family in their backyard garden.

Acknowledgements

Grateful appreciation is given to the many friends who have encouraged and helped with this undertaking. Special thanks go to my wife (and assistant), Annette, and to Edwin G. Wells, Jonathan Schmuhl, Trevor Howard, Ron Williford, Candy Glendenning, Carol Williams, Perry Johnson, Clark and Karen Doxey, David Evett and Chris Solomon who helped with the proofreading and photography. Special appreciation is also expressed to Helen Mischka for her drawings and advice as well as her skill in doing the layout for this book and to Mary Lou Wells Chaffin for additional drawings included in the new edition. Thanks must also be extended to the University of California, Division of Agricultural Sciences, for the great body of published material made available for easy reference.

It is easy to grow delicious fruits and vegetables in the garden once you learn a few basic principles.

Contents

Forward

Home Gardening should be fun. The process of planting and watching the small miracles which occur as the plant grows is inherently exciting. To be able to make plants produce delicious fruits and vegetables by providing the proper nutrition and cultural environment is very satisfying.

Home Gardening is a lot more enjoyable if you succeed. You don't have to experience failure to discover what will or will not work. If you understand the basic principles and practical methods of growing a garden, you can have a successful experience with this endeavor the very first time you try.

A careful attempt has been made in the process of writing this book to include only proven, scientific principles and to avoid the many "old wives tales" which seem to be common in this field. There has also been a serious attempt to avoid vague, abstract and philosophical concepts and to give instead actual proven "how-to-do-it" methods of growing things. Many of these methods are used by commercial growers to produce the food you buy in the market. The author is committed to the idea that amateur home gardeners can produce excellent food – better food than is available on a grocer's shelf – because they can use the best varieties and methods available and let fruit ripen on the vine.

A successful home garden does not have to take a lot of time. If it takes too much time, it becomes discouraging and ends up being abandoned. Because many people make gardening too complicated and difficult, this book suggests many practical gardening methods which, if followed, will greatly simplify the entire process.

Many home gardening manuals are full of facts about the odd and unusual, but fail to give the basic instructions needed for raising an excellent vegetable garden. This book avoids the odds and ends, the expensive methods and gimmicks, and concentrates on basic principles, basic methods and basic crops. In a step-by-step process it provides the beginner with everything he needs to know to grow his/her first garden as well as giving more advanced horticultural concepts and labor-saving ideas which are of interest to the experienced gardener.

This book was not written by a committee or boards of editors as are many home gardening books. It is actually written and edited by an expert home gardener who has many years of experience and practical gardening know-how as well as a Masters Degree in vegetable and fruit crops from the University of California, Davis. It is a labor of love. It is hoped that the author's enthusiasm about home gardening will be felt as you study these pages.

Dedicated to my father, Edwin G. Wells

Why Garden?

SAVE MONEY

The obvious answer in this day of rising food prices is that vegetable and fruit gardening saves money. For that reason the garden should be practical and designed in every way to grow usable food in an inexpensive manner.

FOOD QUALITY

If you are an experienced gardener, you know that the quality of the food produced in your own garden far exceeds the quality of vegetables and fruits purchased at the grocery store. This is true because your objectives are different from those of the commercial grower, and you are better able to control the conditions which promote top quality. The food is also fresher and you can choose better tasting varieties.

Varieties

For example, when a commercial grower chooses a variety of vegetables to be planted, he is mostly concerned about two things. He wants a variety which will produce the maximum yield per acre, and he wants to produce a crop which will look attractive on a grocer's shelf. For the most part, the vegetables are shipped to distant markets, and they are not later identified with his particular operation. Thus he is not as concerned about taste since the better tasting varieties may not ship as well, have good shelf life or be adaptable to mechanical picking. These issues may mean the difference between making a profit and just breaking even, so he must choose the variety which will give him a profit. Also, the crop must look good on the grocer's shelf which means that it must be firm enough to hold up well in shipping and lengthy storage. It may taste like soap, but if it looks good to the housewife, it will sell.

That's funny, it doesn't look like soap!

On the other hand, the home gardener's primary concern is food quality in both taste and nutrition. He is not so much concerned about appearance, if the taste and nutrition of the vegetables and fruits are superior. A good example is 'Sugar Queen' cantaloupe. It does not have the heavy net and firmness to ship long distances, but the overall quality and taste are unexcelled. The same is true of tomato varieties which do not have the firmness or green shoulders which give them good shipping and holding qualities, but they may be far superior in flavor and nutrition.

You very seldom see a Nantes type carrot on the grocer's shelf even though they are unexcelled for eating qualities. They do not have the eye appeal of the long, thin, tapered Imperator type carrots. Some new crosses between 'Imperator' and 'Nantes' (like 'Sugar Snax') are also excellent. The quality of pole green beans (e.g., 'Kentucky Wonder', 'Blue Lake', and 'Kentucky Blue') are far superior to bush beans, but bush beans can be harvested by machine, thus avoiding expensive picking by hand, so it is now difficult to buy pole beans at a store.

Freshness and Prime Quality

Another reason that the food quality from your own garden is better is your ability to pick the crop at its peak, rather than leaving it a few more days for maximum yield. It is also a notorious fact that such crops as tomatoes and cantaloupes must be picked green in order to hold up during shipment and look good on a grocer's shelf, but they really don't taste very good and they are lacking in nutrition. The taste, texture and nutrition are never the same when fruit is picked green and allowed to ripen in cold storage. There are crops such as corn in which the natural sugars turn quickly into starch after picking. If they are not eaten, bottled or frozen within a few hours after picking most of the sweetness and flavor are gone. This is true to some extent with almost all garden fruits and vegetables.

For prime quality, it must be fresh.

FOOD STORAGE

Many vegetables, such as carrots and beets will hold in the ground for many months during fall and winter as part of a food storage program. Their quality is not diminished by months of storage in cold soil. Winter squash, onions and potatoes will keep for 6-8 months in a cool dry place.

FAMILY AFFAIR

Another important reason for a home garden is to have a pleasant project in which the family can be involved and work together. The author's children talk all week about Saturday when "Daddy will be home," and they can work with him in the garden. They have a part in everything that is planted and enjoy working at it together. They know where their food comes from and learn principles of hard work and industry.

Gardening should be a family affair.

ENJOYMENT AND SATISFACTION

Most gardeners dearly love the process of making things grow. It is a way to unwind and relax after a hard day at the office. A person may feel "mean as snakes" when leaving the office, but after a few minutes in the garden be fit to live with. There is something very fundamental about the smell of good earth, and the process of bringing delicious food from the garden to the table is very satisfying. It is also fun to have something to give away to friends and neighbors.

Children enjoy helping in the garden.

Make it Practical

You don't want a fussy garden, particularly for your first one. You might be led to chuck the whole idea as "too much trouble", so plant the kinds of vegetables and fruits which are easy to grow (especially the kind you enjoy eating), and lay it out so that it does not demand a lot of attention. You will find in the pages that follow many practical suggestions for the busy gardener who does not have time to make his garden a career.

When you find that many crops are better off not watered too often, that healthy plants are resistant to both diseases and insect damage, that there are easy ways to control weeds and that a few weeds don't destroy a healthy garden, you will enjoy gardening a lot more.

EASY-TO-GROW CROPS FOR THE BEGINNER

- Zucchini squash ('Italiano Largo', 'Spineless Beauty')
- Corn ('Luscious', 'Honey Select', 'Brocade')
- Green Beans ('Kentucky Wonder', 'Blue Lake', 'Bush Blue Lake', 'Bush Kentucky Wonder')
- Beets ('Perfected Detroit', 'Detroit Supreme')
- Carrots ('Sugar Snax', 'Magnum', 'Scarlet Nantes',)

- Peppers ('King Arthur', 'Karma', 'Revolution')
- Tomatoes ('Jetsetter', 'Big Beef', 'Porterhouse Beefsteak')
- Cucumbers ('Sweet Slice', 'Sweet Success')
- Swiss chard ('Large White Ribbed', 'Discovery')
- Strawberries ('Albion', 'Ventana')

Save the fussy crops until later when you become more experienced.

Soil Types

There are basically three types of soil: sand, silt and clay, each being distinguished by the size of particles of which the soil is composed. Loam is a combination of sand, silt and clay and has the best characteristics of each.

Plant roots need to get water, air and mineral nutrients from the soil. The soil must be structurally able to store and supply these basic needs at all times. Plant nutrients come from decomposing minerals, organic matter and fertilizers dissolved in the water which are held in pores in the soil until needed by the plant. Large pores are quickly drained after irrigation and are the source of air for plant roots.

CLAY	
SILT	
SAND	
LOAM (MIXTURE)	

Relative Size of Particles of Basic Soil Types

SAND

Because the particle size is large with sand, it breaks and works easily and is easily penetrated by roots and by water. The air spaces between the particles are large and water drains through quickly so that air, necessary for root health, is also present in the soil. With these advantages go some serious disadvantages. The large air spaces also allow quick drainage and evaporation of the water so that water retention in sandy soil is poor. When rain and snow come, water goes right through the coarse sand taking the soluble nutrients with it down to the subsoil beneath the root zone. For this reason sandy soils are always low in nitrogen, the most soluble nutrient.

CLAY

Clay soils are at the opposite extreme. The soil particles are so small that they are able to pack very close together without very much air space between them. In heavy clay, the pores are very small. This makes most clay soil very poor for root and water penetration. The aeration is also poor because the particles can become tightly packed, especially if they are compacted when they are wet. This leaves the supply of air in the soil inadequate for healthy roots and makes root penetration difficult. It also has poor drainage and tends to become water- logged during

	1" OF WATER ON SURFACE	SECONDS LATER	STILL LATER
S A N D			
	SAND IS EASILY PENETRATED BY AIR AND WATER, BUT DOES NOT RETAIN EITHER WATER OR NUTRIENTS VERY WELL.		
C L A Y			
	AIR, WATER AND ROOT PENETRATION IS SLOWER IN CLAY, BUT IT RETAINS BOTH WATER AND NUTRIENTS.		

WATER   SAND PARTICLE   FLOW OF AIR
CLAY SOIL   FLOW OF WATER AND SOLUBLE NUTRIENTS

Water Penetration in Sand vs. Clay

rainy weather. Water standing for long periods around plants (especially trees) can leave the roots without oxygen causing serious injury or death. It also induces the plant to get diseases such as phytophthora root rot which causes sickness and usually a slow death.

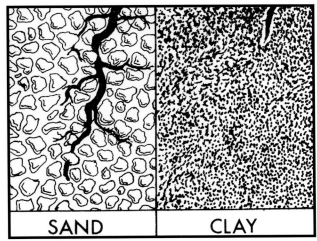

Roots penetrate more easily in sand than in clay and are usually more extensive.

On the other hand, Clay soil has some advantages. It has very good water retention. And the soluble nutrients have not been leached out by rain and snow, so it is usually richer in all of the elements necessary for plant growth, especially nitrogen. Obviously, a mixture of sand and clay will improve both of them, but it is often very expensive and difficult to haul in enough new soil to make any substantial improvement.

The important thing to remember is that almost any soil can be made to be good soil by proper

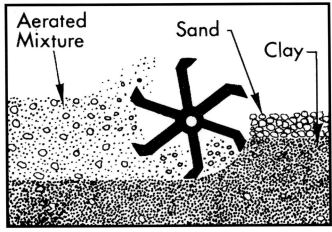

ROTO-TILLING SAND LAYER INTO CLAY SOIL. Mixing sand and clay is helpful, but it is hard to haul in enough sand to make a difference.

handling and by the addition of an adequate amount of **organic material.** It is interesting that the same process which improves the texture of clay soil for penetration of water, air and roots also improves the moisture retention qualities of **sandy soil** and makes the soil better able to hold plant nutrients. The addition of organic material separates the tiny clay particles and holds them apart, making the soil easier to work and less inclined to become compacted or crust on the surface. In **clay soils** the decomposed organic material, or humus, becomes mixed with the soil particles forming aggregates ("crumbs") which completely change the structure and the various characteristics of the soil. It greatly increases the size of the "pores" for root and water penetration, improves aeration and drainage. By the gradual addition of

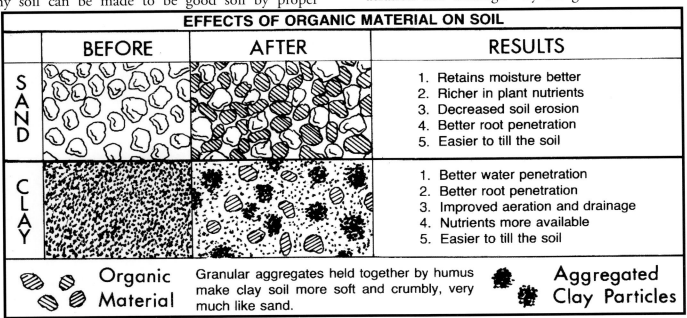

EFFECTS OF ORGANIC MATERIAL ON SOIL			
	BEFORE	AFTER	RESULTS
S A N D			1. Retains moisture better 2. Richer in plant nutrients 3. Decreased soil erosion 4. Better root penetration 5. Easier to till the soil
C L A Y			1. Better water penetration 2. Better root penetration 3. Improved aeration and drainage 4. Nutrients more available 5. Easier to till the soil

Organic Material — Granular aggregates held together by humus make clay soil more soft and crumbly, very much like sand. — Aggregated Clay Particles

large quantities of organic matter over a long period of time, almost any soil can be made into good garden soil. (See below for more details regarding this process of improving soil condition with organic matter.)

NUTRIENTS IN THE SOIL

Sixteen elements are essential for healthy plant growth. The first three of them (carbon, hydrogen and oxygen) the plant takes from water and air. The other six major elements and seven minor ones come from the soil. They are as follows:

Major Elements		Minor Elements	
Nitrogen	Sulfur	Iron	Chlorine
Phosphorous	Calcium	Zinc	Boron
Potassium	Magnesium	Manganese	Molybdenum
		Copper	

Other elements that can sometimes be helpful are cobalt, sodium, vanadium and silicon.

Most western soils are rich in all of these elements except for three major elements: nitrogen, phosphorus, and potassium, and two minor elements: iron and zinc. Of the major elements, the main deficiency is almost always in nitrogen with phosphorus and potassium to a much smaller extent. With regard to the minor elements, the soil may contain normal quantities of iron and zinc but the presence of lime or some other alkaline substances makes these elements unavailable to the plant. They become "fixed" in the soil. Because iron and zinc are not found in most mixed fertilizers, the home gardener should be aware of those possible deficiencies and add the proper fertilizer if it occurs. (See PLANT FOOD section for detecting these and other deficiencies.)

Improving the Soil with Organic Matter

As mentioned earlier in this book, almost any soil can be made into good soil by following a few good gardening practices. (See illustration on page **5** for specific effects of organic material on soil structure.)

SOIL BUILDING MATERIALS

From the Garden

Return everything to the soil. Carrot tops, corn stalks and cobs, and generally whatever plant parts are left in the kitchen should be accumulated and returned to the garden. Only diseased plants should be eliminated.

Leaves and grass clippings cost nothing and are excellent soil improvers.

From the Yard

All available grass clippings, leaves, sawdust and wood chips of any kind should be worked into the garden. These excellent organic sources are often found in abundance in your own and your neighbor's yard. Leaves are an especially good amendment. They contain a waxy, paraffin-type substance which causes certain portions of the leaves to remain in the soil for years without disappearing completely. Grass clippings are a high nutrition source of organic material. There are only a few organic sources which can be toxic to plant growth. Redwood, Eucalyptus and black walnut products are toxic to plants when worked into the soil. Regular walnut and pecan leaves are somewhat toxic at first but are helpful after a few months of decomposition. When large quantities of selective herbicides like Weed and Feed (2-4D) are put on your lawn, the grass clippings which are worked into the soil are toxic to plants in your garden for a period of several months.

All available organic material should be worked into the garden to improve the soil.

From the Nursery

There are many brands of soil amendment available from the local nursery. Some are only decomposed sewage sludge which is gone from the soil in a relatively short time. Others contain decomposed pine, spruce, fir and other kinds of tree materials which remain in the soil for several years and are helpful. Peat moss is especially helpful because most western soils are excessively alkaline (basic) and peat moss being acidic makes the soil more neutral. These commercial organic amendments are valuable additions to your soil, but they are expensive and not entirely necessary for a successful home garden. Avoid redwood compost which has toxic substances that are harmful to plants.

From the Soil (Green Manure)

"Green manure" is a term used to describe a crop to be worked into the soil for soil improvement. It is a cover crop usually grown in an off season when the land is not otherwise being used.

WHEN TO PLANT COVER CROPS

Wherever possible these green manure crops should be grown during the winter season. They should be planted as soon as your vegetables are gone in the late summer or fall. You might want to designate one portion of the garden for a cover crop each winter. If planted by early September, a cover crop such as annual rye grass will be ready to work into the soil by late January or early February in warm winter climates and by April in cold areas. Green manure crops which require more heat can be planted in the early summer in an area used for an early spring garden.

In preparation for planting, roto-till and level as described in the PLANTING YOUR GARDEN section. The seeds should then be broadcast (sprinkled) onto the ground by hand or mixed with fertilizer and applied with a lawn fertilizer spreader. Rake the planted area to cover the seeds with soil and water regularly until seedlings come up.

COVER CROPS (GREEN MANURE)	
1. Annual Rye Grass – Grows fast in cool weather. Fills the soil with great quantities of hair roots.	4. White Clover – A legume, therefore high in nitrogen, but small and quite slow growing.
2. Buckwheat – Grows fast, but requires summer heat. Produces gigantic quantities of organic material.	5. Sudan Grass – Fast growing hot weather grass which sometimes reaches 6 feet tall and produces great quantities of organic material.
3. Yellow Blossom Sweet Clover – As a legume, it adds nitrogen to the soil bit it does not grow as fast as the rye or buckwheat.	6. Grains – Oats, barley and wheat grow fast in cool weather and make good fall, winter, and early spring cover crops.
Cover crops are grown in order to put large quantities of organic material into the ground to improve soil texture and fertility.	

WHAT TO PLANT

There are many crops that can be planted as green manure to turn under for soil improvement. The legumes add more nutrition to the soil but, for the most part, do not grow as fast as the grasses. **Alfalfa** is the best of the legumes for large amounts of protein and nitrogen, but it grows too slowly to be practical for a cover crop. Other legumes such as **yellow blossom sweet clover** and **winter vetch** grow fast enough in warm winter areas to be planted in September and worked into the soil in the late spring. Vegetable legumes such as **peas, beans** (lima, green and soy beans) and **peanuts** are excellent soil builders and can serve a dual purpose in the garden. (See pages **14-15** for details about legumes.)

For an abundant quantity of organic material in a relatively short time, probably the best cover crop is **annual rye grass.** It also grows fast in the late fall and winter when the garden is idle. Besides the abundant top growth, it produces incredible quantities of small hair roots which break up the soil, decompose quickly and add humus to the soil. It grows knee high and becomes a favorite place for the children to romp and play.

Buckwheat is also an excellent green manure because of the gigantic quantities of organic material which it produces. Both buckwheat and rye grass grow quickly enough to smother most weeds so that the weeds don't go to seed in your garden. As you follow these principles and add all available organic material to your garden on a regular

basis, your soil texture and nutrition will become better year after year.

SOURCE OF SEED

Seed for annual rye grass is available at most nurseries, garden shops and seed companies. Seed for the other cover crops mentioned above (buckwheat, winter vetch, white clover, Sudan grass and yellow blossom sweet clover are available in most feed and seed and grain stores in an agricultural area.

Grass clippings and other soil building materials can be put into the garden even before the present crop has been harvested. These materials are later worked into the ground along with the corn stalks or other plant residue.

TEMPORARY NITROGEN DEFICIENCY

As discussed in detail on page 16, the addition of large amounts of un-decayed organic material to your soil can cause a temporary nitrogen deficiency. The soil bacteria which multiply to break down these materials use nitrogen as food. Either allow a three or four week delay after working materials into the soil before planting for the nitrogen to again become available or add nitrogen fertilizer before planting to avoid this temporary shortage.

COMPOSTING WITHOUT BINS

Compost bins are usually a waste of time and energy because they require unnecessary hauling and handling of organic materials. A good compost pile needs to be fed, watered and turned on a regular basis. This process creates heat which dissipates a portion of the plant nutrients into the air. The material must also be hauled to the bins and from the bins to the garden. Besides these problems, compost piles often have a noxious odor and breed huge quantities of flies.

All of these problems can be avoided by putting the organic material directly onto the garden. There is almost always some section of your garden which is not in use or where the crop, such as corn, has almost reached maturity and these organic wastes such as grass clippings can be dumped into the furrows without affecting either the irrigating or picking procedures. At the end of the crop, the organic material can be worked into the soil without further handling. It usually decomposes much faster there than in a compost pile because good garden soil is full of bacteria and fungi which immediately go to work turning the raw compost into humus. Unless your garden is tiny and you have lots of spare time, **this method is far better than composting in bins.**

In order to make this method work, it is important to have a roto-tiller handy or be prepared to turn the compost under with a shovel. Getting the organic material worked into the soil quickly avoids the odor and fly problem and gets the decomposition process started so the soil will be ready for the next crop.

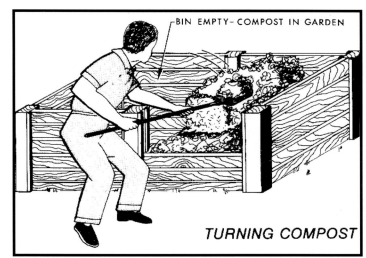

TURNING COMPOST
BIN EMPTY- COMPOST IN GARDEN

Composting in bins and compost piles is usually wasteful of time, energy and valuable nutrients. It should be avoided if possible.

COMPOST BINS

If your situation requires a compost bin (or pile), follow these basic rules:

1. To decompose quickly, the organic matter needs adequate quantities of air, water, micro-organisms (bacteria and fungi) and nutrients.

2. Put organic material into a bin with air spaces on the side for adequate circulation.

3. Add micro-organisms by layering the pile of organic material with garden soil or by buying micro-organisms in soluble tablets and watering them in.

4. The micro-organisms thrive on a diet high in nitrogen. Some of this comes from the organic material itself, but the decomposition process goes faster if a small amount of nitrogen fertilizer like ammonium sulfate or urea is sprinkled onto the pile occasionally and watered in.

5. Keep the compost pile moist but not wet. It also speeds up the process to turn or mix it occasionally with a pitchfork or shovel because the microorganisms need air as well as moisture and nutrients to grow.

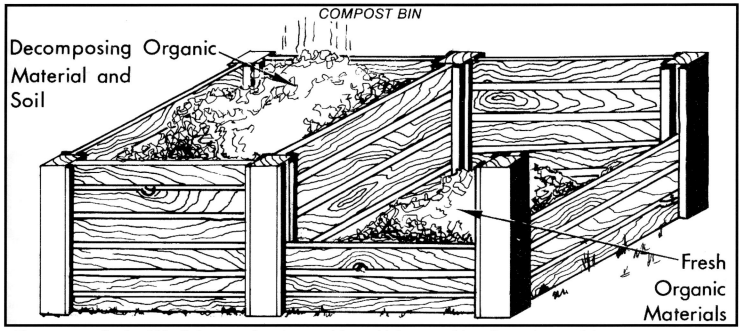

COMPOST BIN

Decomposing Organic Material and Soil

Fresh Organic Materials

The compost pile should be fed, watered, and aerated for rapid decomposition of organic materials.

A barrel mounted on a stand with a handle for turning can be purchased. This method of composting speeds up the decomposition process because turning it regularly keeps it aerated and the heat prevents odors. Except for the expense, this is **far better than a compost pile.**

EFFECT OF GREEN MANURE AND OTHER ORGANIC MATERIALS

By following this kind of program regularly for a period of years, you will be amazed at the quality and productivity of your soil. The soil nutrients which are present in your soil will be released and will become available for plant use.

All of the various kinds of organic material which you mix into the soil will quickly begin to decay when attacked by the various kinds of soil micro-organisms, particularly bacteria and fungi. As this decomposing process continues, the organic material will break down into a product called humus which, when mixed with the soil, improves aeration, drainage, water penetration, water retention, and ease of root penetration. It gives the soil a spongy quality which keeps it from compacting. It gives a good, soft,

crumbly texture which makes it easy to work. At the same time, it makes nutrients more accessible for healthy plant growth and makes the plants more resistant to disease. As explained in the table on page 5, humus makes the sand richer in plant nutrients and able to retain moisture better. It creates aggregates in the clay which gives it larger pores so the water and air and roots can penetrate and it is easier to work, more like the texture of loam. Not only does the humus make nutrients more available to plants, but so do certain types of soil fungi. (See page **90** for effect of earthworms on soil condition.)

Beneficial Fungi

It has been estimated in several text books that a thimble full of good garden soil has over a billion microorganisms. Most of these are beneficial to plant growth. In fact some plants will hardly grow without the presence of the soil organisms known as **mycorrhizal fungi.** These fungi colonize plant roots and extend system into the surrounding soil greatly enhancing the absorptive surface area of root systems. One author states that several miles of these mycorrhizal filaments plants. These filaments greatly enhance the rooting capacity of the plant thereby extending from plant roots exist in less than a thimbleful of soil associated with vigorously growing substantially expanding the nutrient and water uptake and vigor of the plant's growth. Not only do these fungus roots increase the water and nutrient absorption, but they also form a protective barrier around the roots to protect them against the invasion by pathogenic disease organisms such as Pithium, Phytophthora, Fusarium and others.

Because much of the topsoil around many houses gets stripped away in the building process, and that is the portion of the soil which naturally was filled with these beneficial fungi, and especially in desert soils some soils were lacking in the first place, it is often extremely beneficial to add mycorrhizal fungi when planting a garden.

If seeds or the roots of small plants are inoculated, i.e. sprinkled, with the powder or water containing these spores, then these fungi go with the roots wherever they spread. Because there are a number of species of both endo and ecto mycorrhizal fungi and it is necessary to use the one which is compatible with the plant involved, it is helpful to use a mix which has a number of different species. Then, whether you are planting a tree or a tomato plant, you are covered. The author has found that Myco Apply Soluble or Myco Gro Soluble with 20 different types of mycorrhizal fungi (both endo and ecto) is easy to use and effective. It can be mixed with the water in a squirt bottle and sprinkled on the roots before planting. The spores are microscopic in size so a very small amount of the product goes a long way. See source list, numbers one and two, for companies which carry this product and your local nurseries.

Plant Food (Fertilizer)

PLANT HEALTH

Healthy plants, like healthy people, are resistant to diseases and external problems caused by wind, weather and insects. Health in a plant, again like people, is primarily dependent upon proper nutrition which is controlled by proper application of fertilizer (plant foods) and water. The most serious gardening problems occur as a result of improper feeding and watering. In this section, the proper use of fertilizer, both chemical and organic, will be discussed. Watering methods and problems will be reserved to the next chapter.

NUTRIENTS MOST COMMONLY ADDED

As discussed above, even though there are sixteen essential plant elements, most of these are found in abundance in most soils. For this reason, we will only concern ourselves with those elements which are frequently too scarce for good plant nutrition.

IMPORTANT FERTILIZERS FOR WESTERN SOILS	
MAJOR ELEMENTS	MINOR (TRACE) ELEMENTS
Nitrogen Phosphorus Potassium	Zinc Iron Manganese

In western soils, the most frequent nutrient deficiency is in nitrogen. The other two major plant elements which are often needed are phosphorus and potassium. Deficiencies in two trace elements, iron and zinc, are also found in many western soils.

MAJOR ELEMENTS

Nitrogen

Even though 78% of the air we breathe is composed of nitrogen gas, that nitrogen is not usable by plants until converted into a nitrate or an ammonium compound. In nature, nitrogen gets into the soil in a usable form from rainfall, nitrogen fixing bacteria and through decaying plant and animal matter rather than as a by-product of the decomposition of rocks and soil particles as do other soil nutrients. For that reason most soils in the arid western states are low in nitrogen. Therefore, for good healthy crops in these soils, the addition of nitrogen is essential.

WHAT IT DOES

The plant uses nitrogen in the process of making proteins and in the formation of new cells. Nitrogen is the plant nutrient which causes rich, green foliage and vigorous growth. To a great extent you can control the rate of growth and size of most plants by the amount of nitrogen you add. By applying an adequate amount of nitrogen, without an excess of water, most plants will take on a healthy, deep, dark green color. It is the most important fertilizer addition to most soils, and if used with discretion, it will have extremely beneficial effects.

With some crops like corn, onions and berries, a small second application of nitrogen will increase the quality and yield. These nitrogen loving plants will go into the fruiting and rooting stage in spite of the abundant green foliage and vigorous growth. Even with the root crops, the importance of green healthy leaves must not be overlooked. The food that we eat is manufactured in the leaves and stored in the roots or fruit so an adequate supply of nitrogen is important to give the plant large green leaves for good food production.

In cool summer coastal areas, nitrogen is especially important. Just as nitrogen fertilizers will keep a lawn green and growing all winter, even in cold areas, it will encourage growth in cool spring and summer weather when your garden just seems to sit and sulk.

Some caution must be used to avoid too much nitrogen fertilizer with many vegetable and fruit crops. If added in excessive amounts with a plentiful supply of water, the lush green growth will become so abundant that the plant will not set fruit, produce

Symptoms of nitrogen deficiency include lack of vigor, small plants and yellowish-green color of foliage.

A nitrogen-rich diet gives corn a healthy, dark-green color, vigorous growth and an abundant yield.

seed or grow good roots in carrots or other root crops. They will stay in the vegetative or growth stage rather than going into the fruiting or rooting stage. But even with tomatoes, a reasonable application of nitrogen is necessary for healthy plants in most soils.

SYMPTOMS OF NITROGEN DEFICIENCY

The deficiency is recognized by the yellowish-green coloring of leaves and stems, the absence of plant growth and vigor, and by small, stunted plants whose leaves and branches tend to die and fall off. It should be distinguished from zinc and iron deficiencies (called chlorosis) which cause yellowing between the veins, the veins themselves remaining dark green so that you can see the skeleton of each leaf. With nitrogen deficiencies the yellowish-green color is more generalized.

SOURCES OF NITROGEN

Organic Matter

The basic organic source of nitrogen is the protein structure of living things which breaks down into ammonia and nitrates as the organic matter decomposes. It thereby becomes available as a plant nutrient. When the various plant and animal materials (organic matter) decompose, nitrogen is gradually released into the soil. Through this gradual process the nitrogen is converted by soil organisms into ammonia, then into nitrates which can be absorbed and used by plants. Although some small amounts of ammonia are absorbed by some plants, until organic nitrogen goes through these stages to become a nitrate, not much is available to the plant as a source of immediate nutrition.

Temporary Nitrogen Shortage

It should be noted that when a large quantity of any raw un-decomposed organic material (such as sawdust or leaves) is worked into the soil that the first result is a nitrogen shortage. The various kinds of microorganisms which break down the organic material require nitrogen as a substantial portion of their diet. As they quickly multiply in order to decompose the large quantity of plant growth which has been worked into the soil, the amount of available nitrogen is soon reduced below minimum levels required for adequate plant nutrition. As the organic material becomes decomposed and the microorganisms begin to die, the nitrogen is gradually released and again becomes available for plant use.

Avoid the Problem

There are three ways to avoid this problem. The first is to add nitrogen fertilizer such as ammonium sulfate (21% nitrogen) immediately before working the large amounts of raw organic material into the ground. This encourages the growth of useful bacteria and fungi and breaks down the organic matter into humus much more quickly. If a crop is planted immediately, there will be enough nitrogen available for both the plants and the microorganisms.

The second method is to water the area after working in the organic material and then wait a month for the organic material to go through the first stages of decomposition. Then you can put on the regular fertilizer, work the ground again and plant the crop without serious nitrogen deficiencies. By combining these two methods you will have improved soil texture as well as providing a plentiful supply of nitrogen.

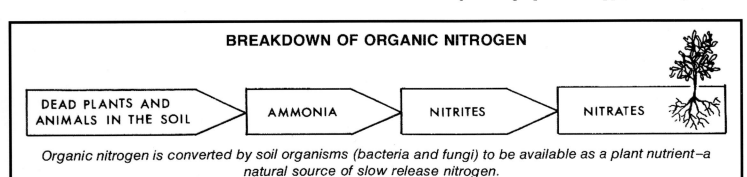

BREAKDOWN OF ORGANIC NITROGEN

DEAD PLANTS AND ANIMALS IN THE SOIL → AMMONIA → NITRITES → NITRATES

Organic nitrogen is converted by soil organisms (bacteria and fungi) to be available as a plant nutrient—a natural source of slow release nitrogen.

A third method would be to decompose the organic material in a compost bin or barrel in a separate area of the yard and add it to your soil after it has decomposed. This humus will not rob the garden of nitrogen.

Other Organic Nitrogen Fertilizers

There are many products available at the local nursery that are made from decomposed organic materials. They constitute excellent soil amendments and have an adequate supply of nitrogen. Some, like blood meal, can be used as a nitrogen fertilizer, but they are a very expensive source of nitrogen for the home garden.

Legumes

There are some plants which have an added significance in increasing the nitrogen content of the soil. They include alfalfa, clover, peas, beans and peanuts, and are called **legumes.** Certain types of soil bacteria (called "nitrogen fixing" bacteria) invade the

LEGUMES		
Peas	Clover	Lentils
Beans	Vetch	Lespedeza
Peanuts	Indigo	Trefoil
Alfalfa	Lupine	Locust
By the use of nitrogen-fixing bacteria, these crops add nitrogen to your soil.		

roots of these legumes causing nodules to form. The bacteria live in these nodules and use energy from the plant to take free nitrogen out of the air and convert it into a form (nitrate) that can be assimilated and used by the plant to build protein.

Some soils have grown legumes for many years and have sufficient quantities of nitrogen fixing bacteria for the legumes which you plant. If you are not sure that your soil has an adequate supply of the right kind of bacteria, you should "inoculate" (see illustration) the legume seeds with a nitrogen fixing bacteria before planting them. Nitrogen fixing bacteria powder (sometimes called "legume aid") is available from most seed companies. The plant tissue of legumes is also very high in protein which is a natural source of nitrogen.

INNOCULATION OF LEGUME SEEDS

1. Pour powder containing nitrogen-fixing bacteria into a small paper bag.
2. Pour seeds into sugar water.
3. Put wet seeds in paper bag containing powder.
4. Shake seeds in bag.
5. Plant coated seeds.

Legumes need nitrogen-fixing bacteria to do their beneficial work.

Manure

Animal wastes (manure) are excellent sources of both plant nutrients and organic matter. They contain all three of the major plant foods, but are often highest in nitrogen (up to 3%). They must be used with **some caution** because manure will **burn plants** if not used properly.

Aged or rotted manure is the safest because the caustic substances have broken down or been dissipated into the air. But, if the manure can be worked into the soil before it gets too old, the plant nutrient value is greater. Generally speaking, the fresher it is when worked into the soil, the more nutrients are added to the soil.

Manure should be allowed to decompose in the soil for a period of time before planting, to avoid any danger of burning new plants or seedlings. If small amounts are used (less than one inch on the soil) or

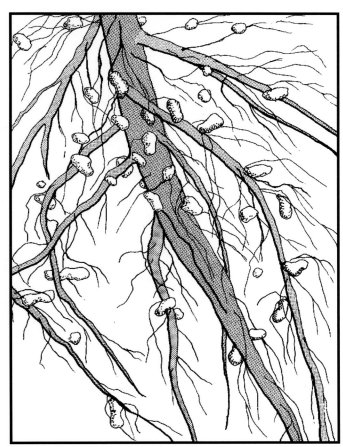

Nodules are formed on roots of legumes by nitrogen-fixing bacteria. They produce useable nitrogen.

Poultry manure is higher in nutrients and usually contains no weed seeds, but be careful not to add very much.

it is well rotted in advance, waiting before planting is not necessary. If three to four inches of relatively fresh manure is added, at least four to six weeks should be allowed after working it in before planting. If it is mixed thoroughly into the soil, and you water the ground at least once during this period, it will speed up decomposition.

All types of manure are beneficial, but some are better than others. Horse and cow manure are usually the easiest to get and can be added in larger quantities if they are available. They are often full of weed seeds, which makes for more hoeing, but your crops will also be healthier. Avoid so-called "steer manure" which usually comes from stock yards where the high salt diet used for the fattening of beef cattle leaves unwanted salt in the manure and damages your garden.

Poultry manure is the highest in plant nutrients and it usually does not contain as many weed seeds. Because of its high potency, this chicken and turkey manure must be allowed plenty of time to decompose

in the soil and should not be added in large quantities or they will burn your crops. Poultry manure is often excessively high in potassium which can raise the pH of the soil and create iron and zinc deficiencies.

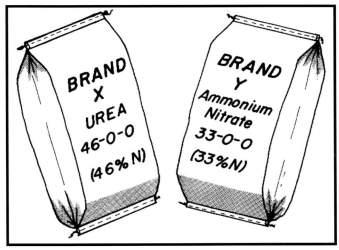

These may burn your crop.

Commercial Nitrogen Fertilizer

There are many benefits of organic gardening besides the "slow release" nitrogen process discussed in this section. Improvements in soil texture as a result of organic matter in the soil are also important benefits. (See IMPROVING THE SOIL section.) This does not mean that the gardener should not go to inorganic sources for plant nutrients.

The problem with using organic materials as the only source of nitrogen is that they do not have a high enough percentage of nitrogen to solve the serious nitrogen deficiency which exists in many soils in the West. They generally run between .2% nitrogen (sawdust) and 3% nitrogen (alfalfa hay, chicken manure). Organic nitrogen fertilizers such as blood meal are very expensive. Most home gardeners and commercial growers as well, cannot economically come up with enough high nitrogen organic matter to get the job done. Commercial (chemical) fertilizers which run as high as 46% nitrogen (urea) must be used as well. Organic materials must break down into an inorganic form (see illustration on prior page) before they are available to be absorbed by the plant, so the basic effect on plant growth is the same regardless of the original source. Also, there are some plant nutrients which are just not available in sufficient quantities in an organic form to supply the needs of everyone. We should combine the best of both organic and inorganic fertilization for maximum quality and yield.

Types of Nitrogen Fertilizer –The commercial (chemical) nitrogen sources are:

Urea. . . . . 46% Nitrogen

Ammonium Nitrate . . . . .33% Nitrogen

Ammonium Sulfate . . . . 21 % Nitrogen

Calcium Nitrate . . . . 16% Nitrogen

It should be noted that some of the above chemical nitrogen sources are more immediately available for plant use than others. The ammonium nitrate, being in a nitrate form, can be used immediately for the plant's nutritional needs. Most of the ammonium in ammonium sulfate breaks down into a nitrate ion in the soil before it is absorbed by the roots, but this happens relatively quickly. The urea constitutes an even slower source of nitrogen. Urea is an organic compound even though it is commercially manufactured. It is broken down by soil organisms and converted into ammonia and finally to a nitrate which is the major source of nitrogen to the plant. It, therefore, releases nitrogen

to the plant over a longer period of time which has some advantages and some disadvantages. Calcium Nitrate is used in acid soils because it makes the soil more alkaline.

Good source of nitrogen which is also a good source of acid.

Ammonium sulfate, usually the cheapest source of nitrogen, is almost as fast acting as the ammonium nitrate. It can be used with less danger of burning the plants than can either ammonium nitrate or urea, so it is the source used most often by home gardeners. More importantly it has the highest acid potential of any fertilizer so it is helpful for acid loving crops, especially in alkaline soils.

Watch for sales on nitrogen fertilizer. There are large variations in price from different sources.

Nitrogen fertilizers are more easily applied than other kinds of plant nutrients because they are soluble in water and therefore can be watered into the root zone with a sprinkler or by rain or snow. Because they are soluble, excessive amounts will burn your plants more quickly than other fertilizers. Too much nitrogen will also keep fruit crops and root crops in a vegetative stage so the roots and fruit will be poor quality and tiny.

Slow Release Fertilizers

Nitrogen fertilizers are used up, leached out, or volatilized out of the soil much more quickly than other fertilizers so that the application which is made may not last long enough for plants like grass in a lawn. For this reason, "slow release" fertilizers have been developed which break down more slowly and make their nitrogen available to the plant over a much longer period of time, usually three to six months. Besides the advantage of feeding the lawn over a long season and avoiding the work and inconvenience of a second or third application in order to get regular growth, the slow release nitrogen fertilizers are also safer to use because there is less chance of salt burn which can come from excess of available nitrogen in the soil at any one time. In sandy soils, slow release nitrogen is especially important to avoid having the nitrogen leached out by watering or volatilized into the air, especially in alkaline soils. **But for use in the garden the regular nitrogen products mentioned above are far better than slow release.**

Natural Slow Release Fertilizers

A much more acceptable form of slow release fertilizer is achieved by the breakdown and release of nitrates from organic material. This happens gradually as the soil organisms (fungi and bacteria) break down the organic material into a usable nitrate form, so that the nitrogen gradually becomes available throughout the life of the crop. Besides the "slow release" advantage of this natural fertilizer, the organic material has the beneficial effect of acting as a soil amendment and improving the texture of the soil.

Phosphorus

This element, usually referred to as "phosphate" (in compound) is often identified with the production of fruits, flowers and seed crops as well as the growth of healthy roots and stems. If the soil supply is inadequate, plant growth is also retarded and spindly. It is particularly important in crops such as

Some good sources of Phosphorous

tomatoes, peaches (fruit crops) and the various kinds of root crops. Phosphorus is used in the process of photosynthesis and energy transfer within the plant.

DEFICIENCIES

Phosphorus deficiencies are not easily identified by looking at the color of plant growth. (Sometimes a bluish or purplish color is noted if the deficiency is extreme). But the smaller size of plants is much more frequently noted. The best way to make certain that you have an adequate supply of phosphorus is to work small amounts into the soil as part of a "complete" fertilizer at least once a year.

APPLICATION

Phosphorus moves very little in the soil and is only absorbed by the plant when the root tips grow into contact with the phosphorus ions in the area where the phosphorus was deposited. It should therefore

Increases production of flowers and fruit.

be worked thoroughly into the soil before planting so that the plant roots will come into contact with it wherever they grow.

Phosphorus is available in superphosphate (Phos 20%), ammonium phosphate (N 16%, Phos 20%), or bone meal (N 1%; Phos 23%), but is usually applied as part of a mixed, complete fertilizer. This will be discussed hereafter.

Potassium

Often described as "potash," potassium is found in muriate of potash, sulfate of potash, ashes and other sources. It is important in the manufacture of starches and sugars in the plant and is necessary for the formation of strong, healthy roots and stalks. It encourages the growth of sturdier, stockier plants as opposed to tall, spindly ones. It is also important to root and fruit crops. It is sometimes used with crops like tomatoes to encourage the growth of a shorter plant with heavier stems and branches, as well as with root crops for heavier yields.

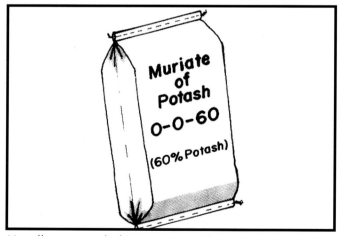

Usually not needed in western soils.

Potash is found in adequate quantities in most western soils, so it rarely poses a problem to the gardener. It is usually difficult to detect any appreciable difference in plant growth as a result of added potassium. It should only be added in small quantities once a year as part of a complete fertilizer in order to avoid potassium deficiencies in the future. In areas where the soil is too alkaline (basic) excessive potassium will exacerbate the problem, so be careful

not to use too much. Also avoid using ashes which will raise the pH of your soil.

MINOR (TRACE) ELEMENTS

Iron, Zinc and Manganese

Although the quantities of iron, zinc and manganese used by plants are very small, all plants must have an adequate supply in order to develop and fruit normally. Iron and zinc act as catalysts, in the enzyme systems, and in chlorophyll formation and cell division.

Until recently, zinc deficiencies were thought to be relatively isolated and unusual problems. It is now known that they occur quite commonly along with iron deficiencies in western soils, sometimes because the soil is actually low in iron or zinc and other times because they are "locked" in the soil by excessive quantities of other substances. Iron, zinc and other trace elements can be present in adequate quantities in the soil but unavailable to the plant because the soil is highly alkaline (higher pH) causing the iron, zinc, manganese, etc. to be "fixed" in the soil. This is usually caused by an excess of lime (calcium carbonate) which occurs naturally in many western soils. It has also been found that the application of excessive quantities of both potassium and phosphate fertilizers can also cause iron and zinc deficiencies in some soils.

SYMPTOMS OF DEFICIENCY

Iron, zinc and manganese deficiencies cause a condition called "chlorosis" which is characterized by prominent dark green leaf veins with yellow interspaces. They also cause small or deformed leaves with generally stunted plant growth. Zinc deficiency is sometimes identified by rusty brown blotches and a leathery texture on the leaves of various kinds of beans. It also causes a condition called "fern leaf" on potatoes, which is detected by curled stunted leaves, "little leaf" on peaches and a yellowing between the veins of the older leaves.

Zinc, iron and manganese deficiencies often delay maturity and limit the yields of vegetable and fruit

This green bean leaf shows classic symptoms of chlorosis from zinc deficiency. Notice the dark green veins with yellow-brown interspaces.

Other symptoms of zinc deficiency are seen in the rusty brown blotches and leathery texture of the older leaf. After side-dressing with zinc sulfate, the bean plants put out new leaves. Notice the healthy dark green color of the leaf which grew after the zinc deficiency was alleviated.

crops. They may even cause the plant to die before maturity. The crops which have shown the most striking symptoms of zinc deficiency are corn, beans (all kinds), onions, tomatoes, potatoes and peaches. Iron deficiencies are most common in fruit trees and berries. If it is an iron or manganese deficiency both large and small veins stand out with a dark green color and the interspaces are light green, tan, yellow or white depending on the crop. Plant yields and health are seriously affected.

TREATING THE DEFICIENCY

Iron deficiency is treated by either spraying the foliage with a diluted solution of chelated iron or adding chelated iron or iron sulfate to the soil. Zinc deficiencies are treated by either spraying the foliage with chelated zinc or mixing zinc sulfate or chelated zinc into the soil.

Since there is almost no movement of iron, zinc and manganese **sulfate** in the soil, they should be mixed thoroughly with the soil before the crop is planted to get maximum contact of the roots with the fertilizer. The **chelated** forms of these trace elements, iron, zinc and manganese are more soluble and more easily "watered in" to the soil.

There are also products like Ironite containing iron, zinc, manganese and other trace elements, which can be incorporated into the soil before planting to solve these problems. Because the availability to the plants of these and other trace elements is usually tied directly to the acidity or alkalinity of the soil, you must read the following materials to completely understand treating these deficiencies.

ACIDITY – ALKALINITY

Most crops do not grow well in soil which is on either extreme of the acid-alkali scale. (See chart) They do well in soils which are neutral or only slightly acidic (pH 6.0-7.0 (pH 7.0 is neutral)). As mentioned previously, many western soils contain an excessive amount of lime (calcium carbonate) and other minerals which, together with the small amount of rainfall, cause them to be on the alkaline side of neutral. Although most plants do best between pH 6.0 and pH 7.0, some handle a broad range between 5.5 and 7.5. Acid loving crops like berries do best on the acid side of neutral with blueberries needing a pH between 4.0 and 6.0. Not only iron, zinc and manganese but all of the other nutrients needed for healthy growth are more available to the plant in that 6.0 – 7.0 pH range.

SOIL ACIDITY (pH) SCALE

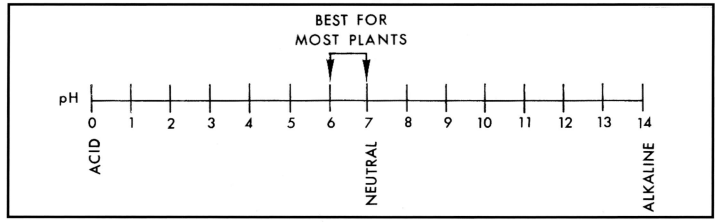

Most fruits and vegetables do best if the soil acidity range is between 6.0 and 7.0.

WHY NOT ADD LIME?

Many gardening books recommend the application of lime to the soil. These recommendations are written for eastern soils where excessive acidity is a problem and lime, being strongly alkaline, is used to correct this problem. In the West where soils are already too alkaline, and excess lime in the water and soil is often a serious problem, it is a mistake to add lime. There are a few isolated examples of acid soil in the West, mostly on the northern coast of California and in the Pacific Northwestern states of Oregon and Washington where there is much rainfall, but these are rare exceptions. Along the east coast there are many examples of acid soils where the regular use of lime is helpful.

Not recommended for alkaline western soils.

REDUCING ALKALINITY

Because the excessive alkalinity causes the iron, zinc, manganese, and other elements to become tied up or fixed in soil compounds and unavailable to the plants, it is important to discuss the various ways of reducing alkalinity. Most organic materials help to acidify the soil. Tilling large amounts of organic matter into clay soil helps form granular aggregates improving the drainage and the ability of alkaline materials to leach out of the soil with rain and snow. The organic material itself can also be very acidic. Sphagnum peat moss for example has a pH of 3.0-4.0 so incorporating substantial amounts into your garden will make the soil much more acid.

The use of acid types of commercial fertilizer like ammonium sulfate, Grow More Soil Acidifier and Miracle Gro Azalea Food is also helpful. But the most potent acidifying agent is elemental **sulfur,** also known as soil sulfur. When it is worked into the soil and watered, the soil microorganisms change it into sulfuric acid which is soluble and moves with the water and makes the soil more acid wherever it goes. This process is not immediate but over a period of weeks and months has a great effect in acidifying alkaline soil. (See Application of Commercial Fertilizer hereafter for applying the right amounts of sulfur.)

COMPLETE FERTILIZERS

The term "complete fertilizer" applies to mixed commercial fertilizers which contain the three major soil nutrients: nitrogen, phosphorus and potassium (in various proportions). The numbers that appear on the sack of fertilizer, usually immediately under the label, represent the percentages of these three elements and are always listed in this same order. If a fourth or fifth number appears, it often represents the presence of trace elements in the fertilizer, usually iron or zinc. For example, the numbers 16-16-8-4-1, in that order, on a sack of fertilizer, would usually mean a mixture of 16% nitrogen, 16% phosphorus, 8% potassium, 4% iron and 1% zinc.

Using a complete fertilizer in the right proportions before planting each crop is the safest way to be certain of adequate nutrition for a healthy garden. Adding other fertilizer during the life of a crop is usually not needed. See specific crops later in the book for a few exceptions. It is beneficial to add a complete fertilizer to your soil at least once a year to avoid future soil deficiencies, even though your soil may be adequate for the particular crop now growing.

An ideal complete fertilizer for many crops in western soils would be a mix of 16-16-8 (16% N, 16% Phos, 8 % Pot.). Because iron and zinc and other trace elements are not available in this so called "complete fertilizer" it is necessary to add these elements to the mixture of 16-16-8 from another source. The best source now available at a reasonable cost is Ironite, which is 1% nitrogen, 0% phosphorous, 1% potassium, 4.5% iron, 0.10%zinc, 0.10%manganese, 12% calcium, 10% sulfur, .02% boron, and .0005% molybdenum.

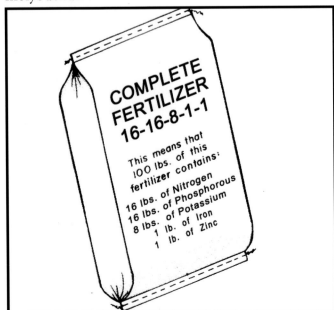

A good Complete Fertilizer.

This complete fertilizer should be worked into the soil before planting. Except for nitrogen, these elements do not move much in the soil (not very soluble) so they need to be thoroughly mixed with the soil by roto-tilling or spading before planting in order to be distributed throughout the root zone. There are some soluble forms of the phosphorous, potassium, iron, zinc and manganese but they are much more expensive so roto-tilling the 16-16-8 and Ironite into the soil before planting your garden is by far the best way to go. (For the much more expensive water soluble sources go to companies like Grow More and Miracle Gro. These would be used for annual fertilizing of established plantings like berries or orchards because they can be watered into the root zone by the rain or snow in late winter or early spring).

Testing Soil Fertility

Soil test kits can be purchased to analyze your soil. You can also take a sample to your local county agricultural agent or farm advisor's office. There are also private companies available in your yellow pages for soil testing. For the most part the fertilizer applications recommended below should be followed in normal situations for most crops.

Application of Commercial Fertilizer

With the principles which we have discussed in mind, the most important time to fertilize is **before** you plant, when it can be thoroughly mixed with the soil to a depth of at least 8-12 inches. This gives your seedlings vigor from the moment they emerge from the soil because they are filled with the proper nutrients. In some soils, especially sandy ones, in areas where you have a long growing season or with nitrogen loving crops, it may be helpful to add a second small application of nitrogen fertilizer **but with most crops** it is neither necessary nor helpful. If you **over fertilize** either root or fruit crops it will **reduce** both the **yield** and **quality.**

All of the fertilizers we talk about in this book are **dry fertilizers** with the exception of chelated Iron,

Zinc and Manganese. Dry fertilizers are much easier to store and use than are liquid ones.

The basic application of fertilizer needs to occur before you work up your soil. It can be made with a lawn spreader, a crank broadcaster, or simply out of a wide-mouth quart jar. **For an area 6 feet by 30 feet (i.e. 180 square feet) you should apply one quart of fertilizer.** This would be the same for an area 10 feet by 18 feet or any other 180 square foot area. Of course if you have 360 square feet you will use 2 quarts (twice as much). If your garden spot were 10 feet by 12 feet (120 square feet) you would put on 2/3 of a quart. Multiply the length times the width of your garden area to determine the square footage and then divide it by 180 to determine the percentage of a quart you need.

Four fifths of the quart jar should be 16-16-8 and one fifth should be Ironite (4.5% iron, 0.10% zinc, 0.10% manganese, etc). Cover the mouth of the jar with your hand or put on a lid and shake vigorously, turning the jar several times until it is completely mixed (homogeneous). Then sprinkle it evenly over the 180 square feet. Over-fertilizing will cause salt problems as described below, so be careful.

When using elemental (soil) sulfur to neutralize alkaline (pH above 7.0) soils, add **two quarts (2 qt) of sulfur to 180 square feet** of garden and work it into the soil. This amount of sulfur will, over time, reduce the pH from approximately 7.5 to approximately 6.5 which makes the soil nutrients more available and the plants healthier. If you want to grow blueberries (pH 4.0 to 6.0), you will need to add a lot more sulfur.

SOIL PROBLEMS

Alkalinity (high pH), and salinity (salt) problems exist in many parts of the West because of the lack of rainfall.

Salinity (Salt) Problems

In areas of high rainfall the various kinds of salts which accumulate in the soil are leached down below the root zone so they are not allowed to accumulate in the area where they will injure the plant.

In more arid areas where the rain and snowfall is sparse the salt build-up in the soil can become a major problem.

SALINITY AND OSMOSIS

Osmosis is one of the processes by which water from the soil defies the law of gravity and is drawn from the ground up into the highest branches of the tallest

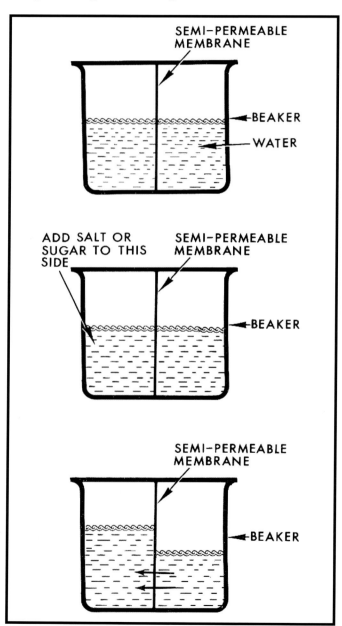

The water is pulled by osmotic pressure into the side with the more concentrated solution.

tree. It is the process by which water is drawn through a semi-permeable membrane from a less concentrated solution into one which is more highly concentrated. It is demonstrated classically by dividing a beaker of water in the center with a semi-permeable membrane. Then by adding salt or sugar to one side of the beaker, thus making the solution more concentrated on that side, water is drawn from the weak solution into the concentrated solution, making the level of the liquid on one side of the beaker higher than the other. This is called an osmotic pump. Any soluble substance can be substituted for table salt or sugar with the same effect.

These soluble substances in the soil are commonly called "salt." It is because the concentration of the solution in the plant is greater than the concentration of "salt" in the soil water that moisture is drawn out of the soil into the plant. If you increase the concentration of the salt solution in the soil until it exceeds the salt solution in the plant, the process is reversed and the water is thereby drawn from the plant into the soil, causing the plant to quickly wilt and die.

In an area of low rainfall the salt from various sources tends to build up in the soil. Some of the sources of these salts are minerals already in the soil, various kinds of dissolved minerals in the water used for irrigation, salt in the manure added as organic fertilizer, and the residue left by various kinds of commercial (chemical) fertilizers used to supply plant nutrients. If not leached out, these various kinds of salts accumulate in the soil until they become so concentrated that the plant cannot draw enough moisture out of the soil into its tissues to supply its needs, and it becomes stunted or wilts and dies. When the salt problem is only minor, it usually causes dead or black areas around the edges or on the tips of leaves which is known as "salt burn." When it is major it kills the plant. See the demonstration on the next page for the effect of excessive salt on tomato plants.

TOO MUCH FERTILIZER

Some soils are so close to an excessive salt concentration that the addition of too much commercial fertilizer may reduce the water intake of the plant enough to cause salt burn. Even with good soils excessive use of commercial fertilizers can be extremely harmful to the crop in the ground as well as to future crops because of the salt build-up and salt burn.

In applying fertilizer, many people feel that "if a little fertilizer will help the plants a lot, then a lot of fertilizer should really make them grow". The opposite is much more accurate. A little fertilizer will do the plant a great deal of good by supplying all of the nutrients which it needs for aggressive, healthy growth, but by doubling the amount of fertilizer, the plant will be seriously injured or caused to die completely from salt burn.

REDUCING SALINITY

The problem of excessive salinity can be handled, not only by careful application of fertilizer, but also by the leaching process. Repeated short applications of water to the surface of the soil can cause salt build-up because as the water evaporates it leaves a residue of

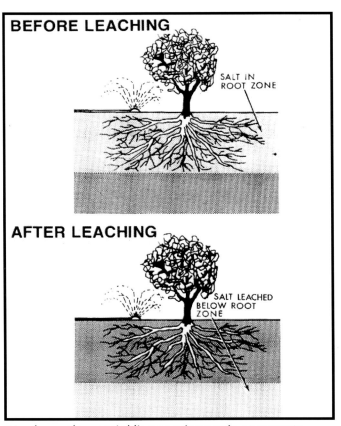

Use long, slow sprinkling or winter rain or snow to leach excessive salts out of the root zone.

EFFECT OF EXCESSIVE CONCENTRATIONS OF "SALT" IN THE SOIL

Pony pack of tomato plants growing in normal potting soil

A concentrated solution of salt (any soluble substance) water is poured onto the soil. This makes the soil water concentration greater than the concentration in the plant.

ONE HOUR LATER

The concentration of salt in the soil is acting as an "osmotic pump" to draw the moisture out of the plants into the soil. (The soil is still very wet.)

FOUR HOURS LATER

The salt water has sucked most of the water out of the plants and they are dying. This process can be reversed by running large quantities of water through the soil to leach out the salt.

These principles should be kept in mind when applying commercial fertilizer to your soil as well as in dealing with salt problems in general.

---

salt on the surface. Less frequent deep watering, on the other hand, wherein the water is allowed to run for a long enough period of time to leach the soluble salts down below the root zone, will have a very beneficial effect on the salinity problem. It is also helpful to have the soil roto-tilled or spaded and in such a condition that it will absorb winter rain and snow. If it comes in sufficient quantities, this salt-free water will leach the build-up of salts out of the root zone into the subsoil. Adding organic material to the soil reduces salt damage to plants and improves drainage making it easier to leach harmful salts out of the root zone.

STEER MANURE

Gardeners should be wary of using steer manure as a soil amendment. It is not the same as dairy or horse manure. Most of it comes from stock yards used for fattening beef cattle. Beef cattle are encouraged to eat as much salt as possible because it helps them retain moisture and fatten more quickly. As a result of this high salt diet, much of it passes through them and accumulates in the manure which is packaged up and sold to unsuspecting home gardeners. Don't use it. It will damage your crops.

Basic Watering (Irrigation) Principles

FILLING EACH PLANTS NEEDS

Irrigation is the life blood of western agriculture. Proper methods of irrigation make the difference between success and failure in home gardening. These methods must accommodate the water needs of each different plant which are many and varied. Some require a more even and consistent soil moisture level. These include the root crops (beets, carrots, turnips, and radishes), as well as the leaf crops (lettuce, spinach and Swiss chard). Others require deep and infrequent watering for good quality and yield. These include the seed and fruit type crops, such as tomatoes, melons and fruit trees. The garden should be laid out to accommodate the moisture needs of each plant. If you inter-mix water-loving vegetables with, heat-loving, deep-rooted vegetables, neither one will do well. To be healthy, the plant must be well-fed (with organic and/or commercial fertilizer), and watered according to its individual needs.

"LEAF AND ROOT" CROPS vs. "SEED AND FRUIT" CROPS

Any farmer knows that in order to get a crop of alfalfa **seed**, it is necessary to stop watering the alfalfa. Apparently the urge to reproduce is greatly increased by making the plant believe it is about to die. This principle that a period of drought encourages reproduction applies to most plants. Therefore most plants that are grown for their seed and fruit are encouraged to produce the desired crop by deep but infrequent watering (every 10 days to 2 weeks).

Other plants are grown for their leaves or roots. You don't want them to go to seed, so you water them more regularly (like twice a week in warm dry weather). This produces beautiful foliage in the leaf

Leaf and root crops need to be watered more frequently than seed and fruit crops.

crop and smooth even roots without cracks in the root crops. When these crops start going to seed, they immediately become tough and strong tasting.

The berries are watered like the leaf and root crops. For example, strawberries which normally reproduce by runners (rather than seeds) are encouraged to produce runners and stop producing berries if they get too dry.

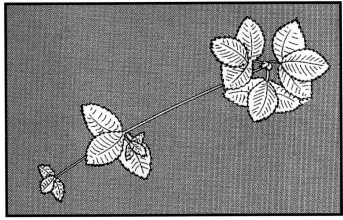

When strawberry plants get too dry, they tend to stop bearing and start putting out runners.

Seed and Fruit Crops

The stages of growth of some plants are dramatically affected by the amount of water which they receive. For example, if you overwater most varieties of tomato plants, they will not go from the vegetative growth stage into the fruiting stage. As a result, you will get large beautiful vines with no tomatoes. These plants respond to water stress (drought) by blooming profusely and setting on fruit.

Some of the early farmers in Goleta along the California coast would give each of their tomato plants a quart of water when they were planted and then not water them again until they began to bear fruit a couple of months later. This is an extreme approach and must have produced some small, dry tomatoes, but it illustrates one method of forcing plants into the fruiting stage so that they will produce a heavy crop in a small space. Once they are in the fruiting stage they will continue to set on fruit with regular, but infrequent watering. By **tempering the extreme method** described above and reducing the watering schedule to watering deeply (10 feet deep) once every two weeks after the tomato plant is established (approximately8-10 inches tall and growing vigorously) you can get an abundant harvest of delicious tomatoes. Most plants do not need to be put into a lack-of-water stress condition in order to produce fruit. For the most part, **infrequent deep watering on a regular basis is a better approach**. If temperatures get up over 100 degrees F. you may want to water every 10 days instead of every two weeks with tomatoes. **Small determinant types** of tomato plants require **more frequent** watering. (See page **146**)

Other fruit crops like melons and fruit trees of all kinds fall into the same classification as the large tomato plants, so they do best with deep but infrequent watering. They should be watered on a 10 day to 2 week schedule.

Intermediate Root Depth

There is an intermediate group of plants, most of which are harvested as immature fruit, such as green

These tomato plants have gone more than two weeks without water. This will encourage them to bloom profusely and set on a heavy crop of tomatoes. Correctly watered tomato plants will have a dark green color.

beans, corn, peppers and summer squash which need to be watered **once a week** in warm summer weather. They are not as deep rooted as the tomatoes and fruit trees but deeper rooted than the leaf and root crops. (See watering schedule for other vegetables.)

Water Loving Plants

Root crops such as radishes, beets, carrots, and turnips, usually require more frequent irrigation. This also applies to leaf crops such as lettuce, spinach, celery and Swiss chard as well as the cole crops including cauliflower, broccoli and cabbage. Strawberries, raspberries and other berries also require more frequent watering. These water-loving crops should be watered **twice per week** in warm weather and should also be soaked fairly well when the water is applied. Under cool weather conditions or in soil with excellent water retention capacity, even these crops only need to be watered once per week. When it is raining a lot you won't need to water at all. Bacteria and fungus diseases thrive under moist conditions, so don't over water.

HOW OFTEN TO WATER

The frequency of watering depends to some extent on the weather and the type and condition of your soil, as well as the rooting depth of the particular crop

Watering Schedule

Leaf and Root Cool Season Shallow Rooted	Immature Fruit Intermediate Rooting Depth	Seed and Fruit Warm Season Deep Rooted
Twice a week	**Once a Week**	**10 days-2 weeks**
lettuce celery spinach Swiss chard radishes beets carrots turnips potatoes peas broccoli cauliflower cabbage strawberries raspberries blackberries	beans corn peppers eggplant zucchini summer squash cucumbers yams peanuts rhubarb onions pumpkins	tomatoes watermelons cantaloupes butternut squash Hubbard squash banana squash peaches/ nectarines pears apples plums cherries grapes asparagus

involved, but some general rules can be stated. Even though the top one or two inches of soil will dry out between watering and the ground can look very dry, if the crop has been watered deeply the rooting zone below can have adequate amounts of water. If your soil is fairly heavy clay with a substantial amount of humus, the soil needs to be watered less frequently for a particular crop than a sandy soil low in humus. Nevertheless, a basic watering schedule (shown on this page) is helpful.

HOW LONG TO WATER

Root Depth Concept

Most home gardeners have no concept of how deep their plants' roots go. For this reason, the biggest mistake home gardeners make is in watering wrong. For example, if you know that a healthy tomato plant in good soil will root down **10 feet** you will water it differently than you will if you think it only roots down 2 or 3 feet. It is also a fact that the first 2 or 3 inches of top soil dry out very quickly, so we waste a

lot of water trying to keep that area wet. The moral of the story is that you should consider the **root zone** as a **reservoir** and when you water you should **fill the reservoir!** Then you don't feel like you have to come back and water again the next day.

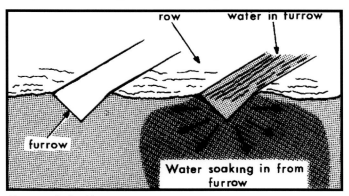
Furrow irrigation.

When you do water, you should allow the moisture to soak deeply. This means that if you irrigate in a furrow, the water should be allowed to stand one hour or more, depending on the type and texture of your soil. If your land is not flat and the water runs down the furrows instead of standing deep in the furrows, then it must run much longer to soak adequately across a row (raised bed). (See pages **53, 64 and 69** for the process of making and using furrows and other watering methods.)

SPRINKLER IRRIGATION. Impact-type (Rainbird) sprinkler on circular stand at the end of a hose.

If you water with a standard size home garden impact type (Rainbird) sprinkler (5/32 inch nozzle) it should be allowed to run approximately one hour if set on a quarter circle pattern to soak deeply on a once a week watering schedule and approximately twice as long if it is set for one half circle in order to soak deeply.

The basic rule of thumb is that **one inch** of water over the surface of the soil will soak **down one foot.** The second inch of water will go down more than one foot because the soil stays wetter down there. The third inch will cover even more territory, more like one and a half feet, depending on the moisture level

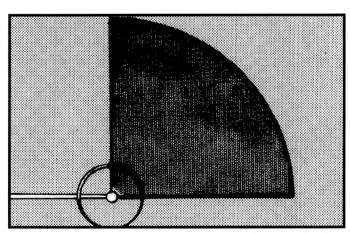

RAINBIRD SET ON QUARTER CIRCLE PATTERN. Soak approximately one hour.

and soil condition. For that reason, **soaking down five feet does not require five inches of water.**

In the thirty years since the author first published this book, the use of **drip/trickle irrigation systems** have become very important to both commercial growers and home gardeners. See page **69** for a discussion of these methods, including the length of time for watering.

DEEP ROOTS

Many gardeners water **too often,** but do not let the water run **long enough to** soak deeply. Most plants are lazy so that if there is a constant and sufficient supply of water right along the surface, the roots will spread out along the surface rather than going deep.

The constant moisture along the surface also means that the soil down a few inches stays very wet. This creates poor aeration of the deep soil so that the roots attempting to go deep become water-logged and do not find sufficient air in the soil for good root health. Plants are also susceptible to bacterial and fungal diseases when exposed to excessive moisture. This over-watering usually causes yellowing of plant foliage and stunting of plant growth.

In some cases it causes phytophthora root and crown rot and other soil diseases which kill the plant involved. Utah State University publication **The Home Orchard Pest Management Guide** states "Over watering is by far more common than under watering. Allow surface soil to dry out before irrigating." This "over watering" problem can be seen among both home gardeners and commercial growers everywhere.

An example of the problem is that trees planted in a lawn which is watered every day may have their roots right on the surface so that it is even hard to mow the lawn. If the lawn is watered more deeply once a week, both the trees and lawn will root more deeply and be healthier. In desert climates in mid-summer, the lawn can be watered deeply twice a week, but go back to once a week as soon as it begins to cool off in the fall. An alta fescue lawn roots much more deeply than bluegrass so it can be watered less frequently on a 10-day to two week cycle. Unless the right grass can be planted, trees are much healthier if not planted in a lawn so they can be watered deeply every two weeks.

Keep furrow full for at least one hour.

Deep, but infrequent irrigation allows more air in the soil and promotes a deep, extensive and healthy root system. The moisture is available to the plant, but as the soil gets drier on the surface, the plant is forced to go deep with its root system in order to maintain its moisture level. This deep, extensive root system also gives the plant a greater capacity to find the necessary nutrition for an abundant crop. Deep rooted crops like tomatoes and asparagus will root down ten feet deep in good soil. Fruit trees will root even deeper. Even shallow rooted crops like lettuce and broccoli will root down two or three feet in good soil.

GROW BOXES

Throughout this book we talk about raised beds, but we are **not** talking about grow boxes. We are talking about the area between the furrows which is used for planting. The problem with grow boxes is that they are expensive and time consuming and waste valuable space as well as water. Grow boxes usually do not take into consideration the rooting depth of regular fruits and vegetables. Those recommending them usually are using artificial soil composed of perlite, vermiculite,

sand and peat moss. This artificial soil has virtually no plant nutrients, so **all** of them have to be added every year. In years when commercial and organic fertilizer may be in short supply, grow boxes would grow very little.

One of the problems is that roots going from one growing medium into another type of soil which is very different tend to stay in the original instead of crossing the line into the new soil. This has been demonstrated untold times and is pictured over and over in soil science textbooks. For this reason, if you feel you must have grow boxes, it is very important to mix the two soils at the interface so the roots grow down beyond the artificial soil. Some who have recommended grow boxes have suggested putting plastic landscaping cloth under the grow boxes (for some inexplicable reason) so the roots can't grow down which is very foolish. Tomato roots in a good garden go down approximately 10 feet. How could you get any kind of quality or yield without an expansive root system? In warm dry western climates you will find yourself watering constantly with a grow box.

It is also very hard to get any kind of equipment into grow boxes to work the soil. It won't have any weeds the first year but after that they will have blown in from other areas. It is also hard to water a grow box by either furrow or drip systems so you end up with constant hand watering which is very time consuming. In a regular garden, once a drip system is set up, it can be quickly turned on for a large area of garden and just as quickly turned off after the area is soaked.

TOUGH STOCKY PLANTS

Most plants, if watered too often, will tend to develop a soft, watery and rank growth. This makes them vulnerable, not only to the wind and weather, but also to insects and plant diseases. You have probably noticed in a crowd of people on a summer evening that the mosquitoes seem to gravitate toward certain members of the group. This is also true with insects on plants, and the plant which is soft and watery is very tempting to the sucking and chewing insects which are frequently present in the garden. On the other

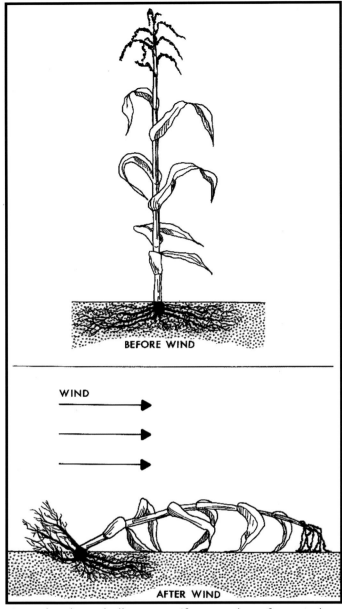

WIND

Corn develops shallow roots if watered too frequently.

The tough, stocky plant is less susceptible to damage from wind, weather, insects and diseases than the rank, watery one.

FUNGUS DISEASES

hand, a plant which is properly watered tends to be tough, wiry and have a more stocky growth habit. They are more resistant to wind and disease and less susceptible to insect damage.

When watered deeply but not too frequently, a crop like corn will be deep rooted and will not blow over in the wind. Deep but infrequent watering should be the rule with most plants. If properly fertilized and watered in this manner, most plants will be healthy. The exception would be the cool season crops mentioned in the **Watering Schedule** above which **need** to be watered more frequently.

As much as possible, avoid watering the leaves of garden plants. Water on the leaves promotes the growth of fungus diseases which thrive in damp places. For this reason, irrigation in furrows or by drip systems is almost always preferable to using sprinkling systems. They also use less water. The use of furrows and drip

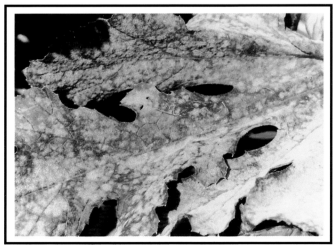

Squash, melons and cucumbers get fungus diseases (powdery and downy mildew) very easily. Leaves should not be watered.

irrigation systems in the home garden (discussed hereafter in great detail) are also excellent for getting water to the roots without wetting the foliage and without wasting water.

Some plants are particularly susceptible to foliage fungus diseases (powdery and downy mildew, etc.) and should never be watered by sprinkling unless you live in hot desert areas. These crops include squash, pumpkins, melons and cucumbers. If **sprinkling** must be used, water the first thing in the morning so that the foliage will dry completely before evening. If the leaves are wet all night, the mildew spores which come from the air will germinate and grow on the leaves which will make your crop sick and/or die prematurely.

If you are watering by sprinkler, the type of sprinkler used should put the water down slowly, such as an impact type (Rainbird) sprinkler. This kind of sprinkler can be allowed to run long enough to soak the soil deeply without losing water by run-off. Once the leaves are wet, the sprinkler should be allowed to run long enough to thoroughly soak the ground. Then the soil can go longer with the leaves totally dry before it has to be watered again and fungus diseases will be less likely to occur. By watering deeply but infrequently, **soil fungus diseases** such as verticillium and fusarium wilt as well as phytophthora root rot will also be less of a problem.

DRAINAGE PROBLEMS

Plants need oxygen to their roots. This is classically demonstrated by putting a healthy tomato plant into a pot without a drainage hole at the bottom and covering the root ball with water. Within 24 hours the foliage of the plant wilts down from lack of water. The cells in the roots are dying from lack of oxygen and this is plugging up the vascular system so the plants can't transport water to the leaves. This is called "wet wilting".

Plants will drown if water is allowed to stand around the roots for long periods of time. As the soil drains air follows the water into the root zone. Poor drainage is

If your soil drains poorly, open the end ditch or use a siphon to drain water off the garden after irrigating.

more of a problem in heavy clay than in sand and can be largely solved by working large amounts of organic material into the soil. You will have to be more aware of this problem if your ground is relatively flat. If you irrigate in furrows on flat ground and your soil tends to be tight, heavy clay, it is beneficial to drain the furrows after the water has soaked adequately. This drainage of furrows can be accomplished by simply opening the ditch at either end of the garden or by using your garden hose as a siphon to take the water into a lower area of your yard. On the other hand, if your soil is very porous (water soaks in quickly), drainage will not be a problem even on flat ground.

COST

If you are watering from a hose in your backyard, your **pocketbook** will also benefit by correct watering principles. A properly watered garden takes less water than a properly watered lawn. For this reason you save money two ways when you turn part of your backyard into a home vegetable and fruit garden.

WATERING METHODS

The methods of watering which should be used to implement the foregoing principles are important. Choosing the proper method saves time and water as well as growing better vegetables. A detailed discussion of these methods of irrigation including both drip and furrow watering systems is found in the **Planting Your Garden section under step six, Watering Methods.**

Temperature and Sunlight
(adjusting to the peculiarities of your climate)

SUN'S ENERGY

Sunlight is the basic source of energy for the manufacture of the food we eat. The plant absorbs the water and nutrients needed as raw materials for the manufacture of this food through its roots, but the actual manufacturing process takes place in the leaves. Here the nutrients and water are combined with elements from the air to produce carbohydrates, proteins, vitamins and other basic food substances which are then stored in the fruit, roots, stems and other plant tissue. Since the food is manufactured in the leaves, it is important that the plant be encouraged to develop a large quantity of healthy leaves and that this leaf structure get the maximum amount of exposure to sunlight. Many processes described in this book are designed for the very purpose of exposing as much leaf surface to sunlight as possible.

Sunniest Spot

You should choose the sunniest spot in your yard for the garden. All garden vegetables and fruits do best in full sun, but some will do quite well if they have at least one half day's sun. Vegetables which do fairly well in partial shade are leaf crops, such as lettuce, spinach, Swiss chard, celery and possibly peas. The heat-loving plants which need maximum sun include melons, tomatoes, peppers, squash, string beans, corn, fruit trees, and grapes. There are various ways to get maximum sunlight for your garden vegetables. These include: not planting the rows too close; using trellises, poles, and fences to elevate, spread out and expose leaf surfaces to the sun, and eliminating unnecessary and non-useful trees. Trees can also be pruned so that they are attractive but do not shade your garden.

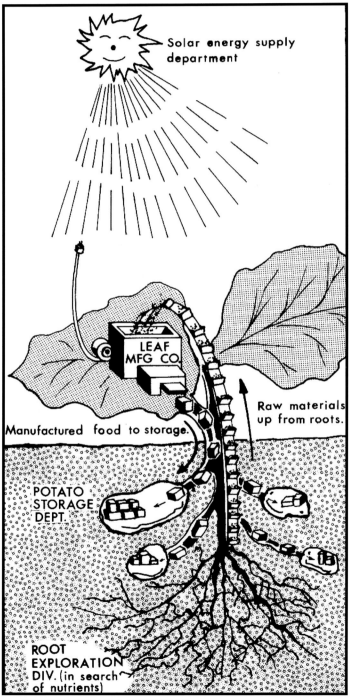

SOURCE SINK RELATIONSHIP

SOURCE SINK RELATIONSHIPS

All of the food which is produced by the leaves including vitamins, minerals, proteins, sugars, flavor compounds, phytonutrients, etc. that flow through the plant in the cell sap are called **soluble solids.** The **source of these soluble solids is the leaves. The place where these soluble solids are either used or stored is called the sink.** The plant has options between using the soluble solids to produce more leaves or to store it in the fruit (tomatoes or melons etc) or roots (carrots, yams, potatoes). This process of switching from one use to another is called **partitioning.** If too much nitrogen fertilizer and too much water is used on fruit crops or root crops the plant will stay in a vegetative growth stage rather than going into a fruiting or rooting stage and the fruit or roots will be small and lacking in sugar and flavor.

In this whole process the plant needs adequate nutrition because it is important that the leaves be large and healthy. The food is manufactured there. **But** it is equally important that the plant is not **over-fertilized or over-watered** because you want the partitioning to work right. At a certain point you want the growth of new leaves to slow down or stop and have all the soluble solids directed into the production of fruit or roots (the sink). If too much fertilizer (especially nitrogen) and too frequent water are applied to the crop, the soluble solids are partitioned to leaves (the leaves become the sink), the plant tries to stay in the vegetative stage and the fruit and roots are tiny and poor quality.

The same process applies to the hardening of plants for the winter. Ocean water does not freeze because of a concentrated solution of salt in the water. The salt acts like anti-freeze. The same thing happens in plants. When watered and fertilized properly they accumulate a concentrated solution of soluble solids in the cell sap as cold weather approaches. This concentrated solution acts like anti-freeze in the tissues preventing damage by freezing temperatures. If the gardener keeps the plant in a vegetative condition by too much nitrogen fertilizer and water right into the fall, the plant uses its soluble solids to produce new leaves (the wrong sink) instead of storing it in the plants branches, limbs and roots.. When freezing weather comes, the plant dies from lack of anti-freeze (soluble solids) in the tissues.

TEMPERATURE

Certain plants have very definite requirements regarding the amount of heat needed or tolerated during the growing season.

Cool Season Vegetables

Some plants are especially adapted to cool weather areas. In hotter locals they should be planted as early as possible during the spring so that they will mature before the hottest part of the summer or they should be planted in the summer to mature in cool fall weather. These include radishes, carrots, beets, turnips, spinach, celery, lettuce, Swiss chard, peas, cauliflower, and broccoli. (See the **Watering Schedule** table for a more complete list of cool season crops.) These crops do not produce good quality fruits and vegetables when they mature during the hottest part of the summer. For example lettuce goes quickly to seed in the heat of summer. There are some warm winter areas where these crops should be planted in January or February but in cold winter areas you will need to wait until mid-March and plant them as part of a **spring garden.**

On the other hand, most cool season crops are best planted at the right time during the summer as part of the **fall garden** so that they mature in September and October when the weather is cool. Ripening in cool weather gives you the best quality of these crops and they remain at top quality for a longer period. Even when light frosts come the quality is still excellent. Carrots will store in the ground all winter in most climates and they continue to get sweeter through early December.

In **extremely hot areas** of the country the cool season perennials like berries can be planted on the east side of the house where they only receive morning sun and are protected from the sun in the heat of the day.

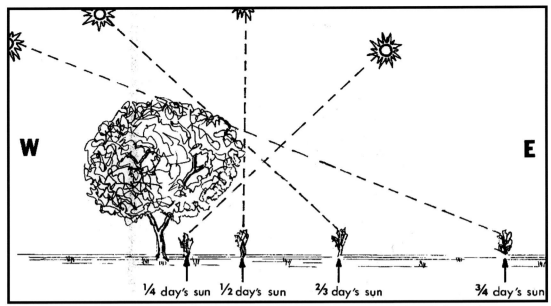

You can determine how much sunlight your vegetables will get each day if planted next to a tree.

¼ day's sun   ½ day's sun   ⅔ day's sun   ¾ day's sun

Warm Weather Vegetables

Some species of fruits and vegetables require hot weather to be healthy and productive. They are the ones discussed in an earlier section which require deep but infrequent watering. The summer heat is about right for most of these plants in the high desert and mountain valleys, but the melons have a particular need for an extremely warm summer temperature. They grow best in the low desert areas like the Imperial or San Joaquin valleys of California, the Moapa and Las Vegas valleys of Nevada, central and southern Arizona and the Dixie area of Southern Utah. They are a little more difficult to grow in the high deserts and mountain valleys such as the Boise area of Idaho and the Salt Lake and Utah valleys of Utah and they pose some special problems for coastal California where the summers are often very cool. The same kind of problem exists in the high mountain valleys such as the Star Valley of Wyoming and the Bear Lake area of Idaho. The high mountain valleys have the additional problem of a very short growing season. Both the lack of heat and short season problems become less serious with the use of black plastic (polyethylene) mulch which is talked about hereafter.

These **cool summer problems** are solved in several ways:

LOCATION

Pick the sunniest spot available. For example it is much warmer in the early spring on the south side of your house, than it is on the north side. The sun goes across the south sky in winter and spring and reflects off the south side of the house creating a great deal of heat. The south side of a hill is also warmer than the north, as illustrated by the fact that snow remains much longer on the north side of a mountain than on the south side. This principle even applies, in small scale, to the south edge of a raised bed of vegetables, which is warmer and grows faster in the early spring than the north edge. Sometimes raised beds have been sloped toward the south to capture more intense sunlight and heat. Sandy soils are also slightly warmer than clay soils.

TIMING

Plant the crop so that it will take advantage of the warmest period of the summer for the basic part of its growing season. This usually means that you plant your melons about the first of May, so that they are up and growing when the warm weather comes in June. They will mature in early August when it is still hot. In some cases you might want to delay your planting until the middle of May in areas where the danger of frost continues that late. In high mountain valleys, it is important with crops like tomatoes, peppers, cucumbers, melons and winter squash to start them inside on a sunny window ledge so they are a healthy plants ready to plant out when danger of frost has passed. Young tomato plants grow very well under hot caps so you can plant them out under the hot caps before danger of frost has passed. The temperature under the hot cap is warmer than ambient air. This brings the tomatoes on earlier giving you a larger crop.

VARIETIES

Some varieties of heat-loving vegetables require less heat in order to produce good quality than others. For example, a banana squash does well during relatively cool summers but a butternut squash does not achieve top quality in either flavor or texture without more summer heat.

As a general rule, the **earlier varieties** of a particular vegetable species do better in cool summer weather than the late varieties. This is not just because they mature earlier, but because they usually have particular characteristics that are adapted to "cold weather". For example, early varieties of tomatoes will set fruit during summer weather when the night-time temperature is below 55°, but the main season varieties require more heat at night to prevent the blossoms from dropping. This is very important in coastal climates and high mountain valleys where the nights may be cool on a regular basis. If you plant only main season and late varieties, you will get fewer

In cool summer areas, the black plastic improves both quality and quantity of melons, cucumbers and squash by heating the vines which lie upon it.

tomatoes. This advantage of early varieties applies to some extent with most vegetables.

Mulching and Heat

Mulches have been used for years for the purpose of preventing weeds, retaining soil moisture and keeping the fruit off the ground. Mulches have been traditionally composed of hay, straw, or grass clippings which are spread in a four to six inch layer down the rows (raised beds) between the plants. Organic mulches are great insulators, so the problem with this procedure in growing some crops is that it makes the soil colder than it would otherwise be. This is a benefit to other crops.

CLEAR PLASTIC MULCH

A number of years ago, strawberry farmers started using a clear plastic (polyethylene) film across the top of the row (raised bed) around the plants in place of the traditional type of mulch. (See pages **78-81** for methods of applying plastic mulches.) It had an advantage over traditional mulches because it not only helped retain moisture and kept the berries off the ground but it also did not attract and harbor insects. It also had one additional advantage. Instead of keeping the soil cold, it warmed it up approximately 15 degrees higher than it would otherwise be. This encouraged root growth during the winter and spring, bringing the strawberry plants out of their dormancy earlier in the spring and the strawberry crop to the table several weeks earlier. A second advantage was that this clear plastic mulch prevented rot in the strawberries where they made contact with the surface.

BLACK PLASTIC MULCH

The big problem with clear plastic is that it does not prevent the growth of weeds. For that reason a black polyethylene film was developed which has the same beneficial effects as the clear plastic in keeping the fruit off the ground and retaining moisture, but it also has the additional benefit of preventing the growth of weeds, very much as organic mulches have traditionally done.

Increased Heat

The black plastic also has one additional advantage. Black plastic absorbs the heat from the sun in the **surface** of the plastic so that the sun's rays do not go through the plastic and warm up the soil beneath. Instead, the surface of the plastic itself becomes very warm increasing the temperature by approximately 15-20 degrees. The soil temperature is also increased slightly (approx. 5 degrees). By planting heat-loving plants like cantaloupe and watermelons in black plastic mulch, and allowing the vines to spread across the hot plastic, the vine temperature is increased to be more compatible with the melon's need for heat.

In the cool summer areas of the high mountain valleys and coastal regions, tomato plants will produce earlier and larger crops with the increased heat developed on the vine by the black plastic. It also reduces fruit spoilage and eliminates weeds.

Most melons crave heat, so unless you live in the low desert, the melons will be improved by this increase of heat. For this reason, black plastic improves both the **quality** and **quantity** of your melon crop by heating up the vines which lie upon it. In tests performed with black plastic on one row and without it on another similar row, the yield of cantaloupe, Crenshaw melons and watermelons have been found to be twice as large with the black plastic. The quality is also improved.

This technique is also beneficial for the growing of tomatoes in cooler climates. The tomatoes come much earlier with the quality and yield much improved and the number of cracked tomatoes decreased. A detailed description of the methods of applying and using black plastic mulch is found in the KEEPING THEM HEALTHY section. It should be noted that the use of black plastic increases the retention of water in the soil and also prevents the cooling effect of water evaporation from the soil.

Too Much Heat

The black plastic must be used with discretion. In the intense heat of the low desert (areas like Imperial Valley in California, Moapa Valley in Nevada and central and southern Arizona) the black plastic becomes so hot that it can burn the plants that spread across it. In areas of extreme heat, the organic mulches of grass clippings, hay or straw are much better because they eliminate weeds without creating any more heat on the vine. These organic mulches also help the soil to retain moisture and have a moderating effect on soil temperatures.

Black plastic has also been used for strawberries because it prevents weeds and keeps the berries off the ground, but the strawberries do not benefit from the added heat. The author has found that **black landscaping cloth** which is made of black plastic which is woven together into a cloth-like material is better for strawberries. It prevents weeds like black polyethylene and keeps the berries off the ground but it does not get as hot which is better for strawberries.

SOURCE OF PLASTIC

The plastic (polyethylene) film, both clear and black, used as mulch, should be at least 3.5 to 4 mil thick so it won't tear and come to pieces as a result of sunshine or bad weather. These are usually purchased at places like Wal-Mart, Lowes or Home Depot in the **paint department.** The landscaping cloth is found in the same stores in the garden shop. Be certain to use enough heavy bricks or rocks around the plastic to hold it down so the wind won't whip it off. Also put a brick next to the tomato or melon plant so the wind will not whip the plant back under the plastic.

Planning Your Garden

SEED CATALOGS

Many seed companies offer free seed catalogs. Once you get on their mailing list, you get a new one each year. They are very colorful and give a great deal of valuable information about the various garden vegetables. They are especially important in listing the disease resistant qualities of the various fruits and vegetables. They also list the qualities of flavor and sweetness. They list the days to maturity which helps in determining when to plant a **fall garden** in your particular area. They feature the new varieties, particularly those which have received the All-American Selection Award in the vegetable judging which takes place each year. Judges from different parts of the country grow the new varieties in experimental plots, and then they are judged and some superior varieties are chosen which receive this award.

It is fun for the family to plan the garden by studying seed catalogs in Family Home Evenings.

By getting copies of several seed catalogs filled with beautiful color pictures of the various vegetables, your family can sit down together in Family Home Evenings during the winter months and plan your garden. It will generate tremendous enthusiasm among children and adults alike as each decides which varieties of vegetable seed should be ordered.

Seed catalogs give a description of each vegetable that they carry as well as specific cultural advice for growing them. These catalogs offer a tremendous number of different varieties in the basic garden vegetables. The author spends many pleasant hours studying these seed catalogs in anticipation of the fruits and vegetables he will grow. It makes a great deal of difference which varieties you plant for your particular climate and needs, and the seed catalogs give you an opportunity to study and compare different kinds. Call any of the companies and other sources of plant material listed below for a free catalog.

Some seed companies do not print a catalog but make their seed available on seed racks in various retail stores and nurseries, but these are usually very old varieties which lack the improved qualities and disease resistance of the newer ones.

SOURCES

Seed Catalogs

www.stokeseeds.com	800-396-9238
www.twilleyseed.com	800 622-7333
www.parkseed.com	800 845-3369
www.burpee.com	800 888-1447
www.willhiteseed.com	800 828-1840
www.tomatogrowers.com	888 478.7333
www.totallytomatoes.com	800 345-5977
www.harrisseeds.com	800 514-4441
www.henryfields.com	513 354-1494
www.vanwell.net	800 572-1553
www.baylaurelnursery.com	805 466-3406

Organics

www.fungi.com	800-780-9126
www.mycorrhizae.com	541-476-3985
www.arbico-organics.com	800-827-2847
www.gemplers.com	800-382-8473

CHOOSING THE SOURCE

From these sources the home gardener will find a large selection of seed from which to choose what he wants for his garden. Many of the catalogs also offer trees, plants, and roots of various kinds in addition to the seed.

After buying seed from a number of these companies for several years, you will develop your own favorite seed sources. The author prefers Stokes Seed Company, Twilley Seed Company and Park Seed Company but he also buys seed from various other sources. Van Well and Bay Laurel nurseries are good sources of fruit trees. These companies conduct extensive plant breeding programs and regularly introduce new, improved varieties as well as carrying those which are developed by many other companies. You will develop enthusiasm as you study the seed and fruit tree catalogs and plan your garden.

OTHER SOURCES OF INFORMATION

For information from the United States Department of Agriculture, write to Superintendent of Documents, Government Printing Office, Washington, D.C. 20250, for a list of available publications of the U.S.D.A. bulletin no. 11. From this catalog you can order a number of pamphlets with information about home gardening.

For information from the University of California, Division of Agricultural Sciences, Agricultural Experiment Stations, write to Publications, University of California, Division of Agricultural Sciences, 1422 South 10th Street, Richmond, California 94804 and request the publications catalog.

For information from Utah State University, write Utah State University, College of Agriculture, Agricultural Experiment Stations Bulletin Room,

UMC #48, Logan, Utah 84322 and request the Catalog of Publications.

Free information is also available at the various other agricultural colleges and state universities, as well as your local County Agricultural Agent's office or the Farm and Home Advisor's Office. Numerous pamphlets about various aspects of home gardening are available.

LAYING OUT YOUR GARDEN ON PAPER

Your garden should be neat and attractive. This is facilitated by laying it out on paper before planting.

During the winter months when things aren't growing, you will also enjoy the process of planning the garden on paper. This helps you make the vegetable garden neat and attractive. It is also helpful to lay out your garden in a bound notebook so that you have a permanent record of what you plant and what varieties have done well in the past. There are many reasons for laying out your garden on paper before actually planting it. They include the following:

1. Avoid watering problems.

2. Avoid shading problems.

3. Avoid overplanting.

4. Decide which seed to order.

Watering

When you plan your garden on paper it is very important to put the various crops together which have similar watering requirements. Otherwise, for example, it might be impossible to water your lettuce often enough to get good quality without grossly

Does the Layout Make Sense "Water-wise"?

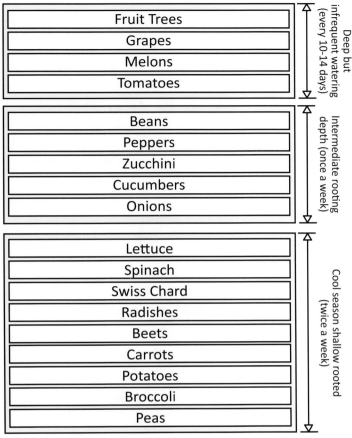

Deep but infrequent watering (every 10-14 days)

Fruit Trees
Grapes
Melons
Tomatoes

Intermediate rooting depth (once a week)

Beans
Peppers
Zucchini
Cucumbers
Onions

Cool season shallow rooted (twice a week)

Lettuce
Spinach
Swiss Chard
Radishes
Beets
Carrots
Potatoes
Broccoli
Peas

If the garden is properly laid out, every vegetable automatically gets the water it needs because of the place where it is located.

overwatering your tomatoes if they are planted next to each other.

If your garden is laid out properly it will take far less time to care for it later because the basic irrigating can be done in one or two simple operations. For example, you will have all of your water loving crops connected to the same valve of the drip system so it only takes two or three minutes to go out and turn that valve to water all of your cool season crops and then another two or three minutes after they have been watered to walk out and turn the water off. It is a waste of time to individually water each kind of vegetable. By planning your garden with all the water-loving plants together in a block, you can water that section without watering other vegetables which require deep but infrequent watering. They are part of a different system. (See illustration of "Water-wise" table.)

Avoiding Shade

All the crops you grow will do better in full sun, but in the home garden you often have to deal with shade created by trees and your home itself, so you will have to make compromises. Generally speaking the crops on the warm season side of the Watering Schedule (see chart) require the most sun and the ones on the cool season side require the least. This means that you can get by with less than full sun with many of the crops you grow. Try to save the sunniest spot for the others.

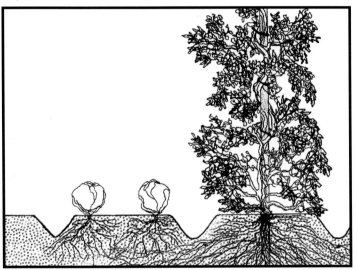

If you plant lettuce and tomatoes next to each other and water to suit the lettuce, you ruin the tomatoes. They become rank and watery with a light green color and no fruit. If you water to suit the tomatoes, the lettuce is no good.

Remember that the sun goes across the south sky rather than directly overhead during fall, winter and spring, so a spring garden can be planted on the south side and even partially under a tree and still receive full sun. Plan the garden so that tall vegetables like corn and pole beans are placed in one area and not intermixed with shorter ones causing more shading.

Don't plant pumpkins or winter squash (banana or butternut, etc.) next to small vegetables because they will soon cover them up. But if you plant a spring garden with radishes, spinach, lettuce, peas, cauliflower, and other things, it is easy to plant the squash next to them a month or so later. Then by the time the squash begins to run the early garden is harvested your garden take into consideration the water, heat, sun and space

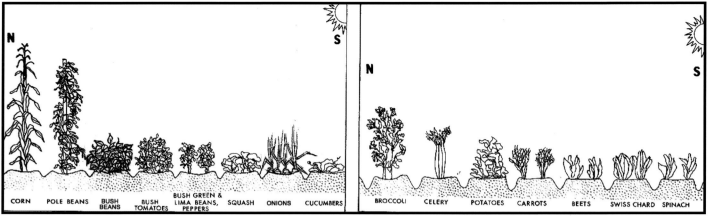

CORN | POLE BEANS | BUSH BEANS | BUSH TOMATOES | BUSH GREEN & LIMA BEANS, PEPPERS | SQUASH | ONIONS | CUCUMBERS

BROCCOLI | CELERY | POTATOES | CARROTS | BEETS | SWISS CHARD | SPINACH

Most plants need maximum exposure to sunlight, so plan the garden to avoid shading smaller ones. Keep in mind that the sun moves across the south sky during fall, winter and spring.

requirements of the different plants. or about gone, so you can train the vines right over the top of these other areas which are not in use. In planning

Too Much Zucchini? Avoid Overplanting

It is easy to over-plant on some easy-to-grow vegetables and then have enough for the entire neighborhood. For example, two zucchini squash plants are adequate for a very large family (with a few left over for the neighbors), so it would waste a great deal of space in a small garden plot to plant 3 or 4 zucchini plants. They grow fairly large and must be given adequate space so they will not shade out some other vegetable next to them. Cucumbers and tomatoes are also very productive plants, so it does not require a gigantic area of your garden to satisfy the needs of the average family. Plan a very small space for vegetables like radishes because they will not store in the ground very long before getting strong and pithy. If you plant a large amount, most of them go to waste. Yellow summer squash are like zucchini and one or two plants are adequate for any family. Even if you follow these suggestions, you will have plenty of produce from your garden to give away.

LIMITED SPACE GARDEN

Even in a limited space the home gardener can grow a tremendous quantity of food. For one thing, he can concentrate the available organic material in a

Don't be a "radish tycoon". Avoid overplanting vegetables which can be purchased inexpensively and do not keep very long in the ground.

smaller space, work it deeply into the soil, and garden more intensively in the space which is available. The same area used for all of your cool weather vegetables in your **spring garden** can be roto-tilled after the crop is harvested in early summer and re-planted with the same cool weather vegetables for your **fall garden.**

The Right Vegetables

The most important factors in maximum production from a small space are to choose the right vegetables and not plant too much of any one thing. There are certain vegetable crops which should be avoided because they spread over large areas or grow tall and shade the smaller ones. These crops, such as winter squash, melons and corn also require more space for the same quantity of food. (See illustration on page **41** for high yield in small space vegetables.)

The Right Culture

These problems can be solved to some extent by planting the taller crops on one side of the garden and by providing trellises for cucumbers, peas and beans. You can grow many crops up instead of out, and thereby get maximum sun without taking up more space.

For example, pole beans produce larger crops over a longer season in the same space as bush beans. The same is true of pole limas. (See bean sections for method of growing beans on poles.) Peas should normally be excluded from a space saving garden, but if you want to grow peas, grow tall peas ('Mr. Big') on a trellis rather than dwarf (bush) peas.

WHEN TO PLANT

In the high mountain valleys and in the extreme northern areas it may only be possible to plant one garden per year, but in the warmer mountain valleys, and all other areas where there is a longer growing season you can plant at least three gardens per year. They may overlap and you will repeat some crops in both early and late garden, but they are most easily

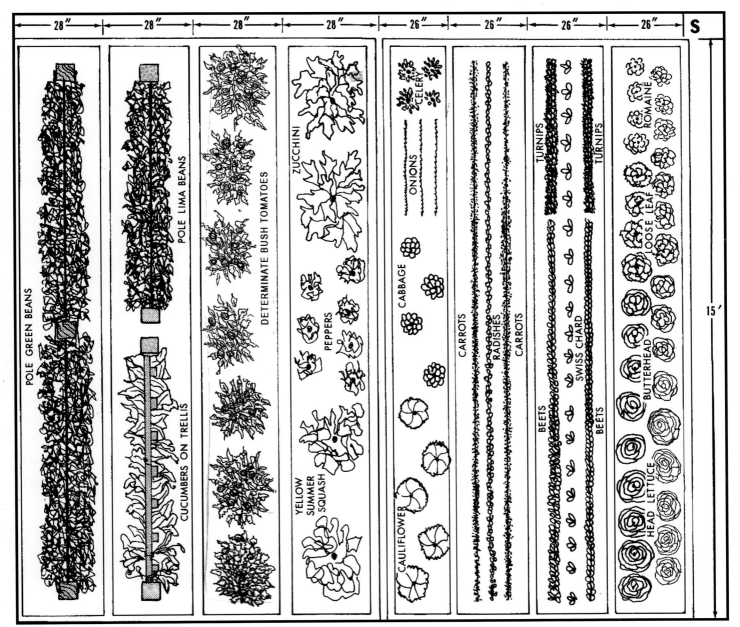

The above layout shows the way to plant a garden for a gigantic quantity of food in a very small space (15 feet by 18 feet). Please note that the crops on the right are cool weather vegetables for a spring or fall garden, but the ones on the left are frost sensitive and must be planted after danger of frost has passed.

discussed as three distinct gardens. Even in short season areas, you may plant these three gardens, but they will overlap.

Spring Garden

Most of these cold weather vegetables stand frost (a light freeze) in the mountain valleys and will thrive in the cool, wet weather of the spring in other areas. The spring garden could include any or all of the following:

SPRING GARDEN		
radishes	lettuce	cauliflower
broccoli	beets	celery
cabbage	carrots	spinach
onions	turnips	Swiss chard
peas		

You will notice that this is basically the same list as the "leaf and root, cool season, shallow rooted, twice-a-week" watering schedule from page **27.** Sometimes in the Utah valley where these crops are planted approximately March 15th they get snowed on but that doesn't bother them much as long as they are hardened up before planting. If you plant them early enough and use early short season varieties, they will mature **before** the intense summer heat. If they mature in the heat, the quality is not good so you plant the spring garden early enough to avoid that problem. If lettuce matures in the heat of summer it quickly goes to seed. The one odd exception in this group which does not mature before the heat of summer is the long season onion. Although planted in the cold, it thrives on the heat of summer and doesn't really mature until September.

GETTING THEM UP

There are certain problems peculiar to an early garden. The soil is cold and often damp, so getting seeds to germinate and come up can be a problem. They germinate (sprout) slowly in cold ground and if they remain in wet ground too long without coming up they will rot.

Using seeds that have been treated with Captan, or other mild fungicides, may prevent rot while the seeds

are germinating. Another way to avoid this problem with cauliflower, broccoli, cabbage, lettuce, celery and onions is to start the seeds inside and transplant outside after the plants are up, growing vigorously and hardened for transplanting into cold weather. They may also be available in a pony pack in a nursery. Even peas can be started inside in peat pellets and moved outside when they are up and growing. Peat pellets are ideal for starting these small plants inside. The peat pellets are very low in plant nutrients so mixing a very small amount (1/16 teaspoon per quart) of fertilizer into the water will produce healthy transplants. (For a description of this process see pages **57-60**) If part of a row, which has been seeded directly outside, comes up too sparsely, you can move plants soon after they come up from a part of the row where they are too thick into the bare areas. Always water immediately after any transplanting to wet the soil and settle it in around the roots.

PICKING THE DATE

Because these vegetables will stand a light frost or even be snowed on without being severely damaged, starting them too early is not a fatal mistake. The important thing is that the weather be warm enough so that the seeds will come up or use transplants instead of seeds. If hardened up adequately they will handle temperatures down to 30 degrees F. but 25 degrees will do serious damage.

In the mountain valleys, the time to plant can be as early as Mid-March, as soon as the snow is off the ground and the soil is dry enough to plant. Talk to experienced gardeners in your area or a cooperative extension specialist and watch the weather reports because the right date for planting will be a little different each year.

In coastal California the time to plant will be early February most years. These plants seem to thrive in cold weather when other vegetables will not even grow.

In the low desert planting dates will vary between late January and the beginning of March depending on the year, the location, and the particular vegetable involved.

STALE BEDS

Farmers worldwide use stale beds for spring plantings. The term simply means the land is prepared in the fall by fertilizing, plowing, disking, leveling and furrowing so that in the spring when the land is too wet to work and prepare, the farmer can go right ahead with planting. In warmer areas where weeds grow in the winter, he may have to spray with an herbicide before planting.

In the case of a home gardener, he/she should put lots of leaves and grass clippings on his soil along with the regular commercial fertilizer (and sulfur where needed to neutralize the soil), then roto-till thoroughly, and make the furrows (which automatically make raised beds between the furrows) and then let the soil lay fallow until he is ready to plant the spring garden. The raw organic matter applied in the fall will be totally decomposed into humus and the beds will be in great condition for planting the spring garden. The soil is usually far too wet to prepare the beds at the time when a spring garden needs to be planted. In warm areas you may need to spray the weeds that have grown in the winter with an herbicide (Roundup), but in cold areas where there has been snow during the winter the stale beds will be clean and ready to plant.

Because some of the nitrogen fertilizer may leach out of the top soil with winter rain and snow, you may need to fertilize the stale bed with a little extra nitrogen fertilizer after the spring crop is up and growing.

Summer Garden

These are the basic crops which require more heat, more sunlight, longer days, and deep but infrequent irrigation. They are killed by frost and thrive in the heat of summer. They include:

SUMMER GARDEN		
beans	pumpkins	tomatoes
corn	squash	cucumbers
watermelon	eggplant	yams
cantaloupes	peanuts	onions
crenshaw	peppers	potatoes

In the low desert where it is extremely hot (up to 120° F. in the shade), the corn, beans, and potatoes do better in the fall garden because they ripen when the intense heat of summer has passed. For example, corn tassels will curl and blight in a hot winds of summer in the desert and pollination will be very poor. The blossoms of pole beans drop until the weather begins to cool. Some varieties of tomatoes do not set well in that kind of heat. In all other climatic zones, these crops grow well in the summer heat. Even in the low desert, they all do well except those mentioned above which need special attention and should be planted as early as possible or later for a fall crop.

Summer garden crops like cantaloupes and Crenshaw thrive in hot weather.

In other areas it is usually recommended that the summer garden vegetables be planted as soon as the **danger of frost has passed.** Along the Wasatch Front in northern Utah the rule of thumb is "after Mothers' Day", but each year is slightly different so you need to follow the weather reports. Each area will also have a normal "last frost date" so check with experienced gardeners or the cooperative extension agent in your area and watch the weather reports to know when to plant your summer garden.

In the longer season areas, vegetables such as corn and beans can be planted several times during the spring and early summer for a continuous supply throughout the season.

Pumpkins and winter squash must be planted in the summer garden in order to mature in the fall.

Fall Garden

The fall garden should include:

FALL GARDEN		
carrots	lettuce	peas
beets	broccoli	cabbage
turnips	cauliflower	radishes

These vegetables are basically the same ones found in Watering Schedule under leaf and root and cool season which you planted in your spring garden. They are crops which do well if they mature after the heat of summer has passed and most of them store well in the garden, often for several weeks or months after they mature. Carrots for example, which mature in October, will store all winter in the ground. They can

The fall garden gives an abundant harvest of broccoli, cauliflower and carrots.

be dug as needed for the table. In cold climates they can be mulched with a heavy layer of grass clippings, hay or straw to keep them from freezing.

In most areas there is a break in the summer heat sometime in September when the nights become cool and the days are pleasant (65-75 degrees F. range). If the fall garden begins to mature at this time, the quality of these cool weather vegetables will be excellent. You need to know when to plant the fall garden in order to have the plants mature at the right time.

Go to your seed catalogs. You will find that the "days to maturity" is listed for each vegetable. Take that figure and count back from the date cool weather begins and it will give you the approximate planting date. For example, if you were planting 'Envy', which is a 66 day carrot, and you live in an area where cool weather begins approximately September 15th, you would theoretically go back 66 days and plant on July 15th. But the author has found that days to maturity in seed catalogs assumes that all of the growing conditions are perfect and that in the real world, he has to add approximately 10 days to the days to maturity to have the crops ripen in the right season, so in the above example he would actually plant the fall garden on July 1st.

It should also be remembered that where he now lives it sometimes begins to cool off in the first week of September which delays maturity. He is also planting on the same day different varieties of broccoli, cauliflower and cabbage which mature in the 60-85 day range. In southern Idaho a person would plant a basic fall garden in June. In Arizona or California it would be planted later in July.

You can find different varieties of broccoli ripening anywhere from 45 days to 100 days. For your spring garden you used early maturing varieties (45-60 days) because you wanted them to mature before the summer heat. For the fall garden you want to choose the very best varieties so you choose the mid-season (75 days) to later maturing (85 days) broccoli. This same thing also applies to cauliflower or cabbage or lettuce. Most areas have a relatively long moderate

Lettuce comes in a multitude of colors and varieties.

period of fall weather, so you would like different varieties maturing between mid-September and the end of November for a continuous supply.

When planting the basic fall garden one must account for the lettuce. Most loose leaf types mature in 40-55 days; the butter head in 55-65 days; the romaine in 65-75 days; and the iceberg type in 80-100 days. As in the broccoli example above, the earlier types (loose leaf, butter head and romaine) are planted in the spring garden to mature before hot weather and the fall garden would only include butter head, romaine and iceberg. Lettuce has **hot weather dormancy** so if you plant the seed directly into the soil in the heat of summer in hotter areas, it will not germinate and grow. Planted in the house into peat pellets it will come up in 4-5 days. The plastic lid on a peat pellet tray should be removed the day they come up and the tray placed out into full sun and watered daily. They should be planted into the soil within 10-14 days.

These cool weather fall garden crops will also handle a light frost without being damaged so you will be picking for an extended period. When night time temperatures go below 28 degrees F. more damage occurs but still some useable vegetables can be harvested. Of course, with the carrots, they are not damaged by these temperatures and can be left in the ground even under the snow and dug when needed until the warmer temperatures cause them to go to seed in the spring. Some prefer to cover them with grass clippings, hay or straw. Others dig and pit them.

In the longer season areas, vegetables such as corn and beans can be planted several times during the spring and early summer for a continuous supply throughout the season. In very hot areas pole beans and sweet corn are best planted as part of the fall garden. Excessive heat will keep the pole beans from setting a crop and the tassels blight on sweet corn. They should be planted in time to produce their crop before frost. Bush beans set their flowers in the shade so they will produce in excessive heat. Pumpkins and winter squash take so long to mature that they must be planted in the summer garden in order to be ripe by fall. **It should be noted that the Spring Garden will be harvested by mid-June so that the same area can be used for the Fall Garden.**

Planting Your Garden

This section is a step-by-step examination of the basic procedures which should be followed in planting a home vegetable garden. If carefully followed, you will have a successful experience with this endeavor. The basic steps in this process are as follows:

1. FERTILIZING
2. ROTOTILLING or SPADING
3. LEVELING
4. FURROWING
5. PLANTING
6. WATERING

BASIC FERTILIZING TOOLS

WHIRLWIND BROADCASTER

QUART BOTTLE

LAWN SPREADER

BUCKET

STEP ONE-FERTILIZING

If you have access to manure or decomposed organic material, it is helpful to put it on your garden in advance. For the most part though, the build-up of organic material is a long-term process. Read the section on IMPROVING THE SOIL for suggestions regarding this process.

If you have soil which has been enriched by organic materials, your job will be easier, but you should still follow the basic steps.

First Application

The most important time to apply fertilizer is before the crop is planted. At that time, it can be thoroughly mixed with the soil and it gives the seedlings vigor because they are filled with the proper nutrients from the time they sprout and begin to grow. It speeds them through the early stages when they are small and most susceptible to insect damage.

In preparation for planting in each section of your garden, before working up the soil, you should sprinkle onto your soil, in the form of commercial fertilizer, the nutrients which your plants will need.

A good balanced complete fertilizer which is right for most soils throughout the west is 16-16-8 (16% N, 16% Phos, 8% Pot) and Ironite. Read the extensive section on **Plant Food (Fertilizer)** and in particular, **Application of Commercial Fertilizer** on page **21** for a complete discussion of all of the plant nutrients and the **specific amounts to apply.**

This first application of fertilizer can easily be sprinkled onto the ground out of a quart bottle. The tilling or spading which follows will work it thoroughly into the soil.

Because in most western soils the main deficiency is in nitrogen and it is often very difficult to notice any effect on your garden of the other fertilizer elements mentioned above, some have thought to save money by only using a less-expensive high nitrogen fertilizer such as ammonium sulfate (21 %N.) and raise an acceptable garden without adding the other elements. But using a balanced complete fertilizer on a regular basis will prevent as well as avoid future deficiencies which would occur by gradual soil depletion. The yield will be larger and the quality better when this complete fertilizer is used every year with each crop. Except for nitrogen, these elements do not move much with the water in the soil, so they need to be thoroughly worked into the soil before you plant. (See FERTILIZER section starting on page 11 for additional information.)

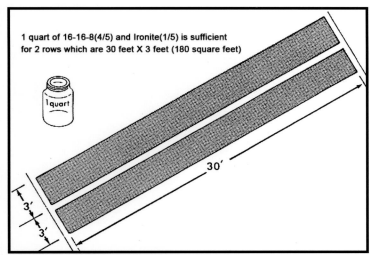

1 quart of 16-16-8(4/5) and Ironite(1/5) is sufficient for 2 rows which are 30 feet X 3 feet (180 square feet)

1 quart

30'

3'

3'

RECOMMENDED AMOUNT OF COMPLETE FERTILIZER. These amounts should be worked thoroughly into the root zone before planting.

HOW MUCH?

See page **21** under Application of Commercial Fertilizer for plant nutrients and the specific amounts to apply. The fertilizer can be applied either with a push-type lawn spreader, a cyclone-broadcasting type spreader or just sprinkled on by hand out of a quart bottle. The latter method is usually the best because it is the most precise. You will know how many square feet of soil you are covering so you can figure the exact number of quarts to apply. If the dimensions of your garden were 15 feet by 18 feet, you have 270 square feet. If you divide that by 180 square feet you will get 1½ so you know you need to cover the area with one and one half quarts of the complete fertilizer talked about above. If you have 10 feet by 12 feet of garden area (120 square feet) you divide by 180 and you know that you sprinkle two thirds of a quart over your soil. It is easy to sprinkle this **dry** fertilizer evenly out of a quart jar over the designated soil. The roto-tilling process mixes it thoroughly with the soil where it is placed.

It should be noted that the quart for 180 square feet is a rule of thumb which is normally followed but there are exceptions. If the soil has a lot of clay and is filled with lots of decomposed organic matter (humus) you will apply less than a quart. If the soil is sandy with very little humus, you will need to apply slightly more than a quart of fertilizer because sand is always lower in plant nutrients than clay. (See section

of the book on Soil.) A little common sense goes a long way in the garden.

Second Application

As noted in the Plant Food section of this book, with most plants under most conditions a crop only needs one application of fertilizer. A second application of fertilizer will actually reduce the yield and quality of most root and fruit crops. There are several exceptions wherein nitrogen-loving crops will benefit by a second small application of nitrogen fertilizer. These include corn, onions, broccoli, cauliflower and berries, especially if planted in sandy soil. Even in these crops a second application is not absolutely essential.

HOW TO APPLY

Nitrogen-type fertilizers are easy to apply to a growing crop because they are totally soluble. They must be applied with caution because they can cause serious damage to the crop if excessive quantities are used or if they are placed on the foliage. (See pages **22-24** for a discussion of salt burn and reverse osmosis caused by excessive amounts of fertilizer.)

This application of fertilizer can be made by putting a band of fertilizer down the length of the plant row 4-6 inches from the plants. For example, this band would be put on both sides of each row of corn when the corn is approximately 8-10 inches tall. Then it is watered into the soil by the use of a Rainbird (impact-type) sprinkler. This is better than a regular lawn sprinkler because it puts the water down slowly and there is no run-off. This way the fertilizer goes into the ground where you want it.

A second method of fertilizer application for growing crops is side-dressing. This is done by making a cut with a shovel about three-fourths of the way down the side of each furrow and placing the fertilizer in this trough. Then cover the trough back with dirt like it was before. When you water in the furrow, the fertilizer gradually dissolves and is carried by the water into the root zone. (See illustration.)

SECOND APPLICATION

BANDING

Approximately 1/2 to 2/3 cup of ammonium sulfate (21% Nitrogen) should be sprinkled in a two or three inch band down each side of a row of corn which is thirty feet long and three feet wide.

WATERING-IN

Pour fertilizer onto a diffuser every 15-20 minutes while watering. It will dissolve gradually and go wherever the water goes throughout the root zone.

The band of fertilizer should be at least four to six inches from the plants. It is watered into the root zone by soaking thoroughly (for one hour set on a quarter circle pattern) with an impact-type (Raindbird) sprinkler.

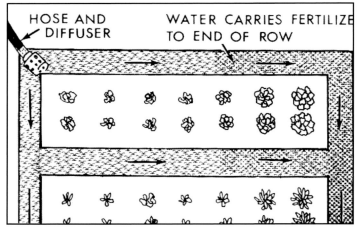

HOSE AND DIFFUSER

WATER CARRIES FERTILIZE TO END OF ROW

Don't pour fertilizer up and down the furrows because it will be carried to the bottom end of each furrow by the water, and the plants at the top will not get very much.

SIDE-DRESSING

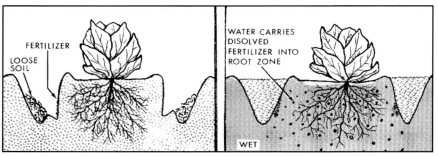

FERTILIZER

LOOSE SOIL

WATER CARRIES DISOLVED FERTILIZER INTO ROOT ZONE

WET

The water gradually dissolves the fertilizer during irrigation and takes it into the root zone.

The trough for the fertilizer is easily made with a shovel. The fertilizer is sprinkled into this trough, then the dirt is pushed back to it's original position.

Whether the second application is by banding, side-dressing, or mixing with the water, the amount should be approximately ½ to 2/3 the amount of fertilizer worked into the soil before planting the crop.

A third method, and the easiest to apply, is to sprinkle the fertilizer onto the diffuser end of the hose as you are watering. It will form a pile on each side of the diffuser head and gradually dissolve in the water as you irrigate. Once in solution, it goes with the water into the root zone. By replenishing the supply with a handful of fertilizer on the diffuser head approximately every fifteen minutes as you irrigate, the fertilizer will spread evenly down the furrows throughout the entire section. Don't pour the fertilizer up and down the furrows before watering because this does not distribute the fertilizer evenly. It will all be carried by the water to one end of the garden and the other end will get little or no fertilizer. (See illustrations on page **48** for further descriptions of these methods of application.)

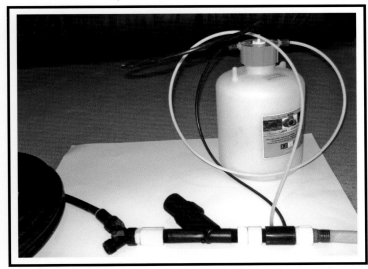

Place a dry soluble fertilizer like ammonium sulfate (21% N) or Grow More Soil Acidifier (30% N) in the gallon tank, fill it with water, and the siphon tubes will carry it into the drip pipes to the plant roots as you irrigate with the drip system.

If you are using a drip system to irrigate, the same dry fertilizer can be placed in a small gallon size water tank (see illustration) designed with siphon tubes which feed the dissolved fertilizer into the drip system where it is carried with the water into the soil to the roots of the plant.

QUANTITY

For this second feeding use approximately one half to two thirds of the amount of fertilizer you worked into the soil before planting, depending on your soil type, the crop involved, and the type of fertilizer used. As mentioned above, if the soil is sandy it is lower in nutrition so the 2/3 quart per 180 sq. ft. would be helpful. If the soil is clay, ½ quart is better. Ammonium sulfate is 21% Nitrogen so it is a good source for this second application. Ammonium Nitrate (33%) and Urea (45%) are so strong that they easily burn the plants so they should not be used.

Fertilizing Established Perennial Crops

Some crops stay in the ground year after year and need to be fertilized once each year. These crops include fruit trees like peaches, apples, and pears, as well as blackberries ('boysenberry' 'triple crown' etc.) raspberries and strawberries. Because you can't roto-till the fertilizer into the ground without destroying the roots, you need to use soluble forms of fertilizer. All nitrogen fertilizer is soluble and many farmers only use nitrogen fertilizer on these crops year after year. In some soils, deficiencies in other elements, such as phosphorous, potassium, iron, zinc and manganese make it necessary to find a soluble form for these plant nutrients that can be sprinkled on top of the soil and watered in.

The soluble forms which are presently available are in smaller quantities (up to 5 pound packages) and are more expensive. These come from companies like Grow More and Miracle Gro. The Miracle Gro Azalea Plant Food is practically identical to the Grow More Soil Acidifier except that the latter is more acidic, which is an advantage. They are both 30% N, 10% Phos, 10% Pot, .325% Iron, .05% Zn, .05% Mn, .05% Copper, 1% Sulfur, .02% boron and .0005% molybdenum.

The author uses a mixture of one third of the above product and one third ammonium sulfate (both of which are completely soluble) and one third Ironite (which is partially soluble) in a quart bottle and sprinkles it onto the ground in the berry patch and orchard in the same proportion as talked about before (1 quart for 180 square feet). If you are sprinkling it on out of the quart jar without measuring the area, pretend you are salting a steak and then you won't apply too much.

These crops need to be fertilized in the late winter or early spring while they are still dormant so the snow or rain will carry the material into the ground. If you fertilize later or if there is no rain, you can water them into the root zone with a Rainbird sprinkler.

STEP TWO ROTO-TILLING OR SPADING

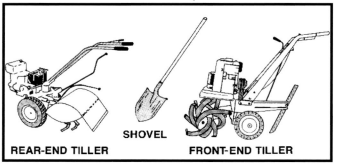

BASIC TILLING EQUIPMENT

REAR-END TILLER   SHOVEL   FRONT-END TILLER

Spading is a very difficult, time-consuming method of working your garden. It gets the job done if you do not have any better way, but unless you are talking about a very small flower bed or a very tiny vegetable garden you should consider a roto-tiller. There are usually several home gardeners in each neighborhood with similar needs who do not feel that they can afford the expense of a roto-tiller by themselves.

Spading, a slow and inefficient method of working the soil, is adequate for tiny gardens, but makes gardening difficult if you are working large areas.

The answer is to go together with three or four other families and divide the purchase price among you. A roto-tiller is much better than spading because it works the soil more thoroughly, completely mixing the commercial fertilizer and organic materials with the soil particles. It also mixes air into the soil and improves the soil texture. Renting a roto-tiller is another possible approach, but it is expensive.

The front end roto-tiller works the garden thoroughly and is affordable to most home gardeners. It is especially good in the smaller areas and tight places of the typical home garden.

How Wet?

If soil is too dry, it will be very hard to work and difficult to make the roto-tiller or spade go deep enough. The more common problem is to attempt working the soil too wet. This is harmful to soil texture and the soil does not break up well. It is gooey and messy and the soil tends to become compacted during the process. As it dries it ends up cloddy. It also doesn't level or furrow very well. The answer is to test the soil by turning over a shovelful. If it is gooey and slick and packs easily, it is too wet. A good rule to follow is: wait at least 4 to 7 days after thoroughly watering before working sandy soil and at least 7 or more days after watering before working clay soil. It should be moist, but not wet.

Work It Thoroughly

Roto-till or spade thoroughly to a depth of at least 8-12 inches. If your equipment will go deeper than 8 inches, that is even better. If there are large amounts of un-decomposed organic materials on the soil where you plan to plant a garden, it is beneficial to work these materials into the ground, then water the soil and let it lay until it is moist but not wet and roto-till it again. Keep the soil moist for a maximum decomposition rate. (See page **6** for a complete discussion of this process.) When you work the soil again after several weeks, you will be surprised how fast these materials have broken down into soil-building humus. Adding small amounts of nitrogen fertilizer will speed the process.

Front End vs. Rear End Roto-Tiller

A roto-tiller functions as both disc and plow in preparing your soil for planting. Either a tiller with tines in front of the wheels or behind them will do a good job. The front-end tiller costs less than half as much and functions better in tight places. The rear-end tiller can be operated with a great deal less effort and does a superior job of working into the soil large quantities of organic materials such as grass clippings, leaves, cover crops and corn stalks.

A tiller with tines at the rear is more expensive, but easier to use on hard jobs and large areas.

A rear end tiller also leaves the soil more smooth and flat without a lot of leveling needed before planting. If it is a larger (at least 8 H.P.) tiller, on the last pass over the soil you can walk beside the tiller and leave no footprints. If you are purchasing a rear-end tiller, look for one that is large enough (at least 8 horse power) and heavy enough to work the soil 8 inches deep. Also buy a roto-tiller with a furrowing attachment

available for the back. This saves the gardener from a lot of work in the process of making furrows. The author has had good experience with both Honda and Troybilt tillers. They are not the cheapest but with three or four families going together, it can be economical. Although the rear-end tiller is better for most purposes, the front-end tiller is adequate for most small backyard-type home gardens.

STEP THREE-LEVELING
BASIC LEVELING TOOLS FOR WATERING IN FURROWS

BASIC LEVELING TOOLS

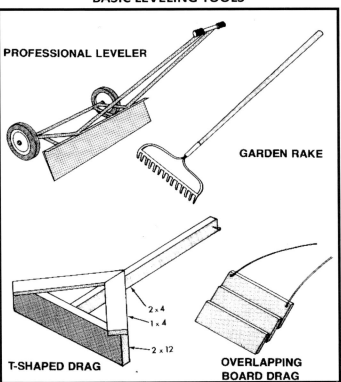

If you are going to irrigate in furrows, the process of making your soil both flat and level is very important. If a drip irrigation system is being used, a totally level garden is far less important. When this section was first written for the first edition, watering in furrows was far more common. It is still important to make furrows for walking but in most gardens you will probably use a drip system on the rows (raised beds) between the furrows for watering.

Leveling can be done with the flat edge of a garden rake or with some sort of leveler or drag which you can easily make at home out of left-over scraps of wood. (See illustration.) A landscaping rake is larger and can be very helpful in leveling. If you get your soil relatively flat and level at this point, you will save time and effort in the irrigation process later. Once you get it basically level so that it waters well, the job of leveling in later years will be easy.

Besides getting it relatively smooth and flat, should you actually try to get it totally level? The answer is that unless you are trying to work a fairly steep slope or hillside, you should try to get it level. It is not as hard as you may think. If you are watering in furrows, you will save a lot of water if the soil is level.

Getting It Level

Either with a homemade drag-type leveler or the more professional leveler-on-wheels which you can get from the local equipment rental, you can move the dirt from a high part of your garden to a lower area. Get a small carpenter's spirit level and tie it to the top of a 10 foot two by four. Lay it in several places in your garden and you will immediately see which direction it slopes and how much. If the slope is extreme, you may want to resort to terracing, but in most backyards a relatively flat spot which can be leveled is available for the garden.

For moving lots of dirt, this rented leveler is best.

Level for Easy Watering

Since your garden will be laid out with a small ditch at each end of the furrows tying them all together, you should run the furrows in such a way that there is no appreciable slope from one end to the other. You can have a small amount of slope on the ditches at each end and still regulate the flow of water from furrow to furrow with rocks, grass, and other obstacles, but each furrow should be basically level so that the water will stand at about the same height for the length of the furrow. By having them this way, you can **fill them very full** and they will soak across the row (raised bed) evenly and quickly.

By placing a carpenter's spirit level on any long straight piece of lumber, it is easy to tell which direction the ground slopes and get it very level.

Even the head ditch can be perfectly level, but a small amount of slope is acceptable. This relatively level garden will save water and make proper irrigation easier. There is virtually no wasted water.

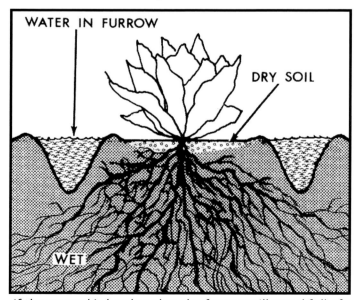

If the ground is level so that the furrow will stand full of water, the moisture moves more quickly across the row into the root zone.

Steeper Slopes

On steeper slopes where it would be extremely difficult to totally level the area, the soil can be terraced or furrowed or watered with an impact-type sprinkler as discussed on pages **68-69** under Watering a Hillside. They can also be terraced and watered with a drip system which will use less water and be more convenient. These methods are much more practical on a steep slope than a massive leveling project.

STEP FOUR-FURROWING

BASIC FURROWING TOOLS

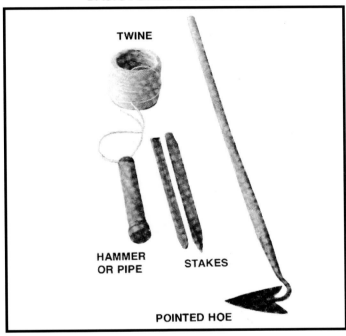

TWINE

HAMMER OR PIPE   STAKES

POINTED HOE

Now that the soil is relatively level and flat, the next step is furrowing. The basic tool is a pointed hoe. If you can get one with a wide spread it will give you a wider furrow which is easier to walk in. With this tool you can make a deep, straight furrow which is the same shape as the one made by a commercial grower with a tractor and other expensive equipment. If you have a roto-tiller with a furrowing attachment, the process of making furrows is very easy. Always fertilize and work the soil thoroughly before furrowing. If the furrows are not wide enough to walk in easily, you can widen them with a regular hoe.

Take two stakes (each 2 feet long) and tie a piece of twine the length of your furrows to each of them. Then drive one stake into the ground at each end

By putting a stake at each end with twine stretched tightly between, it is easy to make your furrows straight.

By using a chopping motion with the pointed hoe as you back up along the twine, you will make a straight, deep well-shaped furrow which will last for the life of the crop and make watering very easy.

of your garden so that the twine is stretched tightly between them about a foot or so from the ground. Then back up along the string chopping with the hoe as you move along. (See illustration.) You will make a nice, deep, straight furrow. Measuring from the stakes the width that you want your row to be, move both of them that distance so that your rows will be even at both ends. When all the furrows have been made the end ditches can be made in a similar fashion with a pointed hoe.

How Far Apart?

For most vegetables such as carrots and beets which will be planted in double or triple rows down the top of the raised bed, you will use a distance of 24 to 36 inches from the middle of one furrow to the middle of the next, depending on the space you have for a garden. For larger crops such as corn, cucumbers and string beans use 36 inch rows. Melons, winter squash and indeterminate (large plant) tomatoes should be planted on larger rows, 48 or more inches across, depending on the amount of space you have for a garden. For these wider rows a drip system needs to be used because in most soil, the water will not soak across a wide bed from the furrows. In many areas of the west, especially in shorter season areas, the melons and tomatoes are allowed to spread across a black plastic (polyethylene) film (mulch) with the drip lines

These furrows for a new bed of strawberries were easily made with a pointed hoe in a very few minutes. These strawberries are planted on 36 inch rows (36 inches from the center of one furrow to the center of the next).

2 ½ to 3 feet apart under the plastic. This brings the crop to maturity much earlier because of the increased heat from the plastic as well as using less water.

Why Use Furrows?
MOST IMPORTANT REASON

Even if you are watering with a drip system on the rows (raised beds) between the furrows, using furrows still offers great advantages. If people walk in the furrows, they stay off the raised beds and off the plants. Even small children can be taught to walk in the furrows. It also avoids compacting the soil in the areas where you want the roots of your plants to grow. Compaction collapses the pores reducing the air, water and root penetration of your soil.

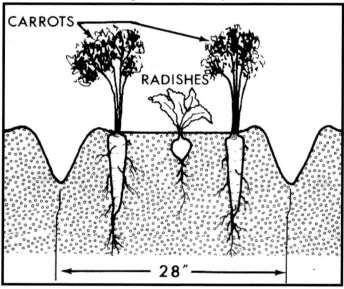

One 28 inch triple planted row (raised bed).

EASIER WATERING

There are many excellent reasons for using furrows. Although it takes some effort to make them originally once they are made it is one of the easiest ways to get the water where you want it. If you are watering with a hose in the backyard, all you have to do is put the diffuser on the end of the hose, put it into the end ditch and turn on the water. It will soon fill up the system of furrows. (See STEP SIX-WATERING METHODS on pages **64-72** for details about this process.) Furrows also, make the application of fertilizer very easy by sprinkling it onto the diffuser during the watering process.

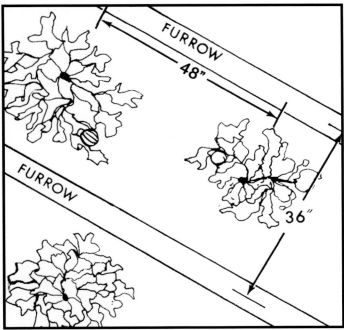
Cantaloupes planted on a 36 inch row should be spaced 4 feet apart down the center of the row.

SATISFY EACH PLANT'S NEEDS

Your garden will be laid out in small blocks of 4 or 5 rows with all of the furrows for the small system interconnected. In irrigating, you will fill the ditches and furrows in that section almost completely full and let the water stand for an hour or more until it has soaked adequately. In most ground you can see the soil get darker on the surface as the water soaks. It doesn't need to soak completely to the center on the surface because it soaks across faster in the root zones a few inches down.

Another system with 4 or 5 rows will start right next to the one just discussed but the ditches at each end should not connect the two systems. They are completely separate. In this way you can put the water-loving plants in one system and the deep, but infrequently watered plants in the next and irrigate each to suit its particular needs. There will be one row between the two systems which will be watered frequently by the furrow on one side and only about half as often by the furrow on the other. Crops like cucumbers and zucchini squash which will tolerate both types of watering can be planted in that in-between row.

DEEP ROOT SYSTEM

Many gardeners have a difficult time soaking thoroughly enough. The use of furrows is conducive to proper irrigation methods. Sprinklers often give the illusion that the soil is soaked when it is really only wet on the surface and the water is turned off before it soaks the root zone. By using furrows the gardener is inclined to soak deeply and thereby encourage a deep and extensive root system.

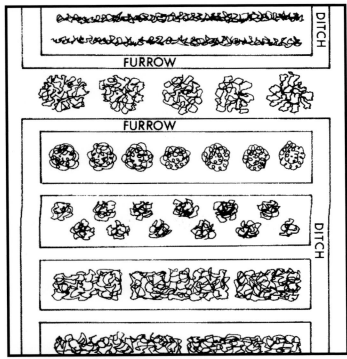
By planting the water-loving plants in a different system of furrows from the deeply but infrequently watered plants, you can easily irrigate to satisfy each plant's particular needs.

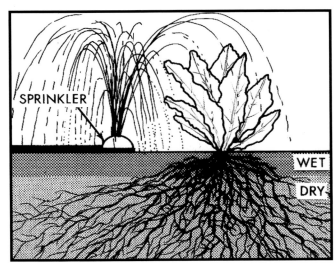
Watering with a sprinkler can give the misleading illusion that the soil is deeply soaked when it is really only wet on the surface. Furrow irrigation is conducive to deep, thorough watering.

AVOID FUNGUS DISEASES

By watering in furrows, you keep the leaves dry and thereby avoid fungus diseases. There are many plants, such as cucumbers, melons, and squash which will get powdery and downy mildew and get sick and/or die before the crop matures if you sprinkle the leaves regularly.

AVOID COMPACTION

Most soils can be packed very easily, particularly when wet. This is usually done by people walking through the garden and is particularly bad if they step near the plants when the soil is wet. Compaction reduces the air and water absorption of the soil and makes it very difficult for the roots to penetrate, particularly with a root crop like carrots. In compacted soil the carrots will be short and poorly formed.

By making furrows and planting on the tops of the rows between the furrows, you can walk in the furrows and totally avoid stepping on the ground which the plant uses for its roots. You can also teach your children (even very young ones) to walk in the furrows. This way, you not only avoid compacting the soil, but you keep them off the plants as well.

It is necessary to walk through the garden many times in the process of planting, weeding, harvesting, etc. If you do not have furrows, you will find that it is almost impossible to avoid the compaction problem. It is also almost impossible to keep the children from tromping down the tender plants when they are young. This system also helps you to get seedlings up because people don't walk over the top of them and make the soil so hard-packed that they cannot push through it.

Once you have started using furrows, whether you water in them or use a drip system and just walk in them, you will see how it solves the fungus disease and compaction problems as well as keeping the children off young plants, and you will never go back to gardening without them.

To avoid walking on plants and compaction problems, use furrows. Even small children can be taught to walk in the furrows.

STEP FIVE - PLANTING

BASIC PLANTING TOOLS

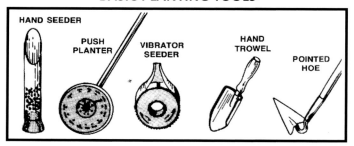

Why Transplants?

HEADSTART

There are several reasons to set out plants rather than seeding directly into the garden. The most important one is to get a head start on the season in areas where frost prevents earlier seeding directly into the ground. For example, by planting healthy tomato plants which are six weeks to two months old as soon as the danger of frost has passed, you gain at least a full month of production in a short-season area. By using hot caps you gain another two weeks.

HARD TO SPROUT

Some seeds require warm temperature for sprouting. If planted in cold, wet soil in the early spring, they just lie there and rot. For that reason, some vegetables such as peppers should be started indoors unless it is warm outside. Others, such as celery, have such tiny seeds that the seedlings will not push through crusted soil outside, and they are so small that they are very vulnerable to insects and fungus diseases for several weeks after they come up. Some crops like lettuce also have a hot weather dormancy but they come up in 3-4 days inside at 72 degrees F.

SPACING

If you are the kind of person who can't bear to pull up those beautiful plants in order to allow the proper space between them, then you should start the plants inside and when you plant them out you can space them properly without destroying any plants.

Celery is usually started as a transplant because the tiny seeds have a hard time coming up outside and it brings the crop to maturity earlier in the season.

Choosing Transplants

If you buy your transplants from the nursery, be **certain** to buy **young**, **healthy** plants and plant them in the garden as soon as possible. If you have had the experience of purchasing celery or lettuce, planting it in the garden, and then seeing it go directly to seed, you know that some plants have been growing in the nursery for a **long** time. Transplants should have a dark green color suggestive of vigorous, healthy growth. It

is also best to choose the stocky plants rather than the tall, spindly ones. Avoid older plants which are blooming or have woody, yellowish or mature-looking leaves, stems and branches. If you are in doubt, ask the nursery man in charge how long it has been since the plants were delivered to his place of business by the grower.

If possible, buy plants that have not been in the pony pack so long that they are "root bound" (the roots are wrapped around and around against the plastic container so they are not inclined to go out into your soil). If this is a problem, carefully pick the outside roots away from the root ball with an ice pick or other pointed object. If you overdo this process until the root ball falls to pieces, there will be so much "transplant shock" that the plant will lose a lot of time becoming established in the ground.

Growing Your Own Transplants

If you grow your own transplants you will know how old they are and can plant them out when they are young. You can also pick the very best varieties available, which is very often impossible if you buy transplants from the nursery. It is also much less expensive to purchase seeds and grow your own transplants. A pony pack of six lettuce plants will cost approximately $3.50 at the nursery. A packet containing approximately 1000 lettuce seeds will cost approximately $3.00 from a seed catalog. They come up quickly and easily under your own plant light and one $3.00 packet will last more than one year.

PLANTING

Containers for growing transplants can be pony pack containers from the nurseries, larger containers purchased for that purpose, the bottom half of two quart milk cartons, the bottom half of gallon plastic milk or water containers or large flats filled with peat pellets. Use **potting soil** (available at nurseries, hardware and home improvement and other variety stores) as a planting medium and be certain that all containers (except for peat pellets) have a hole in the bottom for drainage.

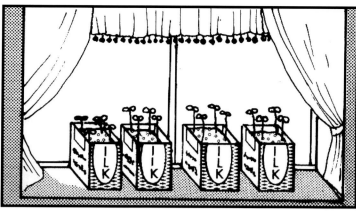

The bottom half of two-quart milk cartons make excellent containers for growing transplants indoors. Keep them moist, but don't over-water. Make a hole in the bottom for drainage.

Lettuce and broccoli in peat pellet trays ready to be planted into the fall garden.

The planting depth for seed in potting soil should be 3-4 times the size of the seed. For smaller plants like lettuce or broccoli which are planted outside within two or three weeks after sprouting, the peat pellets work fine. For plants like tomatoes, peppers and melons which stay in the pot a month or more and grow fairly large before planting out in the garden, the bottom of a two quart milk carton or gallon plastic milk container is better. If the pot is large enough, the plant does not get root bound before planting into the ground.

A quart plastic watering bottle with adjustable spout is helpful for watering. For most plants, the potting medium can be soaked after planting. For melons, squash and cucumbers it is better to soak thoroughly first and plant after 12 hours of drying. After planting, cover the pot with Saran Wrap until plants **begin to emerge**. In a similar way peat pellets in a covered tray are watered first and then planted and covered with the plastic top and not watered again until they come up. Water every couple of days as needed thereafter. As soon as seedlings emerge from the soil, if the weather is moderate, move them into full sun outside. This will keep them from getting tall and spindly from etiolating (tall, spindly, yellowish growth from lack of intense full spectrum light).

Lettuce seed has a "hot weather dormancy". If you plant the seed directly outside into the soil during the heat of summer for a fall garden and the temperature is over 85 degrees F., almost none of the lettuce seed will germinate. If you plant the same seed inside in peat pellets under a plant light at approximately 72 degrees F. it will be up and growing in 3- 4 days. Discard the cover of the peat pellet tray as soon as they come up, water them immediately and move them outside into direct sun. The cotyledons (seed leaves) will handle full sun in the heat of summer without sunburn as long as they are kept wet, watering them at least daily. They will grow fast and can be planted into the soil in 2-3 weeks. The above method can also be used for broccoli and cauliflower for the fall garden. If the weather is hot when they are moved into full sun, you will need to water at least once a day. If they have grown inside for more than a day or two they must be moved out gradually (see hardening).

When you start plants indoors, the lighting is very important. Some heat loving plants do well on a sunny window sill and other plants do better under a plant light. A plant light can be purchased from a nursery or seed catalog or home made. It is basically a 2 foot shop light with legs. It uses 2 foot fluorescent tubes, but they need to be "full spectrum" meaning they are similar to sunlight and have the same wavelengths as natural sunlight. These are available at Lowe's, Home Depot or any good hardware store. The planting container needs to be put close to the fluorescent tube (within 6 inches). This will keep them from etiolating and becoming tall and spindly. If planted inside for a fall garden, the plants should be moved out into full sun the day they come up as described under lettuce above. If started inside for a spring or summer garden, the weather may be too cold for moving outside immediately after germination, so they must be grown inside for a while and moved out gradually when the weather warms up (see hardening).

Some potting soil and certainly the peat pellets are lacking in nutrition. After the plants are up the author adds 1/16 to 1/20 (one sixteenth to one twentieth) teaspoon of fertilizer to the quart watering bottle each time he waters the transplants. The best fertilizer for this purpose is Grow More – All Purpose (15% Nitrogen, 30% Phosphorous, 15% Potassium, .10% Iron, .05% Zinc, .05% Manganese, 1% Sulfur, .02% Boron, .05% Copper, .0005% Molybdenum; OR Miracle Gro-Bloom Booster with basically the same formula.

After they come up, thin seedlings to 6 plants per pony pack or four plants (one for each corner) if you use the bottom half of a two quart milk carton. If this container is used for tomato plants, leave only one plant per milk carton. For melons or pumpkins leave only one plant in a gallon container. Be certain to punch a hole in the bottom of the container for drainage.

HARDEN THEM UP

Plants started indoors and grown there for more than a day or two are easily sunburned when moved outside and also susceptible to damage from wind and cold. They need to gradually become accustomed to the outdoor environment. This process of gradually exposing them to wind, sunlight, lower temperatures and other weather conditions is referred to as "hardening transplants."

HARDENING

This means gradually getting plants used to:

1. Sun (w/o sunburn)   3. Heat (w/o wilting)
2. Cold (w/o freezing)   4. Wind (w/o breaking)

As mentioned above, fall garden crops like lettuce, broccoli and cauliflower started inside in the summer can be moved out into direct sunlight the day they come up, so no hardening is necessary. On the other hand spring and summer garden crops, planted inside in the late winter may have to be kept inside for weeks because of cold weather so gradually hardening them when it is warm enough to move them outside is definitely necessary. These plants which have been grown inside are soft and vulnerable to outside weather conditions, especially if they have been watered excessively inside.

Move them out into the sun onto the south side of the house in stages, for example: one hour the first day, two on the second, three on the third, four on the fourth and then all day. If the weather is extremely windy on a particular day, put them where they are protected from the worst of the wind. After all day exposure to the sun, they are ready to plant into the garden.

The **warm weather** crops like tomatoes, squash, peppers, melons, etc. should always be brought back into the house at night during this hardening process until the night time temperatures stay above 50 degrees F. because they are susceptible to **chilling injury** below 50 degrees F. even without freezing weather. On the other hand, when hardening the **cold weather crops** like lettuce or broccoli for a spring garden, you are not only hardening against wind and sun but against cold also. They might be planted in mid-March in Utah County and be exposed to both freezing weather and snow. This doesn't bother them if properly hardened.

Watch the weather reports. Leave them out into the evening until it gets down to 40 degrees F. and then down to 35 degrees F. for a few evenings and finally against the south side of the house down to about 32 degrees F. overnight for a few nights before planting into the garden. They can then handle down to 28 degrees F. but if it gets down to 25 degrees F. even the cold weather crops will be damaged. In more moderate climates the severe cold hardening regimen can be modified.

In moderate climates most plants can be moved out without as much gradual hardening if they are put against the house where they get some protection from cold at night and only one or two hours of sunlight during the daytime. Then after a week in that location they can be moved into full sun for a day or two before planting.

Tomatoes, peppers, squash, melons and other warm weather crops will be killed by frost (freezing temperatures). They should be hardened gradually before planting out as described above. If the nights become cold after they are in the garden, give them protection from the cold at night (like putting a cardboard box over them).

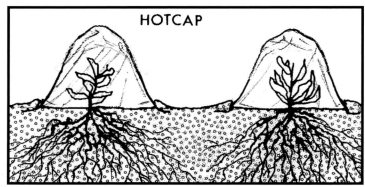

Hot caps keep tomato plants warm in cold spring weather.

HOT CAPS

There are many types of coverings designed to protect plants from cold weather and bring them to maturity earlier in the season. Hot caps work very well on tomatoes. Hot caps are used during the spring after daytime temperatures have begun to warm to approximately 65-70 degrees F. and the nights are not too cold (35-55 degrees F.) but there is still some danger of frost (32 degrees F. and below) and some nights cold enough to cause some chilling injury (below 50 degrees F.) to warm weather crops like tomatoes. The temperature inside the cap is warmer and is much more consistent than outside.

Always water the plant deeply before applying the cap. As is mentioned elsewhere the tomato is planted deep with only about 6 inches being out of the ground. When putting the hot cap over the plant it is important to notice that it has a flange around the bottom which sticks straight out. This flange is to be covered with soil to hold the hot caps down so they

don't blow away in the wind. If the soil on this flange is sprinkled with water right after application, it will stick to the hot cap and even hard winds will not affect it.

After a few weeks, when the danger of frost has passed and the plants begin to push against the inside of the hot cap, cut with scissors north to south from the ground across the top of the cap to the ground on the other side and open it an inch or so. After a day or so, open it 3-5 inches. The sun, going from east to west, will shine on various parts of the plant as it goes across the sky. The plant is thus acclimated to the sun and wind and the cap can be removed after 4 or 5 days without sunburn.

There are many other types of coverings designed to protect plants from the cold weather and bring them to maturity earlier in the season. Wall-O- Waters are a circle of plastic tubes which are partially filled with water and put over the top of plants. They protect the plants from freezing weather and hold the heat even better than hot caps but are harder to use. They tip over in windy areas and in soft soil. They are also harder to remove gradually as we did with hot caps to prevent sun and wind burn.

Seeds vs. Plants

Tomatoes, peppers, eggplants and celery are almost always started as transplants. Broccoli, cauliflower,

Standing in the regular furrows, you can use a pointed hoe to make a tiny furrow for planting down the center of the row.

cabbage and lettuce are started as transplants during early spring weather when the germination would be poor outside. They can also be started as transplants at other times of the year, but some prefer planting the Cole crops out directly from seed in warm weather. Lettuce is also started inside during the summer because of hot weather dormancy.

You may wonder whether it is beneficial to use transplants for such things as corn, spinach, radishes, beets, and beans etc. The answer is no. For example, with spinach and radishes, the seeds germinate well in the cool ground of the early spring, so there are no advantages and a lot of disadvantages to starting them inside. With regard to the rest of these vegetables, they are large-seeded and come up with a great deal of vigor. They have a lot of food stored in the seed which feeds the seedling as it sprouts and pushes through the surface. They come up in a week and grow quickly after they emerge. During this period the roots grow even more quickly than the tops and often go a foot or so deep in the first few weeks. This depth of root system and vigor are lost if you start them inside or buy them as transplants from the nursery and you permanently stunt the plant if you start them in a pot. By planting and watering properly it is relatively easy to get a good stand of these plants and a lot of time is saved by planting them directly outside.

In long season areas, crops like cucumbers, melons, squash and pumpkins should also be planted directly outside. In short season areas where it is important to get a head start on the season, it is helpful to start them inside and then plant them into the soil as established plants after hardening them up. If you grow them in large enough pots, two quart to one gallon milk cartons, they can get quite large without being root bound and there is virtually no transplant shock.

How Deep to Plant

Usually planting depth should be three to four times the diameter of the seed. For example, large seeded crops like corn, beans and peas should be planted approximately one inch deep in sandy or loamy soil and three fourths of an inch deep in clay. Cucumbers, melons, and squash should be planted

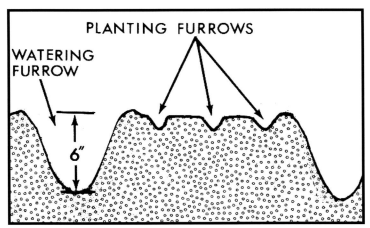

Small planting furrows can be made in a similar manner to the depth needed for the particular seed and in various places down the top of the row. After planting, push the soil over the top of the seeds to the proper depth and firm lightly.

approximately 3/4 inch deep and crops like beets, Swiss chard and spinach should be planted ½ inch deep. Small seeded crops like carrots, lettuce, tomatoes and peppers should be planted approximately 1/4 inch deep (slightly shallower in clay).

Hills vs. Rows

As used in gardening books, the term "hills" refers to groups of seeds or plants in close proximity rather than mounds of soil. You may have been advised to plant some things like corn in hills with the idea of leaving two or three plants to mature in each hill. This is not an efficient use of either root area or sunlight. The plants are too close together and the roots are trying to share the same space and compete for the same nutrients. The plants are over-crowded so that each is deprived of sunlight.

A much better method of planting corn (also peas, beans and other vegetables) is to make a small furrow with a pointed hoe or shovel about 1 inch deep in the center of the top of the row (raised bed) and plant the corn seeds about 2-3 inches apart in that small furrow. When they come up, thin the corn to about 8-12 inches apart depending on the size of plant of that particular variety (early ones are smaller). If you prefer to plant the corn in hills, space the hills 8-12 inches apart, planting approximately 3 seeds per hill, and thin the plants to **one plant** in each hill when they come up. This way you have them well-spaced for maximum efficiency in the use of soil and sunlight.

Cucumbers, squash and melons should be planted in hills (groups of seed) (use a small hand hoe for pulling back the dirt) putting 4 or 5 seeds in each spot. When they come up thin first to two plants, and after they are larger and have started their third set of leaves, thin to one plant per hill.

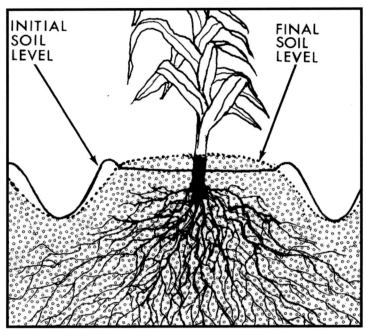

Crops such as corn and potatoes are planted down the center of the row. During the hoeing process when corn is about one foot tall, the furrows can be widened and the excess dirt hilled up around the plant. The potato hills can be higher, providing loose dirt in which the tubers grow.

Where on the Row to Plant

Large, tall-growing plants like corn and pole beans should be planted down the center of a 36 inch row (36 inches from the middle of one furrow to the middle of the next). As you hoe the weeds in the corn, when the plants are about one foot tall, you should widen the furrow using the excess soil to raise the level on top of the row around the corn. (See illustration.) This will make the furrows easier to walk in and the children will have a marvelous time playing games in the tall corn. It also puts the soil where it is needed and helps give the corn stability against strong winds. Wherever the base of the corn stalk is covered with dirt it puts out prop or brace roots which strengthen the plant against the wind.

Plant potatoes approximately four inches deep and one foot apart down the center of the row. When the potato plant is about 6-8 inches tall, the furrow should be widened and the excess soil mounded up around the potato plant, even higher than with corn, because the potatoes are formed on stolens growing off the stem rather than the root portion of the potato plant. They will form in this loose dirt which has been hilled up around the plant. Another method is to put six inches of mulch (grass clippings or straw) down the top of the row on each side of the potato plant. The potatoes will form in this straw as well as right under the surface of the ground and can be easily "dug".

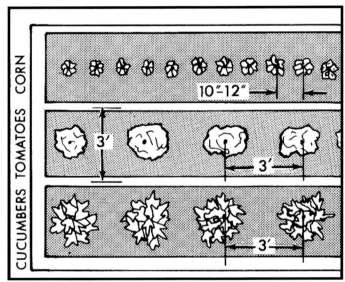

Many crops are best planted down the center of a three foot row. Healthy plants need plenty of space and should be given elbow room

Semi-determinate (bush) tomatoes and cucumbers can also be planted down the center of a 36 inch row. They should be planted at least 3 feet apart to give them room enough to spread. Melons should be planted down the center of a wider bed because they need more room to spread. (For detailed description of planting methods for each vegetable see the CULTURE OF INDIVIDUAL CROPS section.)

Double or Triple-Row Planting

The smaller vegetables should be planted down each side of the row. If transplanting lettuce, for example, plant on each side but stagger the planting so that the plants are not directly across from each other. (See illustration.) The same would be true of cauliflower, cabbage, and broccoli but they need more room than lettuce.

Beets can be planted between rows of carrots and pulled to use as beet greens when very small. This helps the carrots by loosening the soil and giving them room to expand.

After pulling the beet greens the carrots can be weeded with a hoe or knife. As the carrots grow, they provide dense shade which retards and almost eliminates the growth of weeds.

Plant bush peas, carrots and beets in triple rows, as indicated in the illustration. It is recommended, if you like beet greens as our family does, to plant the beets going down the center between the two rows of carrots. When the center row is approximately 6 to 8 inches tall you start pulling the plants in that center row for beet greens. (Carefully wash the dirt off the small roots and cook the whole plant like spinach.) This loosens the soil in addition to giving you an extra crop. By the time the two side rows grow to maturity (carrots or peas) the beets are all gone. Radishes are often planted in the center row in a similar manner. They mature very quickly before the side rows get large and grow over the top of them. For this kind of triple row planting, the distance from the middle of one furrow to the middle of the next should be approximately 30 to 36 inches. For staggered planting of head lettuce a 28 inch row is adequate, but for the larger vegetables such as cabbage, cauliflower and broccoli, a 36 inch row is necessary for staggered planting.

A great advantage of double or triple row planting is that it makes weeding very easy. With either a full-sized or hand hoe you can walk down the row (raised bed) with one foot in each furrow and quickly hoe out all of the weeds on the row as well as those in the furrow. When the carrots, beets, lettuce and other crops get larger they will cover the entire top of the row and also extend out over the furrows, so after one or two weedings, there will be enough shade to almost eliminate future weeds. Because of the orderly spacing between rows of plants when they are young, weeding with a tool such as a hoe is easy.

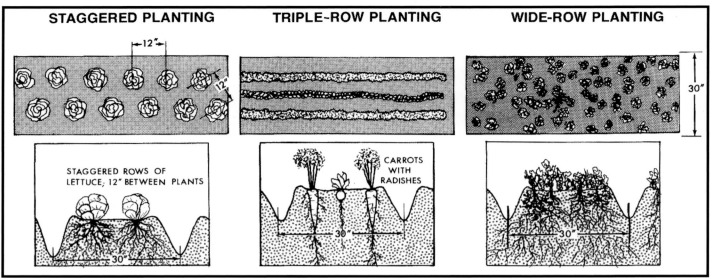

| STAGGERED PLANTING | TRIPLE-ROW PLANTING | WIDE-ROW PLANTING |

Staggered planting is designed to get maximum exposure of the plant to sunlight and root areas without crowding them. With triple row planting, the center row is usually a crop that can be removed earl, allowing the other two rows to expand as they grow. You can then mulch between the double rows. Wide row planting allows a lot of plants in a small space, but it is hard to weed and impossible to mulch.

Wide-Row Planting

So-called "wide-row" planting has been highly recommended in several gardening books. This method means that you sprinkle your seeds randomly across the top of the raised bed. Then you cover them up with soil by raking them with the tines of a garden rake. When the seeds come up they are thinned by dragging a garden rake, tines down, through the "wide row" which eliminates a lot of the plants. They can be further thinned as they get larger by harvesting them for the table. Others are allowed to fully mature.

In most situations, there are several serious problems with this method of planting. The most serious is the great difficulty which you have in trying to weed this wide-row area. You have to do it almost entirely with your fingers because the plants are not in any orderly pattern and a hoe would eliminate the plants along with the weeds. Most home garden areas have not been carefully gardened for enough years to eliminate the weeds, so the inability to weed with a hoe is a very serious problem with wide-row planting.

A second difficulty with wide-row planting is that it is impossible to regulate the depth at which you plant the seeds because they are just raked into the surface soil so you must plant a larger quantity of seed in order to get a good stand. Even then they can come up in patches here and there with open spaces between.

If the plants are thinned with a garden rake as is often recommended, the roots of the plants which you leave are sometimes damaged in the process of eliminating other plants. There is also a tendency to leave plants far too thick in this wide-row planting because they are not planted in a regular, systematic pattern. Because of this thick planting over a rather wide area, there is limited air circulation among the plants and fungus diseases such as powdery and downy mildew can become a problem.

If you feel that you can solve the above problems, experiment with wide-row planting to see how it works in your garden. The vegetables most often recommended for wide rows are peas, carrots, beets and onions.

STEP SIX-WATERING METHODS

It should be noted that the following section about using furrows was written 32 years ago as part of the first printing of this book before **drip/trickle irrigation systems** became such an important part of modern agriculture. Today in watering home gardens the drip systems discussed hereafter are **more frequently used**

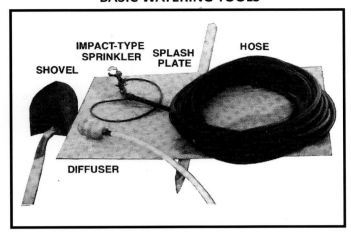

than watering in furrows, but the furrows are still needed to walk in and to create the rows (raised beds) where the fruits and vegetables are planted. **Go to the end of this section for a discussion of drip systems.** In commercial agriculture almost all crops are planted with furrows and raised beds and the irrigation is done with drip systems on top of the raised beds or in the furrows, depending on the crop.

Using Furrows

One of the reasons for choosing furrow irrigation is that it is an easy and inexpensive way to soak thoroughly and to get the water where it will do the most good. It also avoids wetting the foliage thus causing less fungus disease. For these and other reasons discussed in the FURROWING section, home gardeners should consider watering in furrows for their vegetable crops. They are easy to make and

One section can be watered while keeping another section dry.

they simplify the watering process. Furrows make it easy to water one section of the garden frequently while keeping another section dry, and avoid the wasting of water. (See page **53** for easy methods of making furrows.)

DIFFUSER ON A HOSE

To fill the furrows with water, put a diffuser on the end of the hose and place it in the head ditch. The diffuser keeps the water from digging holes when a large stream is used. If the entire system including the end ditches and furrows is level, they will fill to near the top of the furrow with water and you can then turn the water pressure down so the furrows will stay full without run-off and let it soak.

A diffuser on the end of the hose allows you to turn on a large stream of water without digging holes. The pressure should be reduced when the furrow is full. The furrow should be kept full for at least one hour.

If the head ditch is sloped, it is necessary to use some obstacle such as rocks, grass or straw to divert the water into the furrows. (See illustration.) It is best to have the furrows as level and flat as possible for maximum water penetration across the row. If the furrows are sloped too much it is better to use a **drip system** for watering.

LET IT SOAK

The question of how long to let the water run into the furrows depends on several factors. If the soil is sandy it soaks downward much faster than clay soils but more expansive clay soils tend to have more capillarity and soak across the bed faster, especially if filled with organic material. With all textures of soil, clay, silt sand or loam, water penetrates faster if the soil is filled with texture-improving humus. As previously mentioned, if the land is level, so that the water will stand high in the furrows, it will soak faster. Please note that the first time a crop is watered it takes longer than subsequent waterings.

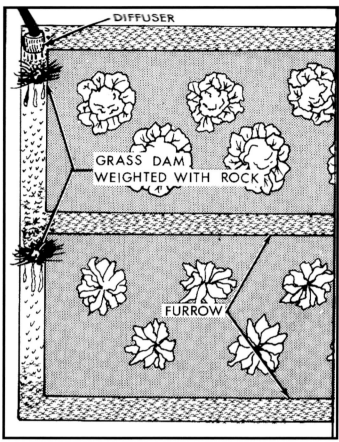

If the ground is not level, you can use rocks, grass, straw, or other obstacles to divert the water into the furrows.

The basic rule is to let it soak at least an hour with the furrow full on level ground in good condition before turning the water off. If the furrows are sloped or the soil is lacking in organic matter or the texture is poor, it will take much longer.

The water soaks faster across the row a few inches down than it does on the surface so it isn't necessary to wait until the surface is soaked completely across the row before turning the water off. It often soaks to the surface during the hour or so after the water is shut off. It also continues to soak across the row after being shut off. The first time you water after planting,

you should let it soak until the darker, wet area on the surface goes over to where the seeds are located. After the seedlings come up, it is usually adequate if the darker, wet area on the surface goes to the plants when you turn the water off.

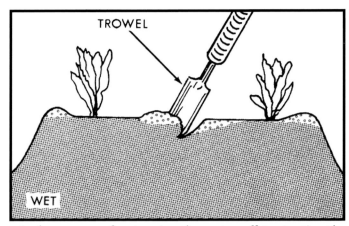

An hour or so after turning the water off, try testing the soil 4-6 inches deep with a gardening trowel to see if it is soaked to the center of the row.

Experiment with your soil by testing the center of the row a few hours after the water is shut off to see if it is wet a few inches under the surface. This will tell you if it is soaked throughout the root zone. Remember that deep watering encourages an extensive healthy root system.

HOW OFTEN?

Many vegetables like beans and corn and other crops picked as immature fruit do best watered about once a week, but this varies with climate and weather conditions, the type and condition of the soil involved, and the type of vegetable being grown. Study the **Basic Watering (Irrigation) Principles** section and specifically the **Watering Schedule** on page **27** for a complete list of the water needs of all the basic fruit and vegetable crops.

There are also cool weather, water-loving plants which do better if watered twice a week, especially in hot weather. These are the leaf crops, such as lettuce, spinach, Swiss chard, celery; the root crops like beets, turnips, carrots, radishes (plus potatoes); the Cole crops like cabbage, broccoli and cauliflower; and the berries. In the cool or wet weather of the early spring even the leaf and root crops will go a week or longer between waterings.

The more deep rooted, hot weather crops like tomatoes, melons, fruit trees and grapes do better on a 10 day-2 week watering schedule. They root down 8-12 feet in good soil (deeper for fruit trees in good soil).

Impact Type (Rainbird) Sprinklers

This type of sprinkler is excellent because it puts down the water softly and slowly without run-off. It is especially good for watering the garden the first two or three times after planting until the seedlings come up. Thereafter, the increased possibility of fungus diseases resulting from overhead sprinkling should be taken into account. (See discussion under FUNGUS DISEASES on page **30.**)

Impact-type sprinkler (Rainbird) puts the water down softly and slowly without run-off.

If the Rainbird sprinkler is put on a circular metal stand and attached to the end of a hose, it can be moved to where it is needed in the garden.

SPLASH PLATES

With any sprinkler, especially impact types, it is difficult to water one area of the garden without wetting the leaves of the row of vegetables next to it with the over-spray. Often the sprinkler is watering the lawn, but the over-spray onto the foliage of nearby squash and melons is enough to promote mildew-type fungus diseases.

Splash plates are easy to build out of scrap lumber. Nail a 4 foot stake onto a 2 foot X 4 foot piece of plywood.

One answer is to put lawn sprinklers along the edge of the garden pointing away from the garden. Splash plates can then be used to avoid the over-spray problem mentioned above. These are constructed with a 2 foot by 4 foot piece of plywood nailed onto a

The stake can be put through (or next to) the wire ring holding the sprinkler. The splash plate keeps the "overspray" from the sprinkler off the leaves of garden plants in order to avoid fungus diseases.

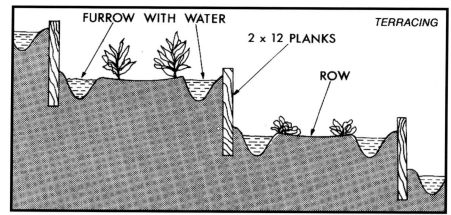

By terracing and watering in furrows, you can soak deeply and keep the foliage dry.

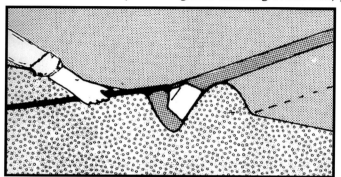

Make furrow on slope with a regular hoe. Pull all of the dirt out on the downhill side of the furrow.

A feeder pipe with a hole for every furrow is one way of watering a slope.

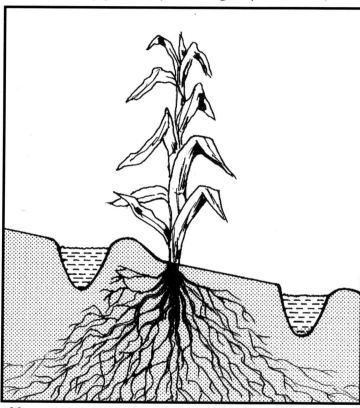

If furrow runs across the slope, the water soaks the root zone quicker because it stands deep in the furrow.

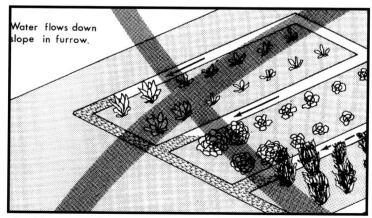

Avoid running furrows down the slope.

4 foot (2 inch x 2 inch) stake. (See illustration.) This can be placed through the wire ring stand or next to it so that the over-spray from the sprinkler is deflected away from the garden.

Watering a Hillside or Slope

Terracing is one solution to hillside watering. (See illustration.) With terracing, the ground can be furrowed and deep watered without wetting the leaves.

Another way, if your slope is not too steep, is to make the furrows run perpendicular to the direction of the slope so that they are relatively flat and level and the water will stand the length of the furrow and soak. If you make the furrows run down the slope, the water will tend to run very fast without soaking in. To avoid excessive run-off and erosion, it will be necessary to make the stream of water very small and the furrows quite close together, but it may still take several hours to soak across the row (raised bed). By watering in furrows running across the slope, you will get good water penetration into the root zone without wetting the leaves. (See illustration.) In order to fill the furrows with water you can use a pipe down one end of the garden with holes cut for each furrow. Another way is to use a small head ditch with straw or grass clippings partially covered with dirt at each furrow outlet in order to back the water up and avoid erosion.

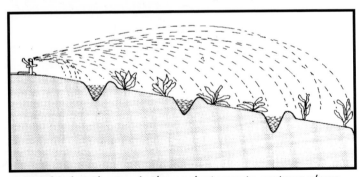

A Rainbird at the top is the easiest way to water a slope.

A third method of watering on a slope is by sprinkling with an impact type (Rainbird) sprinkler. A Rainbird sprinkler on a metal wire platform attached to the hose and placed at the top of the slope is probably the easiest way to water a slope or hillside. It can be easily moved, if necessary, to the proper place for best coverage. There won't be any run-off, even on a steep hillside, because the water is laid down so

slowly over a large area that it soaks in as it comes down. For many crops this is a very successful method of irrigation which can be used without a lot of hassle in re-leveling or terracing a steep area, but fungus-prone vegetables should be watered the first thing in the morning so they dry out during the heat of the day and don't stay wet all night. **A fourth method** of watering is a **drip/trickle irrigation system.** It has many advantages including being the **easiest to use,** using the least **amount of water,** keeping the **furrows dry** for walking, etc.

BASIC PARTS OF DRIP SYSTEM

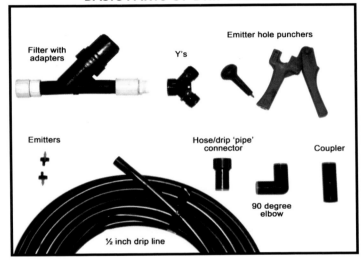

DRIP IRRIGATION SYSTEMS

There are many types of drip irrigation systems. The easiest to use in the garden is a system with one half inch black polyethylene **drip pipe** and an **emitter** inserted every foot along the line. Some systems have the emitters already built into the drip line but they won't last as long because there is no way to replace an emitter that gets clogged up. There are many brands of emitters. The author likes the two-gallon per hour emitters sold by Rainbird which are pressure-regulated, meaning that between approximately 30-50 PSI (pounds per square inch of water pressure) the amount of water coming out of each emitter per hour is about two gallons.

A small tool can be purchased for punching holes into the drip line where the emitters can be pushed in, or another tool hooks right onto the emitter so the sharp side of the emitter can be pushed into the line. It should be noted that the reason for putting one emitter every foot down the drip line is to soak the **root zone.** When people ask "Why not just put one emitter at each plant?" one wonders if that person really believes that the plant only has one root going straight down from the spot where the plant comes out of the ground, which of course is ridiculous. The roots of most plants spread **more extensively than the tops,** so it is necessary to water the root zone for a large healthy plant.

In the process of making the furrows, the dirt is pushed up making a berm (ridge) along each edge of the raised bed. When growing a crop like strawberries, you have two rows of plants, one down each side of the raised bed. The drip pipe with emitters every foot is placed between the berm and the row of plants on each side of the raised bed (See illustration on this page). The emitters one foot apart in the two drip lines down the top of the bed will soak the entire soil profile in about one hour under most conditions on a raised bed about 24 inches across the top from berm to berm.

There are fittings available to connect two pieces of drip pipe (**couplers**). Other fittings turn the pipe around at the end of the row and send it back on the other side of the raised bed (a 90 degree angle **elbow**)

Setting up your drip irrigation system properly can save you hours of time. This entire area of the fall garden (carrots, beets, lettuce, broccoli and cauliflower) and strawberries, raspberries and blackberries is watered by turning on one faucet which runs drip lines (one on each side of each raised bed) for each crop. Notice that the ever bearing raspberries in the background are thick with 5-6 foot canes. They were mowed to the ground in March

and **hose/drip pipe connectors** to hook the drip pipe to a hose.

The drip system is hooked to a regular garden hose at one end, but a **filter** with a 200 mesh screen (75 micron filter) is inserted between the hose and the drip pipe to take out small particles that would clog the emitters. If the filter has pipe threads rather than the standard hose threads, get an **adapter** for each end so that it will screw onto a hose or a **Y** or the drip pipe. The filter may be one that has a pressure regulator built in which keeps the water pressure at approximately **40 PSI** which is about right for the drip system. The author uses a hose Y with small spigots to regulate the water pressure to 40 lbs. The hose Y's can also be used on the drip pipe side of the filter so you can hook up two or three or four or more drip lines from the same hose running through the same filter. At the end of

The hose coming from the faucet is attached to the filter (with adapters on each side) and from the filter through the Y's which divide the water into four drip pipes. Notice that the first two drip lines run down each side of the bed of carrots, lettuce and broccoli. The other two drip lines run down each side of the next raised bed of the fall garden.

the drip line kink the line back on itself and tie it off with electrical or duct tape or green plastic plant tie.

This type of drip system can be used for years because the screen in the filter can be removed and cleaned when necessary and it keeps the emitters from becoming clogged. If they do clog up, a new emitter can be put into the line next to the clogged one. The filter should be cleaned at least once a year, but if your source of water is cloudy or has sand or other debris, clean as often as needed to maintain at least 40 PSI on the emitters. Be certain that the screen in the filter is not larger than 200 mesh in order to keep the emitters clean.

In using a drip system the watering schedule is important so refer again to **Watering Schedule** on page **27.** The frequency of irrigation effects the length of time you let the water run for a particular crop. For example, strawberries are watered twice a week in warm weather so the bed stays relatively wet. For that reason it doesn't take as long to soak the bed as it does for tomatoes which are only watered every 10 days to 2 weeks (the top of the bed down 2-3 feet gets dryer). It is also true that if the drip lines are further apart it takes longer to soak the beds than when they are close together.

For that reason a double row of strawberries (watered **twice a week**) that has the drip lines approximately **12 inches apart** will water in about **45 minutes-1 hour**, whereas if you were watering that same bed **every two weeks** it would take a lot longer to soak. A double row of broccoli with drip lines **22 inches apart** which is watered **twice a week** will take approximately **1 ½ hours** to soak. If you were watering the same bed (drip lines **22 inches apart**) planted to a row of semi determinate (medium bush) type tomatoes being watered every **10 days** it would take **two hours or more** to soak because you are watering less frequently and more deeply.

This row of pole beans is being watered by two drip lines with 2 gallon per hour emitters every foot down each line. The two lines are located just inside the berm (ridge), down the top of the bed. As always, the drip system includes a hose from the faucet, a filter (200 mesh screen), and a Y into the drip lines.

The yellow hose comes from the faucet, through the filter (with adapters on both sides) through the Y's directing the water into three streams which are carried to the drip pipe by yellow hoses. Notice that rebar is connected to the drip line on each end of the tomato patch so that the pipe stays straight in the heat. The drip lines are 3 feet apart under the black plastic.

If you were growing indeterminate tomatoes (large viney plants like 'Better Boy' or 'Big Beef') which are watered **every two weeks** and you have laid out your drip system with three drip lines separated **three feet apart** and the tomato plants spread out 10 feet wide, you will let the drip system run approximately three hours in order to soak the entire root system which is about 8-9 feet wide and 10 feet deep. All of the above calculations are for a drip line with 2 gallon per hour emitters spaced one foot apart and the water pressure is approximately 40 PSI (pounds per square inch). If you don't have a 40 PSI pressure regulator in your filter or inserted separately in the system, you can use a Y to control the pressure to approximately 40 PSI. By observing the emitters as you turn the pressure on and off with the Y, you will notice that the 2 gallon per hour pressure regulated Rainbird emitter goes from a slow drip to a stream shooting out (even beyond one inch if the pressure is high enough). Turn it down with the Y until it is coming out faster than a drip (i.e. a trickle) but not flowing out (if the emitter is horizontal) more than about 1/16th to 1/8th of an inch. It will then be within the range (30-50 PSI) where the emitter with regulate to about 2 gallons per hour.

The above described watering times depend somewhat on the severity of the weather and the type of soil involved but they assume warm summer weather in each case.

Watering by Hand

Avoid watering directly with a hand sprinkler nozzle on the end of a hose. (See diagram.) It will pack your soil, and if you are trying to get seeds up, it will be hard to get them through the crust which is formed by this kind of watering. Watering by hand in this manner does not soak deeply enough to really benefit the plant unless you stand for a very long period of time, and the tendency is to just water the top inch or so and not really soak down into the root zone. Along with the problems of packing the soil, making a crust, and watering too shallow, this method of watering often digs holes and uproots the very seedlings you are trying to protect. Instead, use as a drip system, water in a furrow or use an impact-type sprinkler which throws the water into the air and allows it to settle lightly to the ground in small drops. This will not pack the soil,

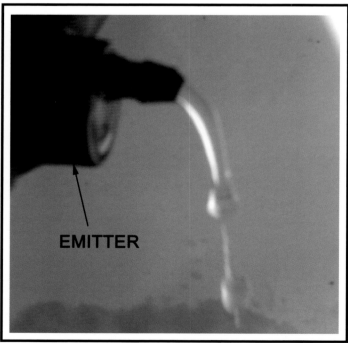

In using Y's to regulate pressure to 40 PSI, water should come out about 1/16 inch in a stream (trickle), not a drip, but the stream becomes fast drops as it falls to the ground.

EMITTER

1.NOT THIS WAY! It digs holes and wets the surface without soaking the root zone. Watering this way with a hose also creates a crust, thus making it hard for seedlings to come up.

will not encourage wasteful run-off of water, and can be allowed to soak long enough to really put the water where you want it.

Watering After Planting

TRANSPLANTS

It is important to water your transplants thoroughly right after planting, preferably by applying water right around the base of the plant. This settles the dirt down around the roots as well as supplying the plant with the needed water. A transplant will need more water than usual because it has probably lost some roots as well as having the soil disturbed in the area around the roots during the transplanting process. In order to avoid wilting, the soil should be soaked immediately after planting. The recommended procedure for tomatoes is to prune off the lowest branches and plant deep enough so that only about 6-8 inches at the top of the plant will protrude out of the soil. The tomato plant will put out new roots all along the buried stem. Most other crops are planted only slightly deeper than they grow in the pot.

This initial watering of transplants can either be done by bucket or a hose turned down to very small stream. It is also very effective, if you have planted a larger area, to use a Rainbird type sprinkler and soak the entire area planted. There are many home gardeners and commercial growers who just water the plants with the drip system from the beginning.

DIRECT SEEDED AREAS

In watering an area planted by seed, it is often easier to water the first two or three times until the plants come up with an impact-type (Rainbird) sprinkler. The first time soaks the ground and settles it around the seeds so that they will sprout. If the Rainbird sprinkler (a standard home garden size-5/32 inch nozzle) is set for one-half circle, it should be allowed to soak approximately two hours this first watering. (Of course, if it is set to cover a quarter circle area, the watering time would be half as long.) It is important that the soil be thoroughly soaked at the time of this first watering. In getting seeds up, you will water more often than usual, but since you have soaked the bed the first day, the successive waterings will only have to be about 10 minutes every day to keep the top few inches damp until the seeds come up.

The soil should be kept damp at the depth where the seed is located until it comes up. With corn, for example, this may only mean watering it right after planting and then again one week later when it begins to push through the surface. With small-seeded

Running water down the top of the row is an easy way to water transplants the first time.

The Rainbird sprinkler is an easy way to water until the plants come up.

vegetables, like carrots, it is necessary to water more frequently because they are planted shallower where the soil dries out very quickly. In hot weather, this may mean as often as every day for seven to ten days until they have sprouted and are up. In order to get a good stand, it is important to water at the time that the seedling is pushing through the surface to soften the crust and allow it to come through.

After They Come Up

Once the plants have come up, you should stop sprinkling and start watering by drip system or in the furrows. This is especially important with cucumbers, melons, squash and pumpkins because continued watering with sprinklers will usually cause powdery mildew. Watering by drip or in the furrows from the beginning has one advantage. Even though it takes a little longer to soak across to where the seeds are planted, there is less likely to be a hard crust on the surface which will keep the tender seedlings from coming up. On the other hand, the easiest way is to water with a Rainbird-type sprinkler until the seeds come up, and then switch to furrow or drip watering to avoid fungus diseases and encourage the right kind of plant and root structures. For a discussion of the principles governing all of the above watering methods, read the BASIC WATERING PRINCIPLES section starting on page **25.**

After plants come up, water by drip irrigation or in furrows. This corn is healthy because correct watering and fertilizing principles are being applied.

Getting Seeds Up

REASONS WHY SEEDS DON'T COME UP

1. Soil gets too dry.
2. Packed soil or hard crust.
3. Cold weather, slow germination, seeds rot.
4. Fungus diseases such as "damping off."
5. Cut worms and other insects.
6. Poor, old seed.

Keep Soil Damp

To get your seeds up follow these basic rules. Keep the soil damp enough so that the seeds can germinate. By laying the garden out properly and avoiding planting on the ridge at the top of a pointed row, you make the job easy. (See illustrations.) Seeds planted in the soil at the bottom of the ridge will stay moist much longer than seeds planted in the soil at the top of the ridge. After a few hours the soil at the top of the ridge may be too dry to sprout the seeds. In hot weather when trying to get very small seeds such as carrots and onions to come up, you can leave the Rainbird sprinkler sitting next to the portion of the garden which you have planted. After soaking the area the first day then turn it on every morning for 5-10 minutes until the plants come up. With larger seeded crops such as corn, green beans, melons and squash, even in hot weather it is not necessary to keep the surface wet because they are planted deeper, but only to soak the ground when planted and then soak it again to soften the crust in about one week as the seeds are coming up.

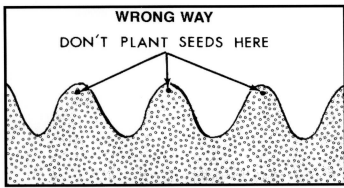

Seeds dry out quickly if planted at the top of a ridge.

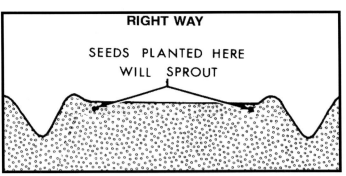

Plant your seeds in a position on the row where the soil stays moist while seedlings are coming up.

Avoid the Crust

Usually the hard crust which forms on soil is created by improper watering. People sometimes stand and water with a hose beating down on the soil until they have created a crust which becomes hard as it gets dry and prevents small seedlings from pushing through. By using a sprinkler which throws water into the air and lets it fall lightly to the ground in small droplets, you can avoid most of the thick, heavy crust. Watering with drip or furrows also avoids the crust.

A compaction problem may be caused by people or pets such as dogs walking across the tops of the rows. You should stay out of the garden as much as possible, particularly when the soil is wet, and when you are in the garden **always walk in the furrows.** Children can be taught early to follow this basic rule and your crops will come up better and grow much better as well because your soil will not be hard and packed. Soils which are filled with decomposed organic materials resist both the crusting and compaction problems, so to get a better stand of seedlings follow the principles laid out in the section on IMPROVING THE SOIL.

So Seeds Won't Rot

Go to seed catalogs for the newer which are usually more resistant to plant diseases. Both the rotting of seeds in cold weather and the fungus diseases such as "damping off" can be drastically reduced by using seed treated with Captan, Thiram or Streptomycin Sulfate, all mild fungicides. By preventing rot while seeds are germinating, you will substantially increase your stand of seedlings which come up in cool, damp spring weather. These fungicides can be ordered separately, but it is much easier to order seed which is already treated. Most seed catalogs will indicate whether or not the seeds which you are ordering are treated. They will be colored pink or blue so that you can identify the treated seeds from untreated ones.

Immediately after the plants come up, watering too often can cause a fungus disease called "damping-off". It usually occurs when the soil is kept very wet at the surface all of the time. By the time the seedlings are up they have a root system going down several inches so they do not need such frequent watering. Thus, immediately switching to a less frequent watering program will avoid "damping off" problems. "Damping-off" also kills transplants you are starting indoors so be careful of too frequent watering.

Control Insects

Cutworms, flea beetles and other tiny insects sometimes eat the small seedlings as they are coming through the surface of the ground. Dusting with garden dust containing Sevin quickly solves this problem.

Poor Quality and Old Seed

Most seed, with the exception of onions, is good to use for at least two years after it is harvested if properly stored in a cool, dry place. The germination percentage will gradually decline as the seed gets older and it will also lose some of its seedling vigor. Seed in the cucurbit family (cucumber, melon and squash) will keep for 3 to 4 years without a problem. It is important to buy seed from reputable seed companies. The safest method is

A tube of Sevin (Carbaryl) garden dust is a handy way to dust vulnerable new seedlings to protect them from grasshoppers, flea beetles, cutworms and other insects.

to buy fresh seed each year. If you buy from a seed rack, make certain the packets have this year's date printed on them. They should also have a guaranteed germination percentage. The problem with seed racks is that they rarely have any of the recently developed varieties. Go to seed catalogs for the newer varieties which are usually more **resistant to plant diseases.**

If you are storing seed, it is best to rotate the seed so that it is not stored for more than two or three years and is kept in a cool, dry place. If the seed comes from a strong, healthy plant and is properly stored, it will produce strong, vigorous seedlings. Check the germination rate which should be printed on the seed packet. Compare your results in the garden with similar seeds from different companies. Some seed companies have higher quality control standards than others.

If necessary, dust to kill bugs which eat tiny seedlings. If the soil is properly fertilized before planting the tiny seedlings will quickly grow to a size which makes them less vulnerable.

Fertilizer

Even though proper soil nutrients do not help the seed to germinate, they give the plant a great deal of vigor as it breaks through the surface of the ground and begins to grow. Tiny seedlings are most vulnerable to insects, diseases, wind, animals and other problems. Sometimes the seeds sprout and push through the surface, but die before you are even aware that they have come up. If the plant is filled with the proper nutrients when it pushes through the surface, it makes amazing growth in the first few days (seedling vigor). This quickly takes it to a size where it is out of danger and no longer at the mercy of every insect that comes along.

Keeping Them Healthy

The most important factors in keeping plants healthy are proper watering and fertilizing. These are discussed on pages 21-22, **25-31, 46-49 and 64-72** as well as in the CULTURE OF SPECIFIC VEGETABLES section.

Other factors are:

1. Weeding,

2. Mulching (organic or plastic),

3. Insect and disease control,

4. Gopher and bird control.

WEEDING

The weed problem is always worse the first year that "new" ground is used for a garden. As the soil is gardened regularly over a period of time, the weed seeds sprout and are eliminated. If you are careful not to let the weeds grow and go to seed, you will have fewer weeds each year.

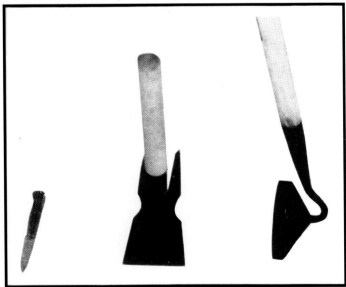

Regular and hand hoes are the most valuable tools for weeding a garden. A paring knife is also helpful.

Hoeing

The basic method for eliminating weeds is by hoeing. A regular full-sized hoe is best for most weeding, but a small hand hoe is important for close quarters. For successful hoeing it is important to have a file and use it regularly to keep the hoe sharp. Having a handle on the file helps you to keep from cutting fingers. (See illustration.) Having an electric grinding wheel on the bench in the garage will speed up the process. In using the hoe, hold the hoe with the blade flat and cut right under the surface of the ground, rather than chopping down at the weeds. This will cut the weeds off right under the crown so that they will quickly wilt and die. The chopping method misses many weeds and leaves others partially covered so that they re-root and continue growing. It also leaves the soil in mounds rather than smooth and flat.

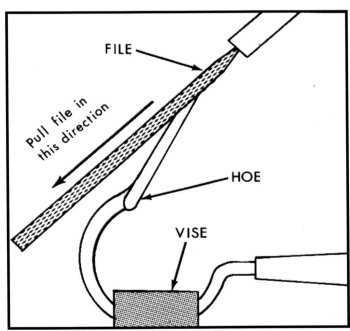

Using a file with a handle, sharpen a hoe carefully to avoid cutting your fingers. It is helpful to put the hoe in a vise and then pull or push the file across the blade at a flatter angle than shown in this illustration.

Under most conditions, hoeing once is enough. The weeds which grow after the first hoeing are almost shaded out by the plants and don't amount to much. If your soil is particularly weedy, it may be necessary to hoe twice in order to control the weeds.

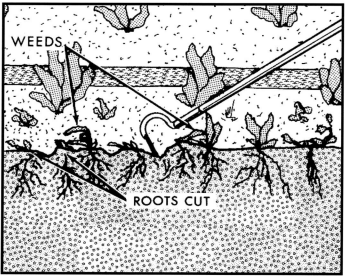

Chopping misses weeds and leaves mounds of dirt.

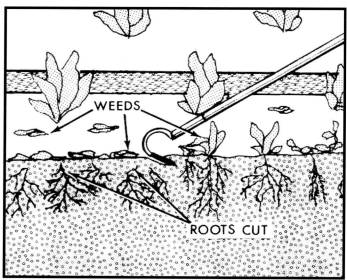

Hoeing kills weeds, cutting them off right below the crown and leaving the ground smooth.

MULCHING

Mulching is a method of controlling weeds as well as retaining moisture and keeping fruit off the ground. Traditionally it has meant placing 4-6 inches of straw or grass clippings around each row of vegetables. Rain water or water from sprinklers will flow right through this mulch, but is retained by the soil underneath because the mulch reduces evaporation. If the mulch is thick enough, it almost entirely eliminates weeds because they are deprived of the light necessary for growth. For root crops which can be injured by drastic fluctuations in the amount of soil moisture or soil temperature, the grass and straw mulches are especially beneficial. (See illustrations.) At the end of the season this organic mulch can be worked into the soil along with the vegetable plant residues to improve soil texture and fertility.

Mulching keeps the ground at a more even temperature and also helps maintain a consistent moisture level.

Types of Organic Mulch

Organic mulch can be almost any organic material which is readily available in large quantities. Alfalfa hay is excellent because its high protein (nitrogen) content adds so much fertility to the soil. Other commonly used mulching materials are: grass clippings, straw, sawdust, wood chips, leaves, cocoa mulch, and ground bark, but grass clippings are the easiest to use. By using a rotary power mower with a grass catcher and keeping your grass growing vigorously with nitrogen-type fertilizers, you will have an adequate supply of grass for mulching a rather large garden. Don't fertilize the grass with Weed and Feed, or other similar fertilizers which have herbicides (2-4 D) which will damage your garden.

When using organic mulching methods, it is easiest to plant the seeds and transplants before applying the mulch. After the plants are up and growing vigorously, then the mulch should be spread throughout the garden between the plants.

Disadvantages of Organic Mulches

The main disadvantage of mulching with organic materials is that they are excellent insulators and keep the soil cold, especially in the early spring as well as attracting insects. For crops which require warm soil for vigorous root and top growth, the organic mulch can be a disadvantage. In order to avoid this problem let the plants get a good start in the spring before applying the mulch. As the weather begins to turn warmer, then the mulch is beneficial.

Mulching with grass clippings around plants and trees will almost totally eliminate the weeds.

In cool summers along the coast and in high mountain valleys, with crops such as melons and tomatoes which require more heat, the organic mulches can reduce the yield. It has also been suggested that organic mulches may tend to promote the growth of various kinds of insects: snails, slugs, earwigs, sow bugs and fungus diseases in damp climates and with susceptible vegetables. For these reasons, it is probably better not to use organic mulches in coastal and high mountain valley areas with melons, cucumbers, winter squash and tomatoes. These problems are solved in those areas by using the black plastic "mulch" discussed below.

It is important to use mulches which are not full of weeds that have gone to seed. They will germinate in the following years and increase the weed problem in your garden.

In spite of the above problems associated with organic mulches, there are many excellent gardeners who wouldn't do it any other way. These disadvantages are far outweighed by the savings in water and the reduction in weeding problems as well as the reduction in spoilage by keeping fruit off the ground.

Plastic Mulch

Although the polyethylene film is not actually a mulch in the true sense of the word, it was developed to take the place of the traditional organic mulch in some situations, so it is usually called by the same name. Any substance which is spread upon the ground to protect the roots of plants from the heat, cold and drought, to keep fruit clean and retain moisture can legitimately be called a "mulch". The plastic needs to be at least **3½ to 4 mil in thickness** so that it will withstand the weather and not tear.

Clear plastic mulch increases soil temperatures in the early spring, as well as reducing evaporation and keeping the fruit off the ground.

CLEAR PLASTIC MULCH

Originally the polyethylene film which was developed for use in the culture of strawberries was clear (transparent). This clear plastic which was spread over the rows next to the ground allowed the sun to shine through into the soil having a "greenhouse" effect and thus increasing soil temperature by approximately 15° F.. This in turn increased root growth, especially in the winter and brought the plants out of their dormancy earlier and also increased the yield. In addition to warming the soil, it kept the soil moist longer by retarding evaporation and kept the berries off the ground. The temperature of the surface of the plastic remained cool so that the berries which lay on top of the plastic were not damaged by heat, moisture, or soil organisms. The only problem with the clear plastic was that it did not restrict the growth of weeds and it made the weeding process very difficult. Clear plastic is still used for strawberries.

BLACK PLASTIC MULCH

The weed problems of the clear plastic are solved by using black plastic mulch. This black polyethylene film solves the weed problem just like organic mulches because the black plastic eliminates the light and weeds cannot grow without light. It has the moisture retention benefits of the other mulches and keeps fruit off the ground.

Soil temperature is about 5 degrees F. warmer with the black plastic as without, but the surface of the plastic gets very warm. Rather than going through the plastic into the ground as they do with clear plastic, the sun's rays are absorbed into the surface of the black plastic so that sometimes it gets quite hot (a 15-20 degree F. increase), even on a cool, sunny day. This means that with heat-loving plants such as melons and tomatoes, the black plastic actually increases the heat on the vines where it is needed as they spread across it at the same time that it is helping to retain soil moisture and eliminating weeds. It also keeps the tomatoes off the ground reducing loss from spoiled fruit.

Unless you live in the low desert where it is very hot, the black plastic will increase both quality and yield by increasing the amount of heat on the vines. This is particularly true of melons but also applies to tomatoes as well. The black plastic has particular value in the cool summer areas of the high mountain valleys and the coastal regions. It makes it possible to successfully grow heat-loving crops otherwise reserved for warmer climates.

The black plastic is cut 36 inches wide to fit the 36 inch row. Unroll enough plastic to go down the length of the row, and then carefully stretch it out. This process should not be done during the heat of the day because the hot plastic can burn the young leaves while they are covered.

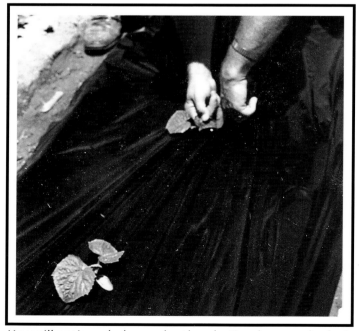

You will notice a bulge under the plastic where each plant is located. Using scissors or a sharp knife, cut a small circle or an "X" above each plant. The plastic is stretchy so the hole does not have to be large. Then carefully pull the leaves of the plant through the hole and push the plastic down to the ground around the stem.

How to Apply

The black plastic should be spread over melons when they are up and have at least four leaves. Tomato plants should be covered approximately one or two weeks after transplanting. It is preferable to apply black plastic in the early morning or late afternoon rather than in the heat of the day because the black plastic sometimes gets hot enough to injure tender young leaves while being put down. **Immediately** after applying the plastic, an "x" or a small circle should be cut over each -plant and the leaves **carefully pulled through**. The plastic stretches somewhat so the hole doesn't need to be too large. Once the plastic is on the ground, the plants can spread across it without damage from increased heat. Black plastic comes in various sizes, so it will fit over the top of a standard 36 inch bed and the plastic will be high enough on the sides of the furrows so that you can walk in the furrows for picking without stepping on the plastic or black plastic can be found in 10 or 20 foot widths for other plants. Of course, you will need to put your drip system down first so that you can water under the plastic. (See illustrations for details about applying plastic mulch.)

Keeping It Down

The wind will go right over the plastic without ripping it off if it is properly applied. The plastic film should go completely across the top of the row and over the edges down three to five inches into the furrow on each side. Then bricks can be placed across the furrow every ten feet to hold down the plastic on each side of the furrow. If bricks are not available, a shovelful of dirt can be taken from beneath the plastic and placed on top of the plastic in the hole that is made (again at approximately ten foot intervals). Bricks and rocks can be used to hold the plastic down with larger plants where no furrows are used. Once the vines have spread across the plastic, they will hold it down.

Sources of Plastic Mulch

There are a great many sources of black plastic, but there is also a great deal of difference in price from different sources. The best prices are usually found

Use bricks, rocks, or dirt to hold the plastic down immediately after application. When the vines grow large, they will hold the plastic in place.

A few weeks after it is laid down, the vines begin to spread across the hot, black plastic. By warming the vines of heat loving crops like cantaloupes, squash and tomatoes, the black plastic improves the quality and quantity of the fruit.

This picture shows the same three rows of cucumbers, cantaloupes and winter squash approximately two months after application of the black plastic. If the size of your garden allows more space between plants, the quality of the fruit will be better.

at stores like Lowes, Home Depot and Wal-Mart. These plastic mulches are usually found in the paint department rather than the garden shop. It should be remembered that plastic mulches do not decompose easily in the soil as do organic mulches so they should be removed and disposed of at the end of the season before working the soil. Black plastic can be left on perennial crops like strawberries for two years and black landscaping cloth, even longer.

Herbicides

Many herbicides are used in modern agriculture to kill weeds. Traces of these herbicides sometimes get into the food we eat, occasionally enough to make people sick. If the person applying the herbicide is not especially trained so he really knows what he is doing, herbicides can be dangerous to the food we eat. Herbicides can sometimes be used properly on one crop to prevent or kill weeds and enough residue be left in the soil to be absorbed into a crop the next year and do damage. For that reason the author does not recommend using herbicides in the garden, with the exception of **Roundup** (glyphosate isopropylamine salt). This product is now out of patent protection so it also may be found under another name.

Roundup has no soil effect. It attaches to particles of soil and is broken down to non-toxic materials by microorganisms. It is only effective in killing plants/weeds when it gets on leaves where it is absorbed into the plant, where it is systemic and circulates to every part of the plant. Because of this systemic action Roundup (glyphosate) is effective in killing even the toughest deep-rooted weeds, but it must be applied in a certain way.

The most difficult weeds like field bindweed (morning glory) have a very deep extensive root system. If the tops are relatively small it is hard to get enough material into the large roots to kill them because of the **dilution effect.** To get the solution of Roundup concentrated enough in the roots to kill the plant, the top of the plant where the herbicide is absorbed through the leaves has to be large enough so that it is balanced (more or less) with the roots. To do this and get a complete kill you may have to fertilize and water

the weed to grow the tops large and healthy before you spray it. It is also true that Roundup will not be absorbed very well by the leaves unless the plant is well watered. On most very dry weeds, the Roundup tends to stay on the surface of the leaves and not very much is absorbed, so again watering and fertilizing a few weeks and days before spraying is important. It is also helpful to spray the leaves thoroughly.

When using Roundup on field bindweed (morning glory), the herbicide is not transported from the leaves to the roots until the plant reaches a certain maturity level, so if you spray too soon, you just kill the tops and they grow right back. Wait to spray until the morning glory starts to bloom and then you will kill the whole plant.

There is one **warning** about the use of Roundup. Because it will be absorbed by any leaf on which it lands, you must be very careful about over-spray onto useful plants of every kind. To avoid this, don't pump up the sprayer with too much pressure because it will cause the herbicide to come out of the nozzle in a fine mist which will float on the breeze to useful plants (both yours and your neighbors). Also avoid spraying in the wind because you will cause unwanted damage to useful plants nearby. You can make a shield out of a large piece of cardboard and staple or tape on a wooden handle and shield your plants from the spray when treating weeds.

INSECT AND DISEASE CONTROL

Plants which are kept healthy by correct watering and fertilizing are vigorous and resistant to insects and diseases. As much as possible it is better to avoid these kinds of problems rather than trying to solve them after the plant is already sick. There are several important ways to avoid the disease and insect problem.

Rotation

Rotation simply means planting a specific vegetable crop in a different area of the garden each year. Certain vegetables are host plants for certain insects and diseases. If they are planted in the same area each year, it doesn't

These beets were grown in soil which was infested with root-knot nematodes. They are microscopic worms which invade the roots of many plants, restricting the flow of nutrients, causing enlarged areas on the roots and limiting the growth of the plant itself.

It is also important to avoid taking dirt from a contaminated area of the garden to one which is free of these diseases. Diseases can be spread by garden tools as well, particularly a roto-tiller which has been used in infected soil should be washed before using it elsewhere in the garden.

TOMATO PLANT WITH TOBACCO MOSAIC VIRUS. After handling tobacco products or removing a diseased plant or tomato, wash hands carefully with soap and water before touching a healthy plant.

Fumigation

The materials that could be used by a home gardener to fumigate the soil to kill weed seeds and diseases have been taken off the market, and the fumigants used by commercial growers must be applied by a certified specialist and are much too expensive for the home garden. For these reasons the home gardener is left with more natural organic methods of killing weed seeds and diseases. **The best way to eliminate these pests is to solarize your soil.**

Solarization

This method of killing weed seeds and diseases relies on sunlight and heat generated by decaying plant materials and the greenhouse effect. Any farmer knows that if he puts up and stores his hay too green

take long for the pests to reach levels which will kill your plants. For example: nematodes live in the soil and invade the roots of many fruits and vegetables. They cause enlargements on the roots called "root knots" which restrict root growth and cause the plant to be stunted and sometimes die prematurely. They cause particularly serious problems with tomatoes, but affect, to a lesser degree, the quality of many garden vegetables. Different types of nematodes attack different plants. By rotating the planting of tomatoes and other susceptible crops, you will avoid the build-up in the soil of this type of problem. Soil-borne diseases such as fusarium and verticillium wilts are also controlled by rotation methods because you avoid a buildup of the race of verticillium or fusarium that affects the particular crop..

(moist) the haystack can get so hot that it catches fire and burns. Try sticking your hand into a pile of grass clippings the day after mowing. It has become hot. This process occurs because bacteria and fungi from the air get into this moist hay or grass clippings causing them to decompose. This is an oxidative process which generates heat.

To solarize your soil you roto-till into the soil large amounts of raw organic materials (grass clippings, leaves, etc.) then put down a drip system for moisture and then cover the area with a sheet of **clear** polyethylene film (plastic mulch). This is best done during the heat of summer when the sun shining through the clear plastic (greenhouse effect) together with the heat from the decomposition of raw organic material which has been watered by the drip system gets hot enough to kill the weed seeds and disease organisms in the soil. The plastic should be held down by bricks and sealed around the edges with dirt and kept on the soil for a month or more during the heat of summer.

Disease Resistant Varieties

Another method of avoiding the insect and disease problem is to choose varieties of vegetables which are resistant to these pests. From many sources, such as university experimental stations and seed companies, new varieties of vegetables are being developed which are resistant to a multitude of diseases as well as nematodes and other insect pests. For example, some new varieties of tomatoes have the letters VFN after their name. This means that the particular variety is resistant to verticillium and fusarium wilts and to root-knot nematodes. A VFFFT variety would also be resistant to three races of fusarium fungus and tobacco mosaic virus. Certain varieties of cantaloupes and cucumbers have been developed which are resistant to anthracnose, fusarium wilt, scab, downy and powdery mildew. If you have had various vegetables die prematurely before the fruit was mature, you should consider the disease -resistant varieties for next year.

Many of the older varieties do not have the disease resistance of the newer ones, so even though the quality of the fruit is excellent under ideal conditions,

it is better to choose a newer variety which is bred for disease resistance so that you won't be disappointed.

Powdery mildew on squash, melons and other plants comes from too much moisture on the leaves. This and other fungus diseases can usually be avoided by not watering the leaves, by allowing enough space between the plants for good air circulation and by planting varieties which are resistant to these diseases.

Hybrids

Many of the new disease-resistant varieties are hybrids. The off-spring of a cross between two different varieties of a vegetable is called a "hybrid". This is commonly illustrated by a well-known hybrid from the animal kingdom. A mule is a hybrid from the cross-breeding of a donkey and a horse. Some hybrids cannot reproduce off-spring.

Hybrids are characterized by increased vigor and uniformity. When adequately fertilized they produce outstanding yields. Many hybrids also have increased tolerance to certain plant diseases. There is a common notion that hybrids in plants can't reproduce or that if you save seed from them, the next generation (F2) will not be anything like its parent. This is true of some plants, but totally untrue of others. For example, the author saved seed from a hybrid cantaloupe and then grew plants from those seeds side by side with plants from new hybrid seed of the same variety and compared the melon. After conducting this trial for three generations he **couldn't find any difference** between the offspring, so if hard times come and seed is not available, save seed from hybrids.

Mycorrhizal Fungi

Mycorrhizae are fungi which form both a symbiotic and synergistic relationship with plant root systems. The mycorrhizal fungi attach themselves to plant roots using food from the plant to live. They grow out from plant roots with innumerable tiny filaments or threads called hyphae. As these fungi colonize plant roots they greatly enhance the ability of the plant to absorb both water and mineral nutrients. In some crops this "fungus root" increases the plant's ability to absorb mineral nutrients and water by more than 10 times. The filaments (hyphae) are much smaller than the tiniest plant root and are therefore able to get between soil particles and extract the nutrients and water. Mycorrhizal fungi are a natural part of any healthy soil, but in many cases in the process of building homes, the contractor has removed and sold much of the top soil thereby virtually eliminating the mycorrhizal fungi. It is also in short supply in many desert soils of the west. There are many species of this fungus and there is not one specie that benefits all plants. For that reason, it is best to use a product that has several species of both endo and ecto mycorrhizae. Then whether you are planting a pine tree or a tomato plant, you have inoculated the roots with the right one.

Mycorrhizae doesn't just increase rooting capacity. It also protects the roots from plant pathogens which would otherwise cause disease or death to the plant. In Plant Pathology, Second Edition, Dr. George N. Agrios states: "The presence of mycorrhizal fungi on and in the roots acts as a protective barrier to infection by highly pathogenic fungi Pythium, Phytophthora, Fusarium and others". One author suggests that the fungi produce antibiotics that retard the growth of soil pathogens.

If the seeds or roots of small plants are inoculated (sprinkled with the powder or water containing these fungal spores), the fungi go with the roots wherever they spread. Refer to sources on page **37** for ways to obtain these products. The author finds that Myco Apply Soluble or Myco Grow Soluble with 20 different types of mycorrhizae (both endo and ecto) is easy to use and effective. It is ground so fine and the spores are so small that 1/8th to 1/4th of a teaspoon full can be mixed with water in a quart watering bottle and squirted onto the root ball before planting. Shake the bottle regularly to keep the material in suspension and inoculate the roots of your transplants right before they go into the ground. (See also page **10** for beneficial fungi.)

Aphids are sucking insects which cause curled leaves and often attract ants. Before the infestation becomes severe, they need to be sprayed with Malathion.

Other Ways of Avoiding Plant Diseases

Adequate sunlight and air circulation are two of the best ways to keep plants healthy. This keeps moisture levels down to avoid fungus diseases and the sun's rays eliminate many disease-causing organisms. To accomplish these and other objectives:

1. Avoid planting in the shade.

2. Avoid crowding plants too close to each other.

3. Keep the garden well-drained.

4. Don't water more often than necessary.

5. Water thoroughly but not frequently.

6. Avoid wetting plant foliage.

7. If sprinkle irrigation is necessary, do it in the morning and avoid overcast, muggy days.

8. Avoid walking and working in the garden when the foliage or soil is wet.

9. Work plant residues into the soil soon after harvest to stop growth of disease-causing organisms and insects and to prevent weeds from going to seed in your garden.

Dusting and Spraying

SPRAYING AND DUSTING EQUIPMENT

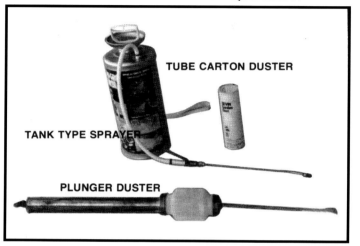

When spraying toxic chemicals on plants to kill insects it is important to know that some material will damage the leaves of your plants if the temperature is too hot when it is applied. For that reason the advice is **"don't spray in the heat of the day."** Dusting and spraying with toxic chemicals should be avoided when possible. Often an excellent garden can be grown without dusting or spraying for insects. Sometimes they make a few holes in some leaves and even some fruit will be affected but the vast majority of your vegetables will not. For example, a few aphids on healthy corn or tomato plants will not, under normal conditions, affect either the quantity or quality of your crop. Similarly, a few worms on corn will not cause much damage if the corn is healthy. The ears will be well-sealed by the husks and few worms get in to do any damage.

On the other hand, you are mostly concerned about not getting any toxic chemicals on the food you eat and not hurting the environment. If you can dust or spray in a limited way without doing either of those things, it is not a problem. For example, when planting carrots, beets, broccoli, and cauliflower from seed during the summer for a fall garden you will sometimes have everything come up and you will have an excellent stand, but tiny flea beetles that are so small that they are hardly noticeable will come and eat the tiny seedlings and the next day there will be no plants. One dusting with a small amount of Sevin dust out

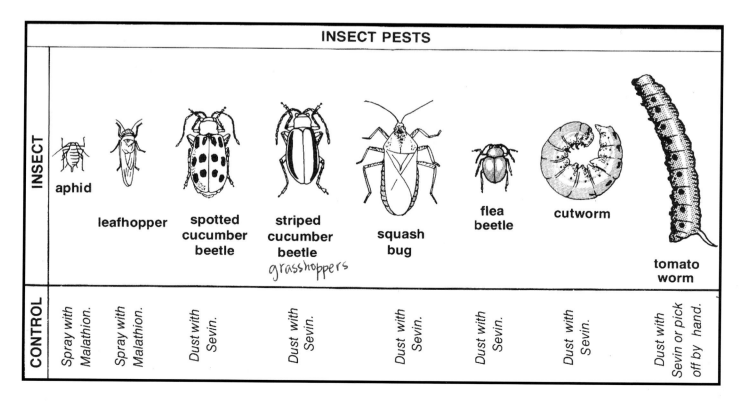

	INSECT PESTS						
INSECT	aphid	leafhopper	spotted cucumber beetle	striped cucumber beetle *grasshoppers*	squash bug	flea beetle	cutworm	tomato worm
CONTROL	Spray with Malathion.	Spray with Malathion.	Dust with Sevin.	Dust with Sevin.	Dust with Sevin.	Dust with Sevin.	Dust with Sevin.	Dust with Sevin or pick off by hand.

of a tube carton duster down the row of seedlings will kill or prevent the flea beetles or other small insects until the crop is large enough to not be vulnerable and will take care of the problem. Within a week or so the Sevin dust oxidizes in the sun and breaks down into a non-toxic material.

Another example is aphids. If they come it is usually in the early stages of the crop and one spraying with Malathion will eradicate them. In the author's experience, they seldom return so you are not spraying at all close to the time of maturity of any crop. The Malathion oxidizes and breaks down to a non-toxic form weeks or even months before picking.

There is also an increasing number of natural organic pesticides which kill the pest and do not put poisons into the garden or harm the environment. An example of this is Bt (bacillus thuringiensis). It is a bacterium which is not harmful to people, pets or the environment, often referred to as a "worm germ" because it kills all kinds of worms. This can be sprayed on tomatoes right up until picking (and beyond) to kill fruit worms and hornworms. It is sprayed on corn silk when it comes out and totally eliminates corn worms. When sprayed on broccoli when the heads are tiny it eliminates cabbage loopers and worms without being toxic to anyone. Neemoil from the Neem tree kills aphids and other insects as well as controlling mildew and other fungus diseases. Protazoan (Semaspore bait) can be purchased in the form of a bait for grasshoppers. Refer to the next page for beneficial insects which can be purchased and placed in your garden to control pests. Check with Arbico Organics or other organic sources listed on pages **37-38** for other natural organic methods of controlling pests.

The Insect Pest Chart shown above lists some of the basic insects and controls but does not mention grasshoppers or Bt (discussed below). On certain crops and in certain specific circumstances, aphids and other insect pests multiply to the point that they must be dusted or sprayed to avoid serious damage. Basically, two substances will control almost all garden insect pests. These are Malathion and Sevin (Carbaryl). Malathion is normally applied as a spray and Sevin

either as a spray or dust. The dust has some advantages with melons and squash because it does not promote fungus diseases such as powdery mildew. The spray is usually more effective in completely eradicating the insect involved.

As a basic rule the best way to control aphids, leaf hoppers and white flies is to spray with Malathion. With many other insect pests, such as cucumber beetles, bean beetles, potato beetles, flea beetles, and squash bugs, as well as cabbage worms, corn worms and cut worms, the recommended method of control is to spray or dust with Sevin (Carbaryl) but use Bt for worms.

A tank-type sprayer can be used for applying either Malathion or Sevin. The Malathion is mixed with water (following the manufacturer's directions on the label) and then the leaves are covered with this mixture. In dusting, the powder is applied either with a plunger-type duster, a bellows-type duster, or just a hand carton with holes in the top.

Bacillus Thuringiensis (Bt)

The chemical insecticides like Malathion and Sevin are often quicker and a little more effective than organic solutions but it is hard to find anything more effective than the organic Bt for worms, even among the chemicals. Bt is not hard to find if you know what to look for. It is sometimes found under brand names like "Thuricide Concentrate" or "Safer Brand" or "Dipel". Read the fine print looking for bacillus thuringiengis or ask in a good nursery for this product. Be certain it is fresh because it contains live bacteria which have a two year life. If it has sat on a shelf for two years it is not good for anything.

Grasshoppers

Grasshoppers are particularly hard to kill. Sevin (Carbaryl) has traditionally been recommended, but Tempo (Cyfluthrin) is much more effective. Because they have an exoskeleton covering it is necessary to mix a surfactant (spreader sticker) with the insecticide to penetrate and kill the grasshoppers. The Tempo has not yet been approved for all vegetable and fruit crops. It is only listed for carrots, radishes, sweet corn, tomatoes and peppers.

Snails and Slugs

The old adage, "an ounce of prevention is worth a pound of cure," applies to these slimy creatures. Put a trail of snail-slug bait completely around the garden right after you have planted and watered it. Keeping them out is much easier and better than trying to get them out by putting poisonous bait in the garden after they get in.

It is often easy to determine the bush or ivy bed where most of the snails and slugs hide out during the daytime. Circle the bush or bed where they hide with a trail of bait in the evening. It is also often helpful to spray the area with water before putting down the bait because the water makes these pests very active. The next morning, you will often find the ground around the bush covered with dead and dying snails and slugs.

Snail-slug bait comes in powder (meal) and pellets. Powder is better because it is safer around children and pets. The pellets are very dangerous because they are easily picked up by curious children and pets who might try to eat them. They are poisonous and should be stored in a safe place out of the reach of children, as should also the other garden pesticides. The active ingredient in this bait is Metaldehyde.

Bait for snails and slugs by putting a trail of bait around the garden at planting time and several times thereafter throughout the season. The meal (powder) is preferable because it is less attractive to children and pets than the pellets.

Sow Bugs and Earwigs

Sow bugs are also known as "pill bugs" and "potato bugs". Sow Bugs and Earwigs are both killed by bait containing Sevin (Carbaryl). You can purchase bait which attracts and kills sow bugs. It is very much like snail-slug bait and should be applied in the same way. There are some baits on the market which combine Metaldehyde and Sevin (Carbaryl) into one product which is designed to kill all four (snails, slugs, sow bugs and earwigs) in one treatment. They have an obvious advantage.

Orchard Pest Control

Many pests in an orchard can be controlled with one spraying which is applied to all orchard trees while they are dormant right before blossoms open and the leaf buds begin to push. This **dormant spraying** is important because it **prevents many problems** before they happen. For example it prevents both fungal and bacterial diseases like mildew (powdery and downey), rust, scab, coryneum blight, gray mold, brown rot and fire blight. It also kills over-wintering insects and their eggs such as aphids, scale, mites, twig borers and leafhoppers.

All three products that make up this dormant spray are mixed into the **same tank** and applied together. The **copper sulfate/fixed copper** is mixed into the tank first. Copper sulfate was the original product but it was made stronger and is called fixed copper and is found under brand names like Microcop, COCS or Copper Hydroxide. These products kill both the fungal and bacterial diseases. Next you mix **Malathion** into the tank. It is an effective insecticide without killing the beneficial insects which Permethrin or Sevin would do. The third ingredient is either a **spreader sticker** like Sta-Stuk which is used in rainy areas to keep the other materials from washing off the tree or **dormant oil** like Volk or Supreme Oil which also sticks the materials to the tree and is used more in snowy areas where there is not too much rain. The oil has the added benefit of smothering over-wintering insect eggs but is not as effective as a sticker in keeping the material stuck to the tree. The spray needs to dry on the tree before rain or snow comes so it won't be washed off. Be certain to put the three products into the tank in the proper order because the sticker or oil would keep the first two from mixing well.

This dormant spray mix is sprayed onto the trees after pruning but when the buds have swelled on the dormant trees and blossom and leaf buds are about to open. It is called the **"pink bud stage"**. On most fruit trees the blossom which is about to open is pink but with some trees like plums it may be white. Shake or otherwise agitate the spray tank regularly to keep the mixture of materials in suspension and spray thoroughly to the point of runoff.

For other pests in the orchard, spray later with Malathion for codling moths (pear and apple worm) as needed. Pheremone traps can be placed in the orchard to capture these moths and to tell you when they are around and you should spray. Codling moth worms can also be killed with Bt. Spraying with Malathion is also effective for peach twig borers during early summer and for aphids. Malathion is also effective for pear slugs on pears and cherries when these small slug-like worms appear. If you have a problem with western cherry fruit fly worms in your orchard, spray with Malathion when the cherries turn from green to salmon color. Also pick up and dispose of all infected cherries that fall on the ground so that you interrupt the life cycle of these pests (they over-winter in the ground, become flies and go back into the tree to lay their eggs in the spring and begin the cycle again).

On July 1st and August 1st spray all stone fruit trees (peach, nectarine, apricot, plum and cherry) for crown borers which can kill the tree. Spray the crown of the tree (from the ground including a few inches of soil up to and including the base of the first limbs with Permethrin. Do not spray the whole tree with Permethrin because it kills predatory mites on the leaves which control two spotted mites. This can cause a spider mite outbreak. If there is an unusually wet spring, the fire blight which was killed by the dormant spray may come back from airborne bacteria. Then you will need to cut off the affected branches 8-10 inches below the blight and spray with Streptomycin.

Ants

Sometimes people worry a great deal about ants in the garden. Ants are usually a symptom rather than the

BENEFICIAL INSECTS

[Larva]

[Larva]

The ladybugs, lacewings, praying mantis, lizard, and toad pictures above live on harmful insects. Your family can encourage them to live in your garden by bringing them in from other sources and protecting those which are naturally present.

cause of your problem. A few ants don't really affect the garden one way or another, but if they are present in large numbers, they are probably only eating rotting fruit or the honeydew residue left by aphids. Aphids are sucking insects very much like mosquitoes or ticks on animals. They take the juices from the plant and secrete a honey-like substance which attracts ants. For this reason, ants can be helpful to the gardener in locating and getting rid of a colony of aphids. On the other hand, large red ants can eat live plant material and need to be killed with a product like Ortho Roach, Ant and Spider Killer or Ant-Be-Gone.

Beneficial Insects

There are certain insects which don't eat plants but instead live on harmful insects. They can eat gigantic quantities of aphids, mites and other insect pests. These beneficial insects include praying mantis, lady bugs, lacewings and tiger beetles. They can be purchased from various catalogs or from local nurseries if they are not naturally present in large enough quantities in your garden. Lizards and toads also live on insects in your garden.

Some of the most beneficial of insects are the earthworms. They improve soil texture as well as making soil nutrients more readily available for plant use. They multiply in direct proportion to the quantities of organic matter found in your soil. These earthworms consume and break down raw organic materials into valuable humus. The digested wastes which they leave in the soil are called "worm castings" which are extremely rich in available plant food. Worms also loosen and aerate the soil leaving pores which facilitate oxygen, water and root penetration.

Gopher Control

An effective method of gopher control is the Macabee-type gopher trap which you place in the gopher hole after you have opened it. The gopher has an obsession about closing off the light in his hole, so if you open the hole so that the light gets in and then place the trap down into one of the tunnels so that he has to cross it in order to close off the hole, he will

get caught in the process of going over it. The tunnels (runs) usually go both ways from the mound so put one trap going each way. Tie the trap to a stake so a cat won't carry off the gopher **and your trap.**

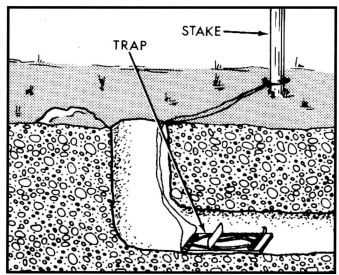

Gopher traps are usually effective because gophers have an obsession about closing the light out of their holes. For that reason, the hole can be opened up and a trap placed down the tunnel. The gopher can't get to the surface to close off his hole without going over the trap, where he will usually get caught.

A second method which is sometimes effective is a gopher bomb. This is a device with a fuse which, when ignited, emits a poisonous gas. Most soils are so porous that the gas escapes into the ground without killing the gopher. To make this method effective,

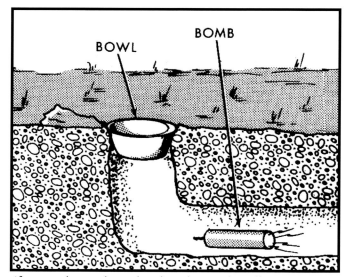

If properly used, gopher bombs can be effective on gophers, moles and other rodents. If the ground is not wet the poisonous gas will leak out through pores in the soil.

especially in sandy soil, you must first water the soil to fill up the pores and then open the gopher hole, light the fuse and quickly insert the gopher bomb into the hole. Take a heavy round-bottomed bowl and push it down into the hole to seal it so that the gas will not escape. It is sometimes beneficial to insert two gopher bombs into a hole before closing it off in order to get the job done. This gopher bomb method can also be effective with moles and other rodents.

An easier way to get rid of gophers is to buy a **gopher bait probe.** The gopher bait which contains strychnine is inserted into the hopper at the top and the probe is pushed down into the gopher mound and around it and between mounds. When it suddenly drops 2 or 3 inches you know you have dropped into a tunnel (gopher run). Turn the handle at the top of the probe which releases poison bait into the tunnel where the gopher eats it and dies below the surface. You will stop seeing new mounds. (See illustration)

Gopher bait probes are the most effective way to kill gophers without endangering children or pets. The probe inserts grain covered with strychnine into the tunnel (run).

Bird Problems

Birds can be a problem, not only in eating the seeds which you plant, but also in eating the young seedlings as they come out of the ground. They are especially active in the garden in the early spring when there is not a lot of other food around. One simple way to protect the seeds and young plants from birds is to construct a large rectangular frame out of 1 inch by 12 inch lumber. Then attach a small size chicken wire over it and place this frame over the plants in the early spring.

For birds eating fruit, cheap nylon netting is available at most nurseries or at Lowes or Home Depot. This netting can be thrown over the trees and bushes to keep the birds away from the fruit. Usually, with most crops, the birds are a problem during the early stages of maturity, but as the fruit begins to ripen faster the amount of damage which they do is proportionately smaller. Birds also have a beneficial effect in the garden because they eat many kinds of harmful insects. Propane canons and firecrackers on a rope which the farmers use to scare away birds do not make the neighbors happy and are not allowed in most cities.

For a small area, this frame covered with small-gauge wire keeps birds away from your vegetables or berries. Netting is even more effective.

Deer Problems

Deer are very destructive in the garden! They eat almost everything including rose bushes. Having tried almost everything he could buy (or that anyone could suggest) to keep the deer out of his garden the author finally resorted to an 8 foot fence around the area. Deer will jump over a 6 foot fence but the 8 foot fence worked and there are no more deer problems.

Culture of Individual Crops

This section contains specific directions for the culture of some of the basic vegetables as well as the commonly grown berries. These directions and the basic principles discussed throughout this book apply as well to other species of fruits and vegetables not discussed in this section. After you have mastered the correct principles involved, you will have acquired a "green thumb" for all sorts of exotic plants which you may want to grow in the future.

By following correct cultural principles you will harvest gigantic quantities of delicious vegetables in a relatively small garden.

Artichokes

A delicacy in ancient Rome, artichokes have been around for a long time. They are grown commercially in the mild Mediterranean climates of the Gulf States and the California coast. They thrive in areas with a mild winter and a cool summer. They can also be grown inland, but they require protection from the winter cold. This is usually done by a heavy mulch of hay or straw applied over the plants in late October after the first light frost. The mulch should be pulled back in the spring after danger of heavy frost has passed.

PLANTING

Artichokes can be planted throughout the spring or summer months and even in the fall in mild-winter areas. They are usually planted from roots, but seedlings are also available in most nurseries in areas where they are easily grown. If they are planted from roots, plant them deep enough so that the crown (from which leaves emerge) is just above soil level. Usually some small new leaves will be protruding out of the crown to make it easy for correct positioning. Artichokes need lots of room to spread and should be planted approximately 4 feet apart down a 48 inch row.

WATERING AND FERTILIZING

It is important to mix adequate quantities of organic material and a good complete commercial fertilizer into the soil before planting. (See sections on soils and fertilizer). Artichokes are perennials, so you will expect them to stay in the same place for several years. Giving them a healthy start will save time and effort later. After planting, they should be thoroughly watered; either by flooding, drip or by sprinkling for a long enough period to thoroughly soak and settle the soil around the roots. Keep artichokes wet for the first few weeks and then follow a watering schedule similar to other water-loving plants. (See details in WATERING PRINCIPLES section.)

A very good way to satisfy the artichokes' need for an even, consistent moisture level and to control weeds at the same time is to put a 4-6 inch mulch of grass clippings (or other organic material) down the row between the plants. As this grass mulch begins to decompose more grass clippings must be added to keep the mulch thick enough to prevent weeds (two or three times each year). Artichokes also thrive on regular applications of high-nitrogen fertilizer. These should be made every six weeks during the fall and spring in mild-winter areas to encourage heavy vegetative growth.

PEST CONTROL

The young artichoke foliage is by nature succulent and therefore a real delicacy for insect pests. Artichokes are especially susceptible to damage by aphids and will probably need to be sprayed once or twice a year with Malathion. They also attract slugs, snails, sow bugs and earwigs so a good snail, slug and sow bug bait should be applied around artichokes immediately after planting and again approximately once per month throughout the fall and early spring season.

HARVESTING

If artichokes (either root or large seedlings) are planted by September and fed and watered regularly, they will produce a good crop the next spring. They normally stop producing when the warm weather comes in late June and should be cut down to the ground to make way for the next crop. If you continue to water and feed the plants, new leaves will soon push through the ground which will produce a small crop in the fall. They will then produce a much larger crop the next spring. After the first year, it is helpful to thin

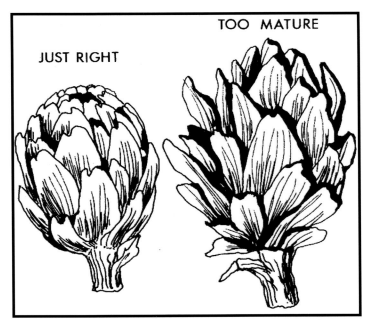

Harvest by cutting about one inch below the bud after it becomes plump and full, but before it begins to open.

the new shoots (which come up in clumps around the original roots) to 3 or 4 of the most vigorous ones.

If you let an artichoke go to seed, you will find that it is actually a thistle with a large blue, violet, and pink blossom. The edible part is the flower bud which should be picked when it is plump and meaty just before it begins to open. After the bracts of the bud begin to open, the edible portions of the artichoke become tough and lose their delicate flavor.

Asparagus

This hardy perennial lives for many years so it should be placed in a portion of the garden where it can remain undisturbed. It is also important to choose a sunny spot where the soil is in good condition or to get it into good condition by adding adequate quantities of organic and commercial fertilizer before planting.

VARIETIES

The major home garden asparagus varieties are: 'Jersey Knight', 'Jersey Giant', 'U C 157', and 'Purple Passion'. The old 'Mary Washington' variety is still good quality but does not have the disease resistance, size or yield of the newer ones listed above. The older varieties put a lot of energy into producing blossoms and seeds which could have been used to store more food in their roots. The newer cultivars listed above are all male varieties which have no seeds. They are therefore more productive of large succulent spears. The 'purple passion' variety is slightly smaller but is sweeter and has purple spears.

PLANTING

Asparagus plants will be in the ground for many years, so it is important to plant them properly. Dig a trench 18 inches wide and 18 inches deep. Add a good complete commercial fertilizer to the soil taken out of the trench. 16-16-8 plus Ironite is a good mix for this purpose. (See application of Commercial Fertilizer on pages **21-22** for the amount to add of each nutrient.) Also add to this soil a large quantity of decomposed, organic material. This should make up approximately 1/4 of the quantity of the finished product. The best organic material for this purpose is something containing peat moss or other decomposed organic material (humus). Carefully mix the organic and commercial fertilizer with the soil removed from the trench and backfill the trench with six inches of dirt. If you are planting roots, a mound should be formed every 18 inches on which to spread each asparagus root.

Make the mounds approximately 4 inches high and spread the asparagus roots over the mounds in the center of the trench. The mound should be high enough so that the crown of the asparagus root is approximately 8 inches below the surface of the ground. Now cover the roots so that only the top of the crown is exposed. If planting plants from the nursery out of a gallon pot, put the root ball out of the pot into the trench on top of 6 inches of soil where the mound would have been. Use an ice pick to pick the outside roots away from the root ball if the plant is root bound but don't pick the root ball to pieces.

Next, run water down the trench, thoroughly soaking the soil around and beneath the roots. Make certain that the roots are still covered, with only the tip of the crown exposed, after being watered. When the

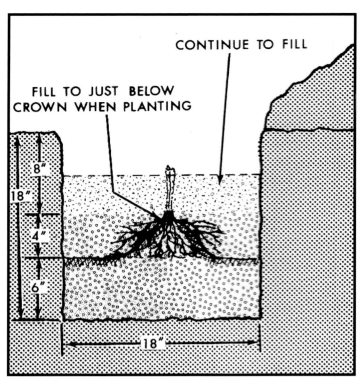

Fill trench gradually as stalks grow.

plant has put up shoots approximately 6 inches long, fill the trench until only approximately 2 inches of these stalks are protruding out of the ground. As they continue to grow, continue filling with the enriched soil which was removed from the trench until it is up to ground level.

If the roots are planted shallower, the asparagus shoots will come up earlier in the spring. In order to prolong the harvest season for asparagus it is recommended that part of the bed be planted 4-6 inches shallower than recommended above.

If planting asparagus seed, instead of roots, follow basically the same procedures as outlined above. The seeds should be planted approximately 1/2 inch deep after you have filled the trench to approximately 8-10 inches from the top with the enriched soil. By planting seeds instead of roots, you will delay your asparagus crop approximately one year.

WATERING

For the first two weeks after planting, it is especially important to keep the asparagus roots damp. Thereafter they should be watered approximately once per week, depending on the soil and the weather.

It is also important to remember that if your soil is very heavy clay with poor drainage, it is possible to kill either roots or seedlings by watering too much or too frequently. If the water were to stand in the trench around the plants for long periods of time, it would cause them to turn yellow and die. Planting in a trench can encourage this problem if the trench is located in a low, poorly drained location or an area where waste water frequently stands. After the trench has been completely filled, you should make furrows at least 28-36 inches apart on both sides of the row of asparagus plant if you plan to water in furrows. Then water the asparagus approximately once per week during the harvest season, allowing it to soak at least one hour each watering. If you will be watering with a drip system furrows won't be necessary. Put the drip lines two feet apart, on each side of the row of asparagus. In the spring and early summer while you are harvesting spears soak the bed for 2 hours every week with the drip system. After you stop harvesting and the spears have grown to ferns, soak the bed for three hours every two weeks with the drip system until the ferns die in the fall.

FERTILIZING

In order to understand the proper application of fertilizer, it is important to know where the food in the new asparagus spears comes from. During the summer, the spears become large asparagus ferns with many tiny leaves. Food is manufactured in these leaves throughout the summer and stored in the roots. Immediately before the leaves turn yellow and die in the fall, large amounts of food are transferred from leaves and stems into the roots for winter storage. As the soil begins to warm in the spring, spears begin to grow from the roots. No food is being manufactured, so all of the growth in the new spears comes from food stored in the roots the previous summer.

For this reason, it is very important to have a heavy, vigorous top growth of ferns during the summer in order to have thick, heavy and delicious spears the next spring. For these reasons, the most important time to fertilize the asparagus is in the late spring or early summer when you are about to stop harvesting

It is important to grow large, healthy ferns for maximum production and storage of food for next year's crop.

asparagus for the table. Then the fertilizer will help the plant to grow large, vigorous foliage (ferns). For this purpose, a high-nitrogen fertilizer like ammonium sulfate is preferable. This is all totally soluble and can easily be watered into the root zone at the proper time. One subsequent feeding should be made in the fall. This is done at the time that the ferns are completely dead in the late fall and you roto-till them into the ground. By planting the asparagus deep as described above, you can roto-till shallowly (2-3 inches deep) over the bed each fall. In that process you roto-till into the bed the complete fertilizer (16-16-8 and Ironite as described in Application of Commercial Fertilizer on pages **21-22**) along with the asparagus ferns and added grass clippings and leaves. This will leave the soil filled with humus for the spring crop of spears so that it is easy for them to push through the surface. Be careful in roto-tilling that you do not go so deep that you cut into the asparagus roots. If you planted normally as described above, 2-3 inches is about the right depth to roto-till.

PEST CONTROL

Dust with Sevin before the new shoots begin to emerge to control asparagus beetle. Scatter snail-slug bait around the bed as necessary.

HARVESTING

After planting the roots in the spring, the asparagus must grow until the next spring before you start harvesting. Then you will only get a small crop because you will need to leave an adequate number of spears to grow into the ferns which produce food for next year's crop. The best rule is to harvest only for a two week period during this second year and then go to a harvesting period of 4-6 weeks the third year and 8-10 weeks each year thereafter. Each year it is important to stop harvesting early enough so that the plant can produce a lot of good healthy ferns.

Like many vegetables, asparagus spears are best when harvested very young. As they get older they get stringy, tough and strong tasting. Use a sharp knife for harvesting asparagus and cut the spears right under the surface of the ground when they are about 4-5 inches tall. Avoid long, deep cuts which will injure other spears which have not yet emerged as well as the plant's root system.

Beans

The members of the bean family, including string beans (also known as snap or green beans), lima beans and soy beans, are all legumes. This means that if there are adequate quantities of nitrogen-fixing bacteria in the soil, they take nitrogen out of the air and change it into usable plant food. Because of this abundant source of nitrogen, beans are an excellent source of protein. (See page 14-15 for information about legumes.)

Pole Beans vs. Bush Beans

Green beans are separated into two categories: pole beans and bush beans. Although they look very much alike, the quality and taste of the two are very different. Pole beans are known for a delicious, mild, nutty flavor. In contrast, bush beans always seem to have a "green" taste, even when thoroughly cooked. Bush beans were developed for mechanical harvesting,

*A child experiences great satisfaction in the way **her** bean plant is growing. She watches it so closely that she can almost see it grow.*

so the whole crop ripens at about the same time. Commercial growers want to grow them quickly, harvest them all in one picking and then put the land into another crop. In contrast, the pole beans ripen slowly over a long season. In a home garden this long season gives you fresh beans over a much longer period of time in addition to superior quality and greater yield.

VARIETIES OF BUSH BEANS

There are also bush beans which have been developed from crosses made with the standard good tasting pole beans. These improved bush beans ('Bush Blue Lake 274' and 'Bush Kentucky Wonder 125') ripen over a two week period and do well in the heat of the summer because their blossoms are placed in the shade and under the canopy of foliage. For that reason these green beans set fruit during the heat of summer when pole beans sometimes drop their blossoms because they are exposed to the heat of the sun.

VARIETIES OF POLE BEAN

'Kentucky Wonder'- This variety has a rich, distinctive flavor which has made it the most popular green bean among home gardeners. The pods are long and attractive. There are both brown-seeded and white-seeded strains of this variety and although they have some slightly different characteristics, both are excellent.

'Blue Lake' - This variety is famous for the freezing qualities of its thick, meaty green beans. The pods are mild, tender, stringless and extremely low in fibrous material, even when quite mature.

'Kentucky Blue' – This variety is a cross between 'Kentucky Wonder' and 'Blue Lake' which has some of the best qualities of each. It is an All America Award Winner and has many excellent qualities.

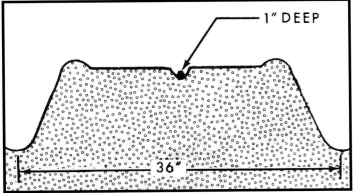

Plant seeds 3 inches apart down the center of a 36 inch row. Thin to 6 inches apart when they come up.

PLANTING

Beans should be planted down the center of a 30-36 inch row. The easiest way to plant is to make a small furrow, one inch deep, down the middle of the row with a pointed hoe. Then place seeds 2- 3 inches apart in the bottom of this furrow-and cover them up so that they are 1 inch deep. In heavy clay soil it is better to plant them shallower than one inch because it is hard for the young plant to push its leaves through

that much hard clay. After they come up, thin plants to 6 inches apart.

Bush beans are a heat-loving plant, so they should be planted in the summer garden to take advantage of the heat which that season provides. This means that the first planting should take place approximately May 1 - May 15 in most areas. Successive plantings once a month until mid-summer will extend your bean crop into the fall. Plant beans in full sun if possible to satisfy their need for heat and light.

As mentioned above it sometimes gets so hot in mid-summer in some areas that the blossoms of pole beans drop without setting fruit because they are up on poles exposed to full sun. In these very hot summer areas the author has found that pole beans are best planted in the heat of summer (by the first of July) so that they begin to mature in the late summer (mid-August) when the weather is not quite so hot. They will then set a heavy crop which will continue for two months if not interrupted by frost. Because pole beans produce for much longer, the crop is much larger. They are also superior in taste.

Planting beans with corn is not recommended. If the corn is healthy, it creates such dense shade that the beans do very poorly. If the corn is planted very thin, planting the beans along with it and allowing them to grow up the corn stalks might be acceptable, but even then the beans will grow clear to the top of the corn and partially shade the corn.

Beans and corn were once planted together because corn needed a lot of nitrogen and beans, being legumes, helped fill the need. Now that an adequate supply of nitrogen is available from other sources, you can get a better crop of each if planted separately.

POLES AND TRELLISES

All sorts of contraptions are satisfactory for pole beans to climb. The important thing is that they need to be 5-7 feet tall and sturdy enough so that they will not blow over in the wind. Pole beans prefer to climb up small diameter objects like twine or small poles rather than large, thick ones. If you have access to a

An inexpensive bean trellis can be constructed with a few 6-7 foot pole or steel posts and a ball of twine.

and beans. The beans climb up by going around and around the poles or trellis, always in a counter clockwise direction.

Whether using bean poles or making a string trellis, a steel post should be driven into the ground every 15-20 feet to support the wire at the top of the poles. The string trellis is made by tying a wire at the top from post to post with enough tension to avoid a lot of sag. Run a piece of twine from post to post approximately 4 inches from the ground and then make a pattern of strings which are approximately 6 inches apart between the top and bottom. This can be done by cutting many individual strips just long enough so that they can be tied between the top wire and the bottom twine and dangle almost to the ground. See the illustration for constructing this pole bean trellis with twine. It is very inexpensive and works fine. Once the bean plant begins to put out runners, they will move with surprising speed up the strings or poles to the top and thereby expose a tremendous amount of foliage to sunlight and good air circulation.

Bean teepees are constructed by putting four one-inch square redwood stakes onto the ground out 4 or 5 feet apart at the bottom with the stakes crossing about 4-6 inches from the top in the shape of a teepee. Use a soft wire like bailing wire at the top to wire all four stakes together. Place 3 or 4 bean seeds in the soil on the inside of each pole at the bottom. Thin the plants to one under each pole when they come up and the plant will climb the pole to the top. The only trouble with the bean teepee is that the beans are harder to pick than the other methods described.

FERTILIZING

A good complete fertilizer should be worked thoroughly into the soil before planting. Refer to Application of Commercial Fertilizer on pages **21-22** for the type and amount of fertilizer to use. Beans are one of the crops which are especially susceptible to zinc and iron deficiencies, so in some areas where the soils have been shown to be low in these elements, it is important to have these as part of your complete fertilizer.

large number of poles without a great deal of expense, push one into the ground approximately every six inches down the center of the row of beans. These can be inserted immediately after planting the beans before watering, or after they are up and growing before they start putting out runners. Six foot bamboo poles from Home Depot are not very expensive and last for years as bean poles.

Tie all of the poles at the top to a piece of wire stretched tight between steel posts at each end of the row of beans. These poles can be tied to the wire with electrical or duct tape so they are secure. The wire can even be electric speaker wire from Wal-Mart which is coated with plastic. Wire is better than string because it does not stretch. The steel posts need to be driven at least 12 or more inches into the ground so they won't blow over when the poles are loaded with vines

A tall trellis makes beans easier to pick and is an excellent way to get pole beans into the air.

As discussed in detail in the plant food (fertilizer) section, beans and other legumes have the capacity to take free nitrogen out of the air and convert it to usable nitrates. For this reason, it is unnecessary to make repeated applications of nitrogen fertilizer with most crops of beans. This assumes that there is an adequate supply of nitrogen-fixing bacteria in your soil or that you inoculate your bean seeds before planting with a nitrogen-fixing bacteria powder. Beans will leave the soil richer in nitrogen than it was before.

WATERING

To get beans up, soak the ground thoroughly with the Rainbird-type sprinkler or a drip system soon after planting. Depending on the temperature, when the beans are planted, they should be watered again in about three days and again in approximately one week. When the seedlings are beginning to push through the surface, water them again in the same manner. This softens the crust on the surface as well as giving the roots the moisture which they need. After the beans come up, it is far better to water in the furrows or by drip system. This helps to avoid fungus diseases on the leaves as well as being much easier. After the beans begin climbing the trellis, it would be very difficult

to water by sprinkler because they are so tall. (See the PLANTING YOUR GARDEN section for methods of using drip and of making and using furrows.)

When watering in furrows, remember to fill the furrows and then turn the water down so that it keeps the furrows full for at least an hour before turning it off. Beans should be watered in this manner approximately once per week in warm weather. (See pages 25-31 and 64-74 for watering principles and methods.)

PEST CONTROL

Insects such as beetles, leaf hoppers, grasshoppers and moth larvae can become a problem on bean leaves. They will make holes in the leaves and eventually shorten the life of the plant. If they become a problem, they should be sprayed or dusted with Sevin. Both spraying and dusting should be done during the earlier stages of growth before the fruiting stage begins in order to avoid contaminating the food. Snails and slugs can also be a problem. Put snail-slug bait around the garden when the plants are young to avoid the problem.

Three reasons for keeping vegetables such as beans, cucumbers, peas, peppers, and summer squash well picked:

1. Crop quality is superior. They become tough and strong tasting as they become more mature.
2. The final maturation process takes a great deal of food and energy from the plant.
3. As these vegetables mature on the vine, the plant's urge to reproduce is satisfied and the plant stops blooming.

HARVESTING

Pole beans will produce over a period of approximately two months. It is important for length of harvest and food quality to pick the green beans before they become too mature. If the pods are allowed to mature on the vine, the plant stops setting on more fruit. They should be picked just as the bean begins to show as a bulge on the pod. If left a day or two, the bulge becomes large and the pod becomes tough and stringy. Use two hands for picking, one to hold the stem and the second to pick the bean. This will leave the young beans and blossoms which are located on the same stem to mature for the next picking.

Bush Beans

The basic planting, watering and fertilizing practices discussed under pole beans apply as well to bush beans. The big difference is that they do not require poles or trellises to climb on, but form a small bush approximately two feet tall and two feet across. They produce heavy yields in a small space and in a very short period of time, maturing a few days earlier than pole beans. They are very easy to grow and require no support. The recommended varieties of bush bean are 'Bush Blue Lake 274' and 'Bush Kentucky Wonder 125'.

Lima Beans

Lima beans, like string beans, come in both pole and bush varieties. The cultural directions are very much like those already given for pole and bush beans. There are some peculiarities with limas which need to be noted.

The soil needs to be quite warm for good germination of lima beans. They have a difficult time coming up because the new leaves are large and often try to push the seed itself through the surface of the ground. It is usually recommended that they be planted one inch deep on edge with the "eyes" down to give them a better chance of pushing through the surface.

The bush type grow larger than regular bush green beans, so they need to be planted at least four inches apart on 24-36 inch rows and thinned to 8 inches apart when they come up. They can either be planted down the top of a 24 inch row or planted on both sides of a 36 inch row.

VARIETIES

There are several excellent quality lima bean varieties in both pole and bush beans. The old favorite

pole lima is King of the Garden. Two excellent newer varieties are 'Prizetaker' and 'Burpee's Best'. In the bush limas, three outstanding varieties are. 'Fordhook 242', 'Burpee's Fordhook', and 'Burpee's Improved Bush Limas'.

HARVESTING

Lima beans should be picked as soon as the seeds become large enough to make the pod look slightly lumpy. The younger they are picked, the more tender and moist the limas will be. Keeping the plants well-picked will also prolong the plant's production.

Dry Beans

These are grown in the same way as bush string beans and bush limas, except that the pods are allowed to remain on the plant until they are mature and begin to dry. The 'Kentucky Wonder'-type of pole beans also make excellent dry beans. Just leave the last of your bean crop on the plant to fully mature. After the plant has died and the pods are dry, the beans are ready to be harvested, shelled and used.

Soy Beans

Edible soy beans are a valuable source of protein and are often used as a meat substitute. They do best in warm weather. Plant them like bush green beans and bush limas. They can be harvested when the pod is green and cooked similarly to lima beans or allowed to fully mature and dry like dry beans. The varieties of soy beans most often recommended are Bansei, Kanrich and Early Green Bush.

Beets

Beets are great food, not only for their delicious sweet roots, but also for their tender stems and leaves. For beet greens, they should be harvested when the root is marble size and the tops are approximately 6 inches tall. Wash carefully to remove all of the grit from the roots, cook like spinach and eat the whole plant. Many families feel that beet greens are better tasting than either spinach or Swiss chard.

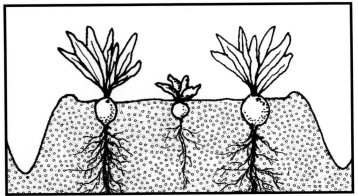

To get maximum yield in a small space, use triple-planted rows with either radishes or beet greens in the center which can be pulled in thirty days to avoid crowding.

VARIETIES

For many years the favorite variety has been Detroit Dark Red. There are now several strains of this variety including Detroit Supreme and Perfected Detroit. Other excellent varieties of beets include Crosby Green Top, Pacemaker II, and Crosby's Egyptian. Another variety of beet, known variously as Lutz Green Leaf, Winter Keeper and Long Season, matures very slowly, but keeps for a long period of time without getting tough and strong. It is very sweet, with a slightly different taste than most beets, and appears to be a near relative of the sugar beet. Although very sweet, the flavor has a hard time competing with the old standard Detroit Dark Red. A fairly recent development is Burpee's Golden Beet which does not bleed like a red beet and has its own mild, sweet flavor.

PLANTING

Beets should be planted approximately ½ inch deep on 24-30 inch rows. For maximum quality and yield in a small space, the easiest way is to triple-plant the top of the row with beets on either side and radishes in the center. The radishes mature very quickly (approximately 30 days) so they can be pulled before the beet tops get large enough to cover them. This gives you an extra crop as well as loosening the soil for the beets. Beets can also be planted in this same way between rows of carrots and then pulled for beet greens in approximately 30 days, giving you an additional crop as well as loosening the soil for the carrots. In any event, with all of your beets, you will find it is very difficult to plant them thin enough to allow them to enlarge properly at maturity. The easy way is to plant them fairly thick and then thin them when they are approximately 6 inches tall and use all of the plants which you remove for beet greens. This gives you delicious greens as well as the 3-4 inch spaces between plants needed for good large beets.

WATERING

Beets do best in cool, early summer or fall weather. They are not injured by light frost and can be planted in the early spring garden. If planted in July or August, they mature in the cool weather of the late fall and will store in the ground for several months.

Like the other root crops, they need a relatively even, consistent moisture level. In the early spring weather, a once a week watering schedule is sufficient, but when the weather begins to get warm, you need to water twice a week for top quality beets.

FERTILIZING

Because beets mature very quickly (approximately 55 days), one application of a good complete fertilizer (like 16-16-8 and Ironite) before planting is adequate to mature the crop. (See Application of Commercial Fertilizer for the kind and amount to apply.) Beets benefit from large quantities of organic material worked into the soil. This improves soil texture and is particularly valuable with root crops.

HARVESTING

Beets are at their best (sweet and tender) when very young. Start harvesting them for the table when they are ½ inch in diameter as beet greens. This should be done by thinning the row so that the remaining beets are at least 4-5 inches apart and have plenty of room to continue to expand. If they mature in cool weather they will continue to enlarge and still taste good for several weeks but they get tough and woody if left in the ground too long.

Berries

Every home garden should include berries. With proper cultural practices, berry plants will produce an abundant harvest of nature's most delectable food.

The three kinds of berries discussed in this section (blackberries, raspberries and strawberries) have vastly different growth habits, but they have several important characteristics in common. They are all perennials which require a certain amount of cold winter weather to give them vigor, good quality and heavy yield in the next year's crop. All three thrive on a regular supply of water and a high-nitrogen diet. Although they produce seeds, each of them reproduces by another means (strawberries by runners and the other two by rhizome root growth with new shoots coming from the ground) although western trailing blackberries also reproduce by pushing the growing tip of each vine into the ground in the fall where they grow new roots and leaves in the spring.

The children always volunteer to help pick the strawberries, but they eat about as many as they pick.

Strawberries

Strawberries are a delight to grow because of their sweet, delicious and tangy flavor, their excellent nutrition (being rich in vitamin C and anti-oxidants) and the abundance of the harvest which they yield. Commercial growers produce up to 30 tons per acre of this delightful fruit in a 4 month fruiting season.

Strawberries are a native American fruit. The modern berry was developed by hybridization of the wild species of Eastern North America and the wild species of South America together with a wild day-neutral (ever bearing) variety from the mouth of Brighton canyon in Salt Lake City, Utah.

VARIETIES

There are many varieties of strawberries and new ones are being developed all the time. In choosing a variety, it is important to pick one which performs well in the climate of your area and is resistant to damage from diseases and insect pests.

Strawberries are divided into June-bearing (short-day) and ever bearing (day-neutral) varieties. (There are technically some differences between the ever bearing varieties and the true day-neutral cultivars, but for convenience they are all grouped together for our discussion in this book.) Generally speaking, in comparing June bearing (short day) varieties with ever bearing types their one advantage in the home garden is that the crop is more concentrated into a shorter period of time which is better when you need a large quantity for putting up jam. On the other hand, the ever bearing (day-neutral) varieties, even though they don't give quite as many berries in the spring (or early summer in short season areas) they give a larger yield overall and a more or less continuous production over a long season.

The June bearing types are induced by the shorter days of fall, winter and spring to bloom and produce fruit. Along the California Coast they start producing in February and keep fruiting until May. In more severe inland climates, they do not start growing until it warms up in the spring and may not start producing until early April and as late as June, depending on the weather. They also produce berries for a much shorter period of time because the hot weather encourages them to stop producing berries and start producing runners. Watering more frequently keeps them producing longer and discourages runners.

Ever bearing varieties of strawberry and particularly the true day-neutral types are not induced by day length, but start producing as soon as they mature enough to bloom and fruit, which is usually about 90 days from the date of planting under good weather conditions. They continue fruiting if the weather does not get too hot or too cold. As was mentioned with the June bearing varieties, watering more frequently encourages continued fruit production and delays the production of runners. Pinching off the runners also encourages the continuation of fruiting and large size strawberries. See the illustration on this page of strawberries picked on July 18th in 100 degree F. weather from 'Albion' and 'Diamante' varieties of day-neutral strawberries. These same plants produced approximately 50-70 berries per plant in late May and throughout June when it was much cooler where the author lives in Utah Valley. The July crop is very small but they come on with heavier production in late August, September and October until heavy frost ruins the remaining berries. The harvest here is much smaller than in coastal California where the weather stays cool.

The **best varieties in the June bearing** (short-day) berries are:

'Ventana'

'Sequoia'

'Camino Real'

'Camarosa'

The **best of the ever bearing (day-neutral) varieties** are:

'Albion'

'Diamante'

'Fern'

'Selva'

'Hecker'

All of the forgoing have excellent eating quality (taste and size) and have excellent disease resistance. 'Albion' and 'Diamante' are especially outstanding and do well over a broad range of weather conditions. It is important that they do not shrivel in the low relative humidity and hot arid conditions of much of the west. 'Albion' is the author's favorite. It is the first to bear fruit in the spring and the last in the fall.

This is the spring/early summer crop of strawberries. It is the largest crop and will run between 50 and 150 berries per plant depending on how the berries are grown and your climate.

CLIMATE

Like many types of fruiting perennials, the strawberry requires a certain amount of winter chilling to give the plant vigor, good quality fruit and an abundant harvest the next spring and summer. This chilling requirement is satisfied in colder areas by normal winter weather.

Warm Winter Areas. In the warm winter climates of coastal California, this need for cold weather is not satisfied in the normal manner with plants in the ground, so strawberry plants are given an "artificial winter." New, young strawberry plants which have grown from runners the prior summer are dug in the winter after some chilling (below 40 degrees F.) and stored at 29-30 degrees F. until planted. They are then carefully planted at the proper time so that the chilling influence of this artificial winter does not wear off before the crop is harvested. This artificial winter is given to the plants by refrigerating them at 29-30 degrees F. for a period of time (several months in most cases). Because the plant vigor and fruit quality given by chilling wear off, the strawberry plants are worked into the soil after harvest each year in these coastal climates and new "chilled" bare-root plants are planted out to take their place. In colder climates, strawberry plants, being perennials, will produce good crops for about three or four years.

In warm winter areas, planting time should be approximately August 1st, but fluctuates to some extent depending on the number of cold days which a particular area has during the winter. Strawberries are planted bare root, without any foliage, having just finished a long, cold winter in cold storage. The speed and vigor of their growth during the next three or four months is almost unbelievable. They then go through a short semi-dormant period in December (the second "winter"), begin to come out of their dormancy in January and start setting on fruit in February. In these warm winter areas, they produce an abundant harvest continuously over a long season (approximately March 15 to July 15) during temperate spring and summer weather.

There is one additional strategy used in the south coast of California where partially chilled plants from mountainous areas of northern California are dug in late October and November and planted immediately. They are kept growing throughout the winter by substantial amounts of nitrogen fertilizer and start producing berries in January. They don't produce the large yields as other methods of planting do but come into bearing much earlier than other strategies.

Cold Winter Areas. In areas of adequate winter cold for chilling, strawberry plants should be planted in the spring as soon as the severe cold weather and snow are gone. This would usually mean planting in early April. If you are planting June bearing (short-day) berries, you will get a very small crop during June from the short-day induction before the berry plants were dug in the late fall or winter. They will not bear fruit again until an abundant crop comes the next June.

If you are planting ever bearing (day-neutral) varieties like 'Albion', you should pick off the blooms that come immediately to let the plants

grow large very quickly. As soon as they are mature enough (approximately 90 days) you will start getting good strawberries. They will keep producing until stopped by cold weather in the late fall. These ever bearers will give you an abundant crop throughout the next season. The cold weather of late fall, winter and early spring give the plants the chilling they need for large vigorous plants and they can be left in the ground for 3 or 4 seasons.

Strawberry plants should be stagger-planted approximately 12 inches apart down each side of a 36 inch row. This photo was taken 8 days after setting out bare root plants without leaves.

PLANTING

The easiest way is double planting on 36 inch rows (raised beds). The plants should be placed 10-14 inches apart down each side of the bed and staggered back and forth to give the maximum distance between plants. Avoid planting too close to the furrows because the fruit grows in clusters beyond the leaves and tends to hang down into the furrows where the green berries are easily stepped on while picking.

Strawberries are planted from bare roots which have been in cold storage, so they are just roots with a crown (leaf buds ready to emerge) and no leaves. Sometimes strawberry plants are purchased in pony packs at a nursery. These were started from bare root plants 3-4 weeks earlier and look better to the consuming public because they now have green leaves and sometimes flowers, but they are usually much more expensive than purchasing plants bare root.

Whichever way you purchase the plants, they should be planted with the roots covered and only the crown protruding from the soil. The crown is the area where the leaves emerge, not the stems of cut-off leaves protruding above the crown. (See illustration). The hole for the roots should be deep enough so that the roots will stretch down full length into the hole with the crown just protruding out of the soil. This is easily done with a garden trowel.

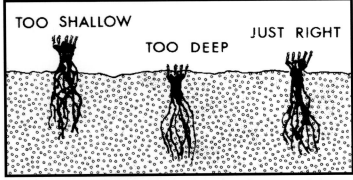

Strawberries should be planted so that the crown is just above ground level. The soil will settle down a little around the plant after being watered, so be careful not to leave too much plant exposed. Don't mistake the base of cut off leaves for the crown.

RUNNERS

Strawberry plants reproduce by putting out runners which grow roots and leaves every foot or so to form new plants. This process may start fairly soon after planting and also occurs each year at the end of the fruiting season as the weather gets warmer (especially if they get too dry).

The runners should be removed to encourage the plant to continue producing berries. If the runners are allowed to remain and grow new plants, the berry patch will soon become too thick (a matted forest of strawberry plants) to produce good berries. Not only will the size of the berries decrease, but the overall quality and yield as well.

FERTILIZING

Because strawberries are in the ground a long time, it is especially important to prepare the soil properly. It is very helpful to work substantial amounts of organic material into the top 8-10 inches of soil before planting. This will improve soil texture and fertility and encourage extensive, healthy root growth. In addition to other sources of humus, sphagnum peat moss is very helpful to the soil when planting a strawberry patch. It not only improves the soil texture but it also has a pH of 3.0 to 4.0 which will help acidify the soil for this acid loving crop. Because most western soils tend to be too alkaline for strawberries, it is also helpful to add elemental sulfur to the soil to make it more acid. Use 4 quarts of sulfur for 180 square feet of area which is double the amount of sulfur for other crops and mix it thoroughly with the soil.

As discussed in detail in the section on Plant Food (Fertilizer) and especially the part about Minor (Trace) Elements, strawberries are very susceptible to chlorosis which is caused by deficiencies in iron, zinc and manganese. The elemental soil sulfur is changed by soil microorganisms into sulfuric acid which lowers the pH of the soil. This process also makes the trace elements iron, zinc and manganese more available to the plant.

Although strawberries are nitrogen-loving plants, it is also helpful to work a complete fertilizer containing all three of the major plant foods (nitrogen, phosphorous and potassium) as well as iron, zinc and manganese into the soil along with the organic matter before planting. Refer to Application of Commercial Fertilizer on pages **21-22** for the type and amount of each element to use. It is important in planting bare root strawberries to not over fertilize on the initial application of the complete fertilizer before planting them. In other words, be careful not to use more than one quart for 180 square feet and if your soil has been well fertilized in the past and has a lot of decomposed organic matter and is not excessively sandy, use a little less than one quart of commercial fertilizer. It is a fact that too much fertilizer will restrict the growth of new roots with any bare root planting so be moderate.

Approximately one month after planting the strawberries, add a second small application of high nitrogen fertilizer to your strawberry bed. By this time the plants will be well rooted and will respond quickly to the fertilizer. This second application should be about half the amount of the first application, i.e. about ½ quart for 180 square feet. You could use straight ammonium sulfate (21% nitrogen) or you could use a mix of 1/3 ammonium sulfate, 1/3 Grow More Soil Acidifier (or Miracle Gro Azalea Food), and 1/3 Ironite. The first two products are totally soluble and the third partially so. After sprinkling this high nitrogen acid type fertilizer down the top of the bed, carefully water it into the soil. This can be done with a Rainbird (impact type) sprinkler. If you are using a hand sprinkler on the end of a hose, turn the pressure way down so the water is coming out slowly enough that it soaks into the soil as you walk up and down along the bed. You want the fertilizer to soak straight down where you placed it and not run off to over-fertilize another spot. After soaking it down a few inches, a drip system can be used for the rest of the watering. This process precedes the putting down of black plastic landscaping cloth over the drip system.

Strawberries are super-sensitive to an excess amount of "salt" in the soil and salt burn can be caused by putting on too much fertilizer in any one application. For this reason, a light application is a better idea.

SECOND AND THIRD YEAR FERTILIZING

In colder areas strawberry plants should last at least three years in the ground and it is important that they be fertilized every year. For raspberries and blackberries where you have no covering over the beds, it is easy to sprinkle the soluble fertilizer over the beds in the late winter or early spring and let the snow and rain carry it into the beds, but the strawberry beds are covered with black plastic or landscaping cloth, so the fertilizer has to be placed under the plastic or landscape cloth over the drip lines so that it can be watered into the soil.

The beds need to be cleaned up each spring by removing all dead leaves so only a few small leaves beginning to protrude out of the crown of the plant are left. For that reason the outside edges of the black plastic or landscaping cloth can be flipped back over the plants and held down by bricks or rocks, exposing the drip line. The soluble fertilizer is then sprinkled down the row over the drip line where it can then be watered with a hand sprinkler on the end of a hose with the pressure turned way down and subsequently water completely into the root zone by the drip system. This is cumbersome but it works and it only needs to be done once a year in the early spring.

A mixture of the fertilizer mentioned in Fertilizing Established Perennial Crops is ideal for this purpose. It contains 1/3 ammonium sulfate, 1/3 Grow More Soil Acidifier or Miracle Gro Azalea Food (30% Nitrogen, 10% Phosphate, 10% Potassium, .325% Iron, .05% Zinc, .05% Manganese, .05% Copper, 1% Sulfur, .02% Boron and .005% Molybdenum) and 1/3 Ironite. One quart of this mixture for 180 square feet will provide healthy vigorous growth of plants.

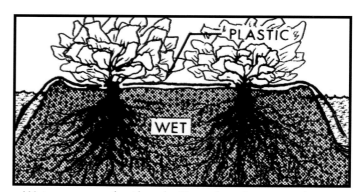

Water goes under the plastic and soaks across the root zone when using furrows.

WATERING

Strawberries need to be watered regularly to keep an even, consistent moisture level in the soil. They have a relatively shallow root system, filling the soil with roots to a depth of approximately 2 feet. Letting them get too dry stimulates the growth of runners for reproduction and stops the plant from setting on fruit.

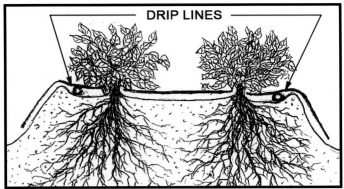

DRIP LINES

Notice that the drip lines run between the berm and the plants down both sides of the bed when using a drip system. The emitters are 1 foot apart down each line.

At Planting Time. The ground should be thoroughly soaked immediately after planting. The easiest way is to use an impact type (Rainbird) sprinkler, allowing it to run approximately one hour if set on a quarter- circle and longer if set for a larger pattern. It is equally effective to use a drip system down both sides of the raised bed. If the furrows are properly made, it is also possible to let the water run down the top of the row around the plants (see illustration on page **73**) and thereby water the strawberry patch row by row as the plants are being put into the ground.

If planted in warm summer weather, strawberry plants should be watered for a few minutes every day for the first week. If planted in cool weather, every other day is adequate, even during the first week. This will keep the root zone very moist and the bare root strawberry plant will put out a multitude of tiny hair roots in a very short time. During the second week after planting, you should water every two or three days, depending on the weather.

Regular Watering Schedule. After two weeks, go to a regular twice-a-week watering schedule which you will want to follow throughout the warm part of each growing season. If you water with an impact type (Rainbird) sprinkler, let it run long enough to soak the root zone. Once the plants are established, it is preferable to water in furrows or by drip system rather than sprinkling because the frequent moisture on leaves and fruit causes fungus diseases and spoilage. It is also necessary to water by drip system or in furrows when using plastic mulch around the plants because

The first strawberries of the season are always the largest, but these berries from day neutral 'Albion' and 'Diamante' plants, held by the author, picked in the heat of summer (July 18th at 100 degrees F.) are also fairly large and extremely delicious. They continue all summer and into the fall if watered and fertilized correctly.

the water can't get into the ground from above through the mulch. The water soaks across from the furrows under the plastic so that the root zone gets soaked. It is usually necessary to keep the furrows filled for at least one hour before turning the water off. (For additional information about irrigation and especially about drip systems, see the sections starting on pages **64, 69--72.**)

If you live in an area where it gets very hot in the summer and your berry patch is mostly ever bearing (day-neutral) varieties, you will want to keep the fruit coming all summer. To do that it is helpful to plant several varieties of day-neutral strawberries. Even though 'Albion' and 'Diamante' may be the best overall, if you also plant a few 'Fern' and maybe even some 'Hecker' and 'Eversweet', they will fill niches when the first two slow down so you will have a more continuous supply. If you want your day-neutrals to keep producing during very hot weather, you will also need to add a third watering every week to your schedule. See the illustration of strawberries picked on July 18th in the Provo area of Utah on a day when the temperature was 100 degrees F. and the relative humidity very low. The berries are large, sweet, and delicious and show no signs of shriveling in spite of the high heat and extremely low humidity. The berry size is **largest** when they **start producing** each season but certain varieties like 'Albion' and 'Diamante' stay fairly large throughout the season.

MULCH

Organic mulches of various kinds have been used for many years around strawberry plants. They help to preserve an even, consistent moisture level as well as keeping the fruit off the ground. They are still recommended for strawberries in some areas.

Grass clippings make an excellent organic mulch and they are almost always available. They should be placed approximately 4-6 inches deep around each plant after they are growing vigorously. This organic mulch will also almost totally eliminate weeds from the area which is covered. The entire row area around the plants should be mulched. Straw is also used for mulching around strawberries. Organic mulches are more commonly used for mulching in the east and midwest where it is important that the regular rainfall be able to filter through the mulch to get to the roots. The problem with organic mulches is that they tend to attract and hide insects that eat holes in the berries. In the west, where rainfall is not an issue and irrigation for strawberries is mostly by drip systems, plastic or landscaping cloth is a much better type of mulch.

Clear Plastic. Clear plastic (polyethylene) mulch is used in coastal areas for strawberries. It is usually applied in the winter when the plants are approximately 5 months old. Planted in early August, they are almost full-size by the first of January. At that time the older leaves around the edges of each plant are trimmed off, all of the weeds in the strawberry patch are removed and snail, slug, sow bug and earwig bait is sprinkled over the entire row. After this general clean-up, the plastic film is placed over the row and small circles or "X's" are cut in the plastic for each plant and they are then carefully pulled through so that the plastic settles down against the ground. The sun shining through the clear plastic increases soil temperature approximately 15°. This helps bring the plants out of their dormancy and causes extensive root growth and early production of the strawberries (beginning to ripen in February and March). The plastic also retards evaporation from the soil and keeps the berries off the ground, thus greatly reducing spoilage. In coastal climates, this method of mulching is the best way to grow strawberries.

The only problem with the clear plastic is that it does not prevent the growth of weeds. In commercial production the soil is fumigated to kill all weed seed so weeds under the plastic are not a problem. In the home garden if the soil is solarized and relatively weed-free, this is not a big problem because one weeding under the plastic in February will take care of the weeds. With the abundant top growth of the strawberry plants pressing down on the plastic, any remaining weeds which tend to grow are shaded out and don't amount to much.

If strawberry plants are healthy, they grow large and are covered with fruit. Notice that this area was solarized to kill weed seeds and clear plastic mulch was used.

Black Plastic or Landscaping Cloth.

In soils with an abundance of weeds, an alternative is black plastic (polyethylene) mulch. It eliminates weeds as well as retaining moisture and keeping the berries off the ground. Black plastic is especially valuable in the culture of vegetables which require a lot of heat on the vine, but with strawberries the excessive heat is not helpful. The black plastic also absorbs heat rather than letting it pass through into the soil, so the soil temperature is not increased as much in winter months like it is under clear plastic. In spite of these problems, black plastic is often used because it controls the weed problem.

Another solution which works very well in strawberries is black landscaping cloth. It is a woven cloth-like material made out of black polyethylene which does not get hot like black plastic but prevents weeds, retains moisture and keeps the fruit off the ground. It is relatively inexpensive at places like Home Depot and Lowe's and lasts longer than the plastic. Black plastic lasts two years and the landscaping cloth should last three or more. It is put over the beds just like the plastic mulch after the second application of fertilizer and is an excellent alternative in the home garden.

(Do **NOT** put landscaping cloth **UNDER** berry plants roots or under anything else you plant in the garden because it will stop the growth of the roots. People who use grow boxes sometimes put landscaping cloth under their plants where the grow box meets the ground and then they wonder why the plants wilt and won't grow.)

HARVESTING

The great advantage of growing strawberries in the home garden is that they can be picked ripe and refrigerated immediately. Most of the sweetness comes in the last two or three days of the ripening process so picking them ripe makes a great deal of difference in berry quality. A straw-berry patch needs to be picked three or four times a week during the fruiting season. Some people think they are getting a good crop of strawberries when they get 15-20 berries per plant per season. They have hardly scratched the surface. If you follow proper cultural practices as described in this section, you should be getting at least 100 berries per plant each year. Along the coast where the winters are not cold and it stays cool all summer you will almost double the yield.

PEST CONTROL

Snails, slugs, sow bugs and earwigs are the most serious insect pests for strawberries in the home garden. Baits can be purchased which kill all four, and should be sprinkled around the strawberry patch immediately after planting to keep them out as much as possible. In the winter or spring, after the patch is cleaned up, as described earlier, the snail, slug, sow bug and earwig bait should be sprinkled around and over the crown of each plant before putting down the plastic mulch. (This is done in January in coastal areas and in March or April in cold winter areas.) If you use an organic mulch, sprinkle the bait on top of the mulch around and into the crown of the plant. Strawberry plants place their berries around the perimeter, usually beyond their leaves, so the bait which is placed right around and in the crown of the plant before it begins to grow in the spring will not contaminate the fruit. It is also helpful to sprinkle bait around the perimeter of the entire berry patch periodically throughout the season to keep these pests out.

Aphids and spider mites can occasionally be a problem on strawberry plants. To kill these pests, spray with Malathion or Neem Oil. Mix according to directions on the bottle and apply with a tank-type sprayer. Neem Oil will also control fungus diseases like powdery and downey mildew and grey mold on berries.

Raspberries

These berries are delightful to eat and fun to grow. Plant them in a spot where they can stay for several years because they are a perennial and take a while to get established.

Raspberries do well in most western climates but are difficult to grow in extremely hot areas like southern Arizona, Imperial Valley in California and the Moapa and Las Vegas Valleys of Nevada because it is too hot and they require frequent watering and cooler weather.

VARIETIES

Like strawberries, raspberries come in both June bearing and ever bearing varieties. As the name suggests, June bearers produce most of their crop in June but in some areas, start much earlier and in others come later. In cold areas like Bear Lake in Idaho, the June bearer 'Canby' produces most of the summer. June bearers need pruning, whereas ever bearers can be easily mowed to the ground every spring and produce their crop on new canes.

Recommended June bearers: 'Prelude' 'Encore' 'Canby' 'Meeker' 'Newburgh' 'Tulameen'.

Recommended ever bearers:

'**Autumn Bliss**' produces large, sturdy, vigorous canes and large crops of large, delicious berries. It is easy to grow and very productive. They start producing berries in July and continue over a long season.

'**Dinkum**' is very much like 'Autumn Bliss' (which is one of its parents). It has large vigorous canes and large good tasting berries which start coming early like 'Autumn Bliss'.

'**Heritage**' is an excellent older variety which has very good quality fruit. The canes are less vigorous than the former two and it starts producing about three weeks later. The berries are excellent quality but smaller than 'Autumn Bliss' with a somewhat smaller yield.

'**Fall Gold**' is a golden colored raspberry which is extremely sweet. It starts producing with 'Heritage' and has berries and yield the size of 'Heritage'.

PRUNING AND SUPPORT

June bearing raspberries produce their fruit on second year canes. This means that they grow the canes one summer which put out lateral branches on which the fruit is produced the second season. The canes are relatively stiff and freestanding, but they tend to lean as they get tall. It is best to put a row of posts down each side of the bed and string plastic coated radio wire about four feet off the ground between the posts on both sides of the raspberries. This will give support to the canes as they become heavy with fruit. In many areas if the plants are healthy, the canes are strong enough that they can be grown **without support.** Some canes on the edge may lean but for the most part the canes are free standing.

In the winter when the leaves are gone, remove all of the canes which produced fruit the prior summer.

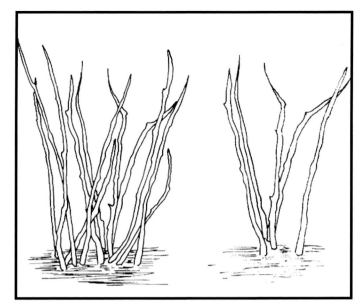

June bearing raspberry plants can be thinned, leaving 5 or 6 or more of the largest, strongest canes around each planting. As the raspberry plants mature and spread by rhizome root growth, the canes can be left thicker than shown in this illustration for a larger crop of berries.

Also remove all of the small, spindly canes and leave five or six strong, healthy canes around each planting. These canes should be topped at approximately 5-6 feet tall. Remove stray canes which have grown between the rows.

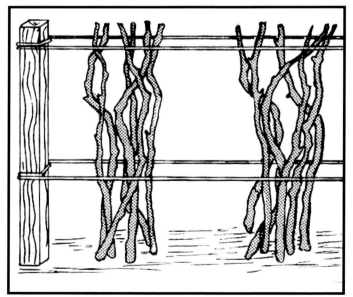

Put wires on each side of the canes for support. Cut the canes back to approximately 5-6 feet.

Another way to handle June-bearing raspberries is to top the canes at 5 feet the first summer and they will branch out with several shorter canes on top. These secondary branches can then be shortened in the winter. This process, which needs to be repeated every summer, makes the canes more stiff and free-standing.

Ever bearing raspberries are much easier to grow than are June bearers. Planted in the early spring, ever bearers will produce a small crop the first year because they produce on **first year canes.** You can cut off the tops of these canes after the season, removing the area of the canes on which they produced berries and they will produce a smaller crop further down on the cane the next spring.

Most people do not bother with this second crop. Instead they will cut the ever bearers clear to the ground with an inexpensive hedge trimmer after the canes have died in late fall or early spring and only produce one very large crop each year. This eliminates all of the time and hassle of carefully pruning them each season. With 'Autumn Bliss' or 'Dinkum' on new canes grown this season this harvest starts by midsummer and continues until late fall so the yield is very large.

PLANTING

You can buy raspberry plants as bare roots with one cane protruding from each plant or in a pot from a nursery. Plant them approximately two feet apart at the same depth as they grew before. If you have a cheap source of plants, put them one foot apart and they will fill in more quickly. Plant down the center of a 2 to 2 and 1/2 foot row (raised bed). They will spread by rhizome root growth putting up new plants every few inches until they fill the bed with canes. **Obviously you will not use black plastic with raspberries.**

PREPARING THE SOIL AND FERTILIZING

Since raspberries are perennials, and will remain in the same spot for several years, pick an area with good soil or fortify it by adding lots of organic material before planting. Like strawberries, raspberries are acid loving crops, so using a lot of sphagnum peat moss with a pH of 3.0-4.0 is helpful in not only improving the texture of the soil but also making it more acid.

Add elemental soil sulfur as needed to bring the pH to between 5.5 and 7.0. Working two quarts of sulfur thoroughly into 180 square feet of soil will lower the pH from 7.5 to 6.5. This is a gradual process because the sulfur has to be changed by microorganisms in the soil to sulfuric acid. If your soil is extremely alkaline, it may be necessary to increase the elemental soil sulfur from 2 quarts to 3-4 quarts when establishing a bed of raspberries or blackberries. This will make your soil acid enough to avoid the chlorosis problems (iron, zinc and manganese deficiencies) in the future.

A good complete commercial fertilizer should be thoroughly mixed into the soil along with the humus and peat moss mentioned above. The amount and formula of this complete fertilizer is discussed on pages **21-22** in Application of Commercial Fertilizer.

A month and one half after planting the raspberries, add a small second application of high nitrogen fertilizer to your raspberry bed. By this time the plants will be rooted and should respond quickly to the fertilizer. This second application should be about half the amount of the first application, i.e. about ½ quart for 180 square feet. You could use straight ammonium sulfate (21% nitrogen) or you could use a mix of 1/3 ammonium sulfate, 1/3 Grow More Soil Acidifier (or Miracle Gro Azalea Food), and 1/3 Ironite. The first two products are totally soluble and the third partially so. After sprinkling this high nitrogen acid type fertilizer down the top of the bed, carefully water it into the soil. This can be done with a Rainbird (impact type) sprinkler. If you are using a hand sprinkler on the end of a hose, turn the pressure way down so the water is coming out slowly enough that it soaks into the soil as you walk up and down along the bed. You want the fertilizer to soak straight down where you placed it and not run off to over fertilize another spot. After soaking it down a few inches, a drip system can be used for the rest of the watering.

The fertilizing of the raspberry bed on the second and each subsequent year should be done as described on page **49** under Fertilizing Established Perennial Crops.

WATERING

The watering should be done with two drip lines about 14-16 inches apart down each side of the raised bed. Raspberries are water loving plants and need to be watered twice a week during the growing season. Soak the bed with the drip system but do not have a water-logged (standing water) condition which will lead to phytophthora root rot (fungus disease) and sick or dying plants. For raspberries it is better not to use furrows on each side of the raised bed. Instead leave a two foot strip which can be roto-tilled 3-4 times a season to eliminate weeds and raspberry plants which grow out of the bed.

Blackberries

The culture of blackberries is similar in most respects to raspberries. The important differences are that they have a more extensive climatic adaptation (doing well even in hotter areas). Blackberries include both the western trailing types and the eastern erect and semi-erect types. The western types grow as a vine (trailing cane) which requires a trellis for support instead of the stiff upright canes of the eastern ones.

Most varieties of blackberries like 'Triple Crown' and 'Siskiyou' produce substantial crops of large berries.

Recommended Western Trailing Varieties:

'**Siskiyou**' is a very vigorous with large canes and berries which are large and delicious.

'**Boysenberry**' is less vigorous with smaller berries which are excellent quality.

'**Thornless Boysen**' produce a smaller crop that its thorny cousin.

'**Marion**' is a marvelous quality berry but is less adaptable than others. It gets chlorosis from iron, zinc and manganese deficiencies when the soil is too alkaline.

Recommended Eastern Varieties:

'**Apache**' (erect) has excellent large berries with very large yields but is more susceptible to chlorosis if the soil is not acid enough like 'Marion'. It is extremely vigorous and hard to keep in a confined area. Thornless.

'**Arapaho**' (erect) is very much like 'Apache' but earlier with slightly smaller fruit. Thornless.

'**Navaho**' (erect) has outstanding quality fruit which is slightly smaller than 'Apache'. Thornless.

'**Triple Crown**' (semi-erect) has outstanding size and berry quality. It produces huge yields (later than the erect types) on plants which are not as vigorous as the erect types. It is easy to grow and is recommended for any garden. Thornless.

'**Chester**' (semi-erect) has fruit quality very similar to 'Triple Crown' but is harvested slightly later. The yields are excellent and it is easy to grow. Thornless.

'**Prime Jan**' (semi-erect) produces a very late crop on first-year, very thorny canes. It is grown to extend the blackberry season and produces fairly good quality berries late in the season.

PLANTING

The planting of blackberries is basically similar to raspberries but they are placed further apart. Normally they are planted 4-6 feet apart down a row (raised bed) which is 2 and ½ to 3 feet across. As with raspberries, the blackberries will be in the ground for a number of years so the bed should be well prepared with lots of humus. Blackberries should be planted at the same depth as they were growing before they were dug. Look at the old stem to determine which part was above and which was below the ground.

WATERING AND FERTILIZING

They should be watered immediately after planting and twice a week there after. Both the watering and fertilizing are **similar to raspberries.** Blackberries should be planted during the spring or early summer for a crop the next year. They like full sun and deep fertile soil. They are a nitrogen-loving plant and should be fed in the manner described in the raspberry section. The fertilizing of blackberries on the second and each subsequent year should be done as described on page **49** under Fertilizing Established Perennial Crops.

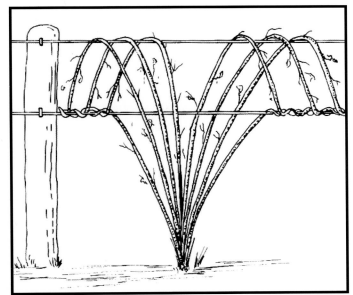

Western training Blackberry vines can be trellised in the form of a fan. Put them over the top wire, tie them to the bottom wire, and remove the tip of the vine.

PRUNING AND TRELLISING

All blackberries, except 'Prime Jan', produce their crops on canes that grew the previous summer. Blackberries produce crops during the late spring and throughout the summer depending on the variety. With **western trailing berries** immediately after the harvest ends in midsummer, all of the canes which produced fruit should be cut off approximately one foot above the ground. This will encourage the plant to put out new canes which should be allowed to grow

The vines can also be wound around both wires in the form of a loose barrel roll. Be careful not to break the vines. This barrel roll can run both directions from the plant.

along the ground throughout the rest of the summer and fall. These new canes will produce next years' crop.

Trellising can be done in the fall, winter or spring in most areas, but in cold climates where the winter will subject the canes to snow and extremely cold weather, the canes need to be **left on the ground** for protection from cold weather until it begins to warm up in the spring. Then choose the 7-8 of the best canes and tie them up to the trellis as shown in the illustrations on this page. It needs to be done carefully because the canes are brittle and will break if not kept relatively straight. The rest of the canes should be cut off approximately 6-8 inches above the ground.

The trellis is usually formed by putting posts about every 6 feet and running two strands of heavy grade smooth wire between the posts. Steel posts are cheap and easy to pound into the ground. At least two wires should be attached to each post, the first about 3 feet from the ground and the top wire about 5 feet from the ground. Plastic covered radio wire is excellent because it will not cut the vines. The canes are either placed on the wire trellis in the shape of a fan (see illustration) or are woven between the two wires in loose spirals, being careful not to break the canes. This barrel roll method goes both ways from the base of the plant and puts more vine into the air for a larger harvest. The end of the cane is tied to the wire with green plastic tie from the nursery. Whichever method of trellising you use, it is very important in tying up the canes that you remove the end of each cane (called "tipping"). This forces the plant to put out lateral branches on which the fruit will be born during late spring and early summer, rather than just going on growing from the end of the cane. If properly cared for, blackberries will yield an abundant harvest of delicious purple-black berries.

The eastern erect and semi-erect varieties do not have to be trellised. During each summer as new canes are produced, as you are harvesting fruit from last years' canes, the new canes should be shortened, forcing each of them to send out several lateral canes. With the erect types, this cut is made about 42 inches above the ground and 36 inches above the ground with semi-erect varieties. During the next spring, while the plant is still dormant, these lateral canes should be shortened to a length of 12-18 inches depending on how large the cane is. In any event, don't leave these canes so long that they produce fruit down on the ground.

HARVESTING

These berries go through shades of pink, red and purple before they get ripe. They are very sour until they get almost totally black. During the last two or three days of ripening they develop most of their sweetness, so don't pick them too soon. A blackberry patch needs to be picked two or three times each week during the fruiting season.

Broccoli, Cabbage and Cauliflower

These three members of the Brassica family (referred to as Cole Crops) have basically similar cultural requirements so it is helpful to consider them together. These vegetables all thrive in cool spring and fall weather. They require a regular supply of both fertilizer and water in order to achieve top quality. They are usually started as transplants in the early spring in order to get a jump on the season so they will mature before it gets too hot. For the fall garden, they are best planted by seeding directly into the garden, but can also be planted as transplants. When planted from seed, the heat brings plants up very quickly but they can be started as transplants in peat pellets and moved out when they start their second set of leaves.

The cluster ripens gradually. Only pick the black ones. They are very tart until fully ripe.

Most varieties of these vegetables should be stagger-planted approximately 20 inches apart for maximum exposure to sunlight and root areas.

When started in peat pellets inside for a fall crop, move the tray of pellets outside the day they come up and water once or twice a day.

PLANTING

Whether using transplants or seed, the best way is to plant on both sides of a 36 inch bed and stagger the planting so that the plants are not directly across from each other in order to allow maximum space between plants. They should be planted approximately 2 feet apart down each side of the row. Earlier (also smaller) varieties should be planted slightly closer, approximately 16-18 inches apart.

When planting outside from seed in the summer, space the groups of seed in the same manner mentioned above. Use a hand hoe or garden trowel to pull back a small two inch swath of dirt and then cover four or five seeds approximately ¼ to ½ inch deep. Water them daily until they come up. When the seedlings come up and are approximately two weeks old, thin to one healthy plant in each place.

Study a seed catalog to determine the approximate number of days to maturity of the variety which you are planting so that you can plant the fall crop to mature when the weather has cooled down. For example, the following are maturity dates for typical broccoli varieties: 'Coronado Crown'–60 days, 'Marathon' - 68 days, 'Goliath'-76 days, and 'Arcadia' – 86 days. By starting some of each of them on July 1st and allowing an extra week for adverse conditions, you will start eating broccoli by mid-September and it will continue until into November. Remember that after you cut the major head of broccoli on each plant, smaller satellite heads will come from each leaf axil so you will eat from each plant over a period of time. Also remember that when the weather cools down, they will mature more slowly extending the maturity date. The Cole Crops don't mind colder weather and it is said that a little frost improves the quality, so you will continue to harvest until night time temperatures get down to almost 25 degrees F.

Notice the size of the broccoli, cauliflower and carrot plants in the fall garden.

WATERING

With both direct seeding and transplants it is important to keep them wet the first week. They need to be soaked when planted by Rainbird sprinkler, drip or furrow and then watered every couple of days for the first week until the transplants begin to take root. Thereafter, they should be watered at least twice a week in warm weather and approximately once per week in cool weather. Refer to irrigation principles and methods earlier in the book.

FERTILIZING

A good complete fertilizer should be mixed into the soil before planting and watering and then a light application of high-nitrogen fertilizer should be made 3-4 weeks thereafter for top quality. (See application of Commercial Fertilizer section pages **21-22.**)

PEST CONTROL

Several kinds of insects, including cabbage maggots, cabbage worms and aphids are very fond of these three vegetables. The worms can be controlled by at least one spraying with Bt when the heads are beginning to form. The aphids need to be sprayed with Malathion when they first appear. They will probably not come back. Neem Oil will also work.

VARIETIES

There are many excellent varieties of these three vegetables, some as early as 45 days and others as late as 100 days to maturity. Some excellent **broccoli and cauliflower varieties** are:

Broccoli

'Early Divided'	45 days
'Packman'	55 days
'Coronado Crown'	60 days
'Marathon'	68 days
'Goliath'	76 days
'Arcadia'	86 days

Cauliflower

'Farmers' Extra Early'	40 days
'Snow Crown'	48 days
'Cassius'	65 days
'Cheddar'	68 days
'Artica'	80 days

Early varieties are usually used for the spring garden so they will mature before hot weather comes. The second early and main season varieties are better quality and should be used for the fall garden.

BLANCHING

Most modern varieties of cauliflower are self blanching. This means that the central leaves of the plant wrap around the white curd as it begins to form and this keeps the cauliflower white and mild tasting. It is really not necessary any more to tie the leaves over the head with string or elastics.

Broccoli and Cauliflower produce marvelous crops in both the spring and fall gardens. The author with one picking from the fall garden.

Cabbage

(See **BROCCOI, CABBAGE and CAULIFLOWER**)

Cantaloupes

(See MELONS)

Carrots

Carrots are high in vitamins and antioxidants and easily grown. They also store well in the ground and produce a large amount of food in a very small space.

VARIETIES

Carrots come in many shapes and sizes, from long and thin to the very small and beet-shaped. Traditionally, the Nantes types have been recommended for the home garden because of their outstanding texture, flavor and sweetness. If you have particularly heavy clay soil, you might want to choose a Chantenay type because they have short, tapered roots with broad shoulders and they are easier to get out of the ground, but in modern carrots there are many varieties which are a combination of the four major types: Imperator, Nantes, Danvers and Chantenay and good quality can be found in each. Some excellent varieties include:

'Sweet Baby Jane'	57 days
'Magnum'	58 days
'Sugar Snax'	63 days
'Envy'	66 days
'Scarlet Nantes'	68 days
'Tender Sweet'	75 days

SOIL TEXTURE

In the culture of carrots, the texture of the soil is particularly important. If you have very sandy or loamy soil, this will not be a problem, but in clay soils, it is very important that the soil be filled with organic material which will make it soft and crumbly so that the carrots can grow deep and expand in it.

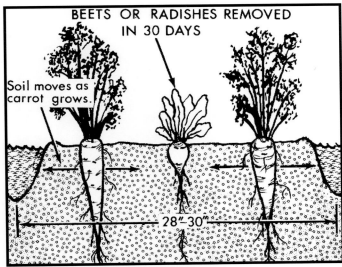

Using deep furrows and triple-planted rows makes it easier for the carrots to expand as they grow.

Because carrots need loose, crumbly soil, it is particularly important to avoid foot traffic on the beds around the young, growing carrots. By using furrows, it is easy to walk in them when working in the garden and thereby avoid compacting the soil around the carrots. If you make deep furrows and tall rows between them, the row can gradually move towards the furrow as the carrot grows and expands, therefore the very shape of tall beds with furrows between makes it easier for them to grow. (See illustration.)

PLANTING

Carrots should be planted on both sides of a 28-36 inch triple-planted row. Radishes or beets (for greens) can be planted down the center of the row between the carrots. The radishes or beet greens are pulled in approximately 30 days after planting before they get too crowded or are shaded by the carrots. This process loosens the soil and gives the carrots room to expand besides providing an additional crop in the same space. The carrots should be planted approximately 1/4 inch deep inside the ridge (berm) on the edge of the row.

It is hard to avoid planting carrots too thick. Using a small clear-plastic tube-type seeder which you hold in your hand may be helpful, but just sprinkling the seed out of your fingers is just as good. Try to put them in a two or three inch band down the row with **three or four seeds** per inch. This is difficult and they usually end up thicker than you want because the seeds are small and rough and tend to fall in clusters. Even though you get the carrots fairly thick, thinning usually isn't necessary. If your soil is relatively sandy, or has an adequate amount of organic materials, the carrots will gradually push themselves apart as they grow. They may take on some peculiar shapes and not be as beautifully smooth and straight as if they had been thinned, but you will get a gigantic yield in a very small space and they will taste good.

GETTING CARROTS UP

Some people have a very difficult time getting a good stand of carrots. The first problem is that the carrot seedling is very tiny when it pushes through the surface of the ground. It is therefore vulnerable to insects such as flea beetles which you may not even notice. It is important to be aware when the carrots come up and dust with a tube of Sevin Garden Dust soon after they emerge if insects are at work. Secondly, if you have fertilized before planting, the seedlings have more vigor during the first few weeks after emerging from the soil and a better chance of survival.

The center rows of beets are large enough to be pulled for beet greens.

beneficial effect in maintaining the consistent moisture level needed.

FERTILIZING

Using the amounts and proportions of the complete fertilizer (16-16-8 and Ironite) described on pages **21-22** under Application of Commercial Fertilizer is ideal for carrots. It has the nitrogen needed for vigorous healthy top growth as well as the phosphorus and potassium needed for healthy roots. This fertilizer is best applied by mixing it thoroughly into the top 8-10 inches of the soil before planting. Carrots mature in approximately 60-70 days, so a second application of fertilizer is not necessary because they mature before the fertilizer is used up or leached out of the soil. In fact a second application will produce larger tops and smaller carrots, see Source Sink Relationship section. Properly fertilizing carrots requires a delicate balance between over and under-feeding. Over-feeding with a lot of high-nitrogen commercial fertilizer or too much fresh manure will cause forking and branching of the roots. Irregular weather and watering will make the carrots rough and hairy.

Thirdly, plant down off the ridge (berm) of the row(raised bed) (see illustration) where the ground will tend to stay damp, and water every day for the first 7-10 days until plants are up. You can water with an impact-type (Rainbird) sprinkler which does not cause a heavy crust or run your drip line between the ridge and rows of seed on each side of the bed. Soak the bed the first day after planting and it will not take so long to water over to the seed each day thereafter until the seedlings emerge. This keeps the soil in the top ¼ inch moist so you will get a good stand. Water them every second day for the week after they come up. The carrot seeds will come up in seven to fourteen days under most conditions and it is particularly helpful to dampen the surface of the ground as the seedlings begin to emerge. It is also important to keep people and pets off the tops of the rows at all times after planting.

WATERING

Carrots need a relatively even, consistent moisture level. Particularly when the carrots are almost mature, getting very dry and then very wet may cause them to crack. It is recommended that carrots be watered twice a week unless the weather is very cool or rainy. Mulching with hay, straw, grass clippings, etc., has a

The same two rows one month later after beet greens are removed and they are ready to harvest as beets and carrots.

HARVESTING

You can start harvesting carrots when they are very small before they become fully mature. They are excellent when relatively young, but they get better and sweeter as they mature in the cool and even freezing weather of the late fall and winter. They will then store in the ground in an excellent condition all winter in all but the most extremely cold areas until they begin to grow again and go to seed in the spring. The high sugar content (soluble solids) of well grown carrots acts like anti-freeze to protect them from the cold and freezing weather of winter. They can be covered with hay, straw or grass clippings if you are concerned. Carrots can be dug fresh whenever needed. In many areas by planting twice a year you can have good carrots stored in the ground almost all year. In extremely hot desert areas, it is necessary to pull them within a month after maturity and refrigerate them in storage. They can also be pitted (in the ground in a plastic garbage can) in the late fall and used as needed during the winter.

Cauliflower

(See BROCCOLI, CABBAGE and CAULIFLOWER)

Celery

Celery is a fussy crop under most conditions. It takes a very long season (100-135 days) and it requires an extended period of cool weather for prime quality.

VARIETIES

Recommended varieties are Tall Utah, Improved Utah 52-70 and Giant Pascal (Summer Pascal). Two good varieties of golden celery are Stokes Golden Plume and Burpee's Golden Self-Blanching.

PLANTING

Celery has extremely tiny seeds and matures very slowly over a long season. For these reasons, it is usually started inside and planted outdoors when it is about 8-10 weeks old. It is \especially important to use transplants for spring planting because this gives you the head start necessary for it to mature before hot weather comes. In coastal areas it can be planted in February and does very well during the long, cool spring and summer season. In areas where the season changes very quickly from winter to summer without a long period of moderate spring weather, it is better to wait and plant celery in the fall garden. The planting should be timed so that the celery will mature during September and October when the weather is cool. When planting during the summer as part of the fall garden, the weather is warm enough so that the celery can be seeded directly outside in the garden. It should be planted approximately 1/8 to 1/4 inch deep and kept moist until it comes up. Whether from seed or transplants, celery should be planted approximately 6-8 inches apart down the row, depending on the size at maturity of the variety which you choose. Plant them on both sides of a 28-30 inch row using staggered planting methods.

WATERING AND FERTILIZING

Top quality celery requires good soil which is fertilized and watered regularly. Start out by working a complete fertilizer into the soil before planting. Then feed with a nitrogen fertilizer at least once a month for the life of the crop. Water celery at least twice a week. Celery should be forced to grow rapidly by feeding and watering frequently.

OTHER CULTURAL INFORMATION

Although the food, water and cool weather requirements of celery are very stringent, it is almost entirely free from insect problems. One other possible problem in celery culture is that of blanching. This is the process of keeping sunlight off the stalks in order to make them white, and more mild and tender. This was traditionally accomplished by heaping dirt up around the stalks as they grew or by tying the heads together at the top. A labor-saving alternative is to put the celery plants close enough together so that as they begin to mature they shade each other and only the leaves at the top of the stalks are exposed to the sunlight. Many people feel that green celery, although slightly stronger, is just as good as blanched celery, so now days, there is very little blanched celery grown.

Corn

Corn is fun to grow because it responds so dramatically to proper care. Even more than most other plants, if it is kept healthy by proper watering and fertilizing procedures, it is practically immune to damage from insects and diseases. For example, healthy corn has extremely tight husks which seal off the silk end of the ear so that it is very difficult for worms to get in. On the other hand, corn which is not kept healthy and vigorous is usually full of worms and often affected by other insects and diseases.

VARIETIES

All of the basic types of corn that we grow now were being grown before Columbus discovered America. By applying normal plant breeding techniques, modern plant scientists have taken from a vast gene pool of corn types being used by Indians and some growing wild in various parts of the North and South American continents to develop the various kinds of corn being used today. So called "Indian Corn" is nice for decoration but doesn't taste anything like the modern varieties of sweet corn. We now have specialized types of corn such as field corn (developed for its large size and tremendous yield), popcorn (developed for its expansion and ability to pop consistently), and sweet corn (developed for its sugar content and excellent flavor).

There are now many types of sweet corn with very different characteristics. The old standard **normal sweet corn** which has been grown for many years is designated with **su** (normal sugar gene). It has an outstanding sweet creamy flavor which is hard to beat if it is cooked immediately after picking. The problem is that if it is picked and not cooked immediately the sugar quickly converts to starch and it loses its flavor.

About 35 years ago plant scientists at the University of Illinois developed **super sweet** varieties of sweet corn. They were extremely sweet (2-3 times the sugar of normal sweet corn) and the sugar did not convert to starch as quickly after picking, but they didn't have the soft creamy texture of the old fashioned sweet corn, did not have as much flavor and were very "crunchy". They also had to be isolated in either time or location from other sweet corn to mature ears normally. The super-sweet varieties are almost like eating a sugar beet in contrast to a regular table beet. The texture of these super-sweets is crunchy and they require longer cooking than regular sweet corn. The super-sweet hybrids are designated with **sh2.**

The next development in sweet corn was the sugar enhanced (se) varieties. They are much sweeter

'BROCADE' (81 days)	'CAMEO' (84 days)	'SILVER QUEEN' (94 days)
'BROCADE' (81 days)	'CAMEO' (84 days)	'SILVER QUEEN' (94 days)

'POLKA' (63 days)	'PRECOCIOUS' (66 days)	'CHIPPEWA' (70 days)	'LUSCIOUS' (73 days)	'HONEY SELECT' (79 days)
'POLKA' (63 days)	'PRECOCIOUS' (66 days)	'CHIPPEWA' (70 days)	'LUSCIOUS' (73 days)	'HONEY SELECT' (79 days)

Plant several varieties in two row blocks for an extended harvest (6-7 weeks) out of one corn patch. In this way you can also experiment with several new varieties each year.

than the normal sweet corn, the sugar does not quickly convert to starch and they have the creamy texture of normal sweet corn. They can either be **se** (heterozygous) where only part of the kernels are sugar enhanced or **SE** (homozygous) where 100% of the kernels are sugar enhanced. This is still considered by many to be the best sweet corn ever developed. It doesn't have to be isolated from other sweet corn to develop normally.

The most recent development in sweet corn breeding is the **synergistic** sweet corn. This is considered by some to be the best of both worlds because it has 25% sh2 (super sweet) kernels and 75% se (sugar enhanced) kernels. The synergystics have the creamy texture, the excellent flavor and the extremely sweet taste. The sugar does not convert quickly to starch and it does not need to be isolated from other sweet corn types.

Sweet corn comes in both the older open-pollinated and newer hybrid varieties. (See page **84** for discussion of hybrids.) The hybrids are usually earlier, more vigorous and more resistant to disease. They also produce more uniform, larger ears with deeper kernels. All of the good varieties these days are hybrids. It is also important to note that **none** of the varieties of fruits and vegetables recommended in this book are **genetically engineered.**

You can purchase corn seed for varieties ripening in anywhere from 45 to 95 days from time of planting. The earlier varieties are always smaller plants with smaller ears and usually poorer quality. When you get to varieties with about 75 days to maturity, they have the same quality as the later corn.

The recommended sweet corn varieties are:

'Polka'	syn, bi-color	63 days
'Precocious'	se, yellow	66 days
'Chippewa'	se, bi-color	70 days
'Luscious'	se, bi-color	73 days
'Ambrosia'	se, bi-color	75 days
'Honey Select'	syn, yellow	79 days
'Providence'	syn, bi-color	80 days
'Sumptuous'	se, yellow	80 days
'Brocade'	se, bi-color	81 days
'Cameo'	syn, bi-color	84 days
'Silver Queen'	su, white	94 days

POPCORN

Popcorn is easy to grow and fun for the whole family. It should be grown just like any other corn, except for the harvesting. Rather than picking it when the kernels are young and tender, let it mature on the plant until the cornstalk turns from green to yellow-brown. Then pull off the husks and put the ears in a warm dry place to become fully dry. When dry (a few weeks after picking) the kernels can easily be pushed off the cob with your thumb and popped like popcorn which you buy in the store. Recommended varieties of popcorn are 'White Cloud', 'Robust 128YH', 'Robust 21-82W', and Strawberry. Strawberry popcorn has a deep crimson color, a delicious flavor and can also be used as a decoration. It should be noted that if your popcorn or Indian corn is planted next to and pollinates at the same time as your sweet corn, your sweet corn kernels will be a mixture of sweet and pop and visa versa.

PLANTING

Although corn is generally a heat-loving plant, it does well in a wide range of climates including the cool summer coastal and high mountain valley areas. For planting in the wet, cold soil of the early spring, the extra early varieties have more vigor. The second early and main-crop varieties should be planted in April or May in most areas to take advantage of the summer heat. In areas where frost is a problem, don't plant any corn until after the danger of frost has passed.

Each strand of silk is attached to a particular kernel of corn and must receive pollen from the tassels in order for the kernel to develop. For this reason, it is usually recommended that corn be planted in blocks so that as the wind blows one way and then another, each ear of corn will be adequately pollinated. At least two rows of corn of the same variety should be planted side by side to give good pollination but three rows are even better.

When planting a corn patch, it is best to take advantage of the broad range of maturity dates in order to have an extended period of harvest out of one corn patch. For example, in planting four rows, plant the bottom half of the first two rows to an extra early variety maturing in approximately 60 days. This variety will ripen its corn over a 10 day period. Plant the top half of those same two rows to an early variety ripening in approximately 70 days. This variety will overlap with the first extending the season for another 10 days. Then plant the bottom half of the next two rows to a main season crop variety maturing in approximately 80 days and the top half of those same rows to a late season crop variety maturing in approximately 90 days. This variety will continue maturing for another 10 days thereafter. You will have corn continuously from this one corn patch for approximately 6 or 7 weeks. (See illustration.)

Early and extra early corn can be planted down the center of a 30 inch row. Main season crop corn should be planted down the center of a 32-36 inch row. (See the PLANTING YOUR GARDEN section starting on page **45** for an extensive discussion of methods of preparing your soil and making and using furrows.) Standing in the furrows, it is easy to make a **4 inch deep** planting furrow down the center of the bed. Plant the seeds approximately 3-4 inches apart and cover them approximately **1 inch deep.** When the seedlings come up, thin them to one plant every 8-12 inches down the row, leaving the largest, most vigorous plants. The small, early variety plants should be left closer together (8-10 inches apart) and the larger, late varieties should be farther apart (10-12 inches).

You still have a small depression on each side of the corn plants because you made the planting furrow **extra deep.** When the plants are 6 inches tall pull

the dirt from the edge of the 4 inch planting furrow in against the corn stalks so it is slightly mounded around the corn stalks. The plant will then put out extra roots in this mounded area called **prop roots** or **brace roots.** They will help to keep the plant from blowing over in a severe wind.

Planting in "hills" (groups of seeds placed together) is not recommended unless you thin each hill to one plant after the seedlings come up. (See pages **56-64** for a general discussion of planting methods.)

FERTILIZING

Corn is a nitrogen-loving crop and will produce tremendous yields of large-eared, delicious corn if properly fed. Before working the soil, you should apply a good complete fertilizer which will be worked thoroughly into the soil to a depth of 8-10 inches. A mix of 16-16-8 and Ironite is excellent for this purpose. (See Application of Commercial Fertilizer on pages **21-22** for the proportions of each element and the amounts.) If corn is properly fertilized, it will be a dark healthy green color, rather than being a light yellow green.(See illustrations on page **12**.)

This corn patch with 63-84 day varieties is being watered down the top of the raised bed. Notice that the water comes from one yellow hose attached to a faucet but is divided into 7 streams of water by 8 Y's. Seven short pieces of hose run from the Y's to pockets at the end of each bed and the water runs down the top of the bed on both sides of the row of corn.

Corn responds dramatically to a second application of nitrogen fertilizer. It should be made when the corn is approximately 8-10 inches tall and watered into the soil. (See pages **47-49** for amounts and methods for applying a **second application** of fertilizer and how to get it into the soil.) This will supply the needed nutrients for a bountiful crop of corn.

Corn does well in soil which has recently grown a crop of beans, or some other legume, because they leave the soil rich in slow-release nitrogen. It is much better to have the corn follow the bean crop rather than being planted with it at the same time. (See pages **14-15** for additional information about legumes.)

WATERING

Basically corn should be watered deeply, but infrequently. In most climates this means that the ground should be soaked thoroughly approximately once per week. This can be done with drip irrigation putting a drip line down each side of the raised bed. If you have enough space to make wide rows (40 inches from the bottom of one furrow to the bottom of the next) and make the furrows large with high ridges (berms) you can water down the top of the beds (see illustration).

You can also water your corn in furrows. In most soils, it is adequate if you keep the furrows full for at least an hour before turning the water off. If your garden is sloped so that the water will not stand deep in the furrows, it will be necessary to leave the water running much longer. (See pages **25-31, 64-74** for a detailed discussion of the effects of different watering principles and methods on corn and other crops.)

If corn is watered too often, it develops a very shallow, along-the-surface root system, so that it will not stand a hard wind without blowing over (lodging). If corn is watered as suggested above (thoroughly but not too often), its root system will be deep and extensive.

In the low deserts where the summer heat sometimes gets as high as 120 ° in the shade, hot dry winds can come while the corn is beginning to put up tassels and cause the tassels to blight (curl and dry up). To avoid this problem, it is some-times necessary to water more frequently than once a week during extremely hot weather. The other alternative in those climates is to plant the corn midsummer for a fall crop.

PEST CONTROL

About the only pest which bothers corn is the earworm. As suggested above, this is not usually a problem if the corn is healthy because the plant produces very tight husks and good tip cover to protect the ear from these worms. Even the occasional ear which gets a worm inside is not ruined. Carefully cut out the bad part and the rest of the ear is not affected. If the worm problem becomes severe, simply spray the silk with Bt once or twice after the silk emerges before the corn matures. Another method is to use a medicine dropper and put a few drops of mineral oil on the corn silk. You can also spray the silk with Sevin.

The tight husks and good tip cover also help to prevent bird damage. Birds usually won't bother an ear of corn unless the kernels are exposed.

WEEDING AND OTHER PROBLEMS

It is easy to control weeds in corn. Corn grows so fast if well fed and properly watered that it provides very dense shade on the ground. If you remove all of the weeds by hoeing when the plants are approximately 10-12 inches tall, the new weeds which germinate and grow thereafter do not have a chance. By the time they come up and start growing, the corn is so large that very little sunlight reaches the ground where the weeds are located, so they don't amount to much. You can hoe a second time but the corn is so large that it is difficult and the second weeding is usually not necessary.

If you have a rear end tiller with a furrowing attachment, you can till shallowly (3-5 inches deep) down the row right along the edge of the corn plants. When you have finished tilling, you can go down between the rows of corn using the furrowing attachment to make new furrows. This process will eliminate almost all of your weeds.

While hoeing the corn, it is easy to widen the furrows, using the excess dirt to raise the level of the row. (See illustration on page 62.) This gives the corn increased stability in hard winds, makes it easier to walk in the furrows when picking and also makes it easier to irrigate in furrows.

It used to be the practice among many home gardeners to remove all of the "suckers" (side branches) from each corn plant and leave nothing but the main stalk. This practice is no longer recommended because it actually reduces rather than increasing the yield.

Healthy corn creates dense shade limiting the growth of weeds. The end product isn't bad either.

HARVESTING

Corn demonstrates the importance of freshness better than any other vegetable. After it is picked, the sugar immediately begins to be converted into starch and it quickly loses its flavor. This happens more slowly in the newer improved varieties. It should be refrigerated immediately after picking and cooked and eaten as soon as possible. If you have never eaten fresh-picked sweet corn, you have missed a real treat.

There are several ways to determine when corn should be picked. The experienced gardener usually does it by color and kernel size. The color gets darker as the corn matures, gradually changing from very pale yellow to a golden-yellow color. The white corn gets a yellow cast as it gets more mature. The kernels grow larger, more rectangular and pack more tightly together. Sweet corn for the table should be picked before the color goes from yellow to gold and before the kernels reach their large, fully-mature size. As the corn becomes very mature, the kernels lose their sweetness and become tough and chewy.

A third method of deciding when to pick corn is to puncture a kernel with your fingernail. The milky juice goes from the watery to a jelly-like stage in a matter of a week or so. If the kernel is plump and the juice is milky, the ear is ready to pick. Experience will teach you exactly when to pick an ear.

Avoid opening a lot of ears to test for maturity because once you pull the husks down to expose the kernels, the ear becomes vulnerable to birds and dries out. You can look at the ear without opening it and notice that the ear is beginning to get fat within the husk. Then open one or two of the fattest ones to see how mature they are inside. After opening them, close them up again.

Most varieties of corn produce at least two ears per plant on the main stalk. When removing the ears of corn, twist as you pull down to avoid breaking the central stalk. It is some-times necessary to hold the stalk with one hand while pulling the ear off with the other. The second ear needs to stay on to finish ripening.

Cucumbers

In spite of some negative comments about cucumbers in a much earlier text (Isaiah 1:8), wherein backsliding Israel (Jerusalem) is compared to a cucumber patch, cucumbers have been grown and enjoyed from antiquity.

VARIETIES

Cucumbers are generally divided into the "white spine" and "black spine" families (spines being miniature stickers which protrude from the warts on young fruit). The white spine varieties turn white and the black spine turn yellow-orange when old. White spine cucumbers have traditionally been grown for fresh table use and black spine varieties for pickling, but there are some exceptions to this division. The pickling varieties tend to have short, blocky, heavily warted fruits and the fresh table types tend to be longer and smoother.

Regular cucumbers along with all other cucurbit vine crops have both male and female blossoms on each vine. They are easily distinguished because the female blossom has a small cucumber at its base when it blooms but the male does not. A new type of gynoecious hybrid cucumber has been developed which has all female blossoms. This increases the production of each vine, but one regular vine must be placed between every three or four gynoecious vines down the row for proper pollination of the cucumbers of the all-female variety.

Basic recommended varieties of cucumbers are:

Slicing	Pickling
'Sweet Slice'	'Eureka'
'Sweet success'	'Pioneer'
'English Telegraph'	'Wisconsin'
'All-season Burpless'	
'Lemon'	

The varieties of slicing cucumbers listed above are all mild, non-bitter and burpless types. There are many other excellent varieties, but cucumbers are susceptible to several kinds of diseases, so look for varieties which are resistant to disease.

PLANTING

Cucumbers are a warm weather vegetable and should be planted in the summer garden. The vines will spread approximately 4-6 feet so they need to be grown on a trellis or given enough room to spread. In a home garden situation where you are cramped for space, they can be planted 2 feet apart down the center of a 36 inch row. Plant directly from seed, pulling back the soil with a hand hoe or some other tool every 2 feet, placing 5 or 6 seeds in an area about four inches square, and then covering them approximately 1/2 inch deep. When the plants come up, they should first be thinned, leaving two strong plants in each place. Two or three weeks after the plants come up, thin to one plant in each place. You can train the vines both ways down the top of the row to keep the furrows relatively open for walking.

Both male and female blossoms are needed for proper pollination and fruiting. Regular cucumbers should be inter-mixed with gynoecious (all female) varieties. All other cucurbit crops (melons, squash, etc.) have both male and female blossoms. Don't worry that your zucchini are blooming but producing no fruit. They usually produce male blossoms first, but the fruit comes on the female ones.

FERTILIZING

A good complete fertilizer (16-16-8 plus Ironite – see Application of Commercial Fertilizer section) should be roto-tilled or otherwise worked into the soil before making the furrows and planting.

WATERING

Cucumbers are extremely susceptible to the fungus diseases known as powdery and downy mildew. The more common powdery mildew causes a whitish growth on the leaf surfaces which will eventually kill the plants. These fungus diseases are caused by moisture on the leaves, so it is very important to avoid all methods of sprinkler irrigation after the cucumbers come up. Cucumbers are best watered by drip irrigation or in the furrows. Keep the furrows full for at least one hour. Soak in this manner approximately once a week. In extremely hot weather, twice-a-week watering is beneficial. (See the furrowing section on pages **53-56** for methods of making and using furrows. Also see the watering principles section on pages **25-31** and the watering methods section on pages **64-72** for further details.)

PEST CONTROL

Cucumber beetles (both the striped and spotted kinds) can cause serious damage to cucumbers. These pests will also invade other parts of your garden. When the plants are young and the beetles begin to multiply, they should be dusted with garden dust containing Sevin. Avoid spraying because the moisture will encourage mildew.

HARVESTING

Pickling cucumbers should be picked very young when they are mild and crisp. Cucumbers mature very quickly, so they should be picked every two or three days. Not only does the younger fruit taste better, but the harvest season and quantity of yield are greatly increased by keeping the fruit picked.

Eggplant

This heat-loving plant is relatively easy to grow. It should be planted when all danger of frost has passed, growing best in hot summer weather, even in the low desert.

VARIETIES

The newer early hybrids are recommended. These include Dusky, Early Hybrid, and Black Magic Hybrid.

PLANTING

Eggplants are usually started as transplants and should be planted out in the late spring. Plant them three feet apart on 36 inch rows to give them enough space to spread out. If you grow your own transplants, plant them 1/4 inch deep and keep them very warm. Put the container on a sunny windowsill for additional heat to help the seeds germinate.

WATERING AND FERTILIZING

Eggplants should be watered (soak thoroughly) approximately once per week in warm weather. A complete garden fertilizer should be mixed with the soil before planting.

PEST CONTROL

Eggplants can be damaged by aphids and potato beetles. Potato beetles are best controlled with Sevin or Rotenone. Spray with Malathion for aphids.

HARVESTING

Eggplants are good when young, before they reach maturity, so you can start picking them when they are about 1/2 of their mature size. The fruit should be glossy and dark purple to black in color. When they lose their glossy appearance, they are too old and should be discarded. Keeping the mature fruit picked will encourage the plants to continue setting on new fruit.

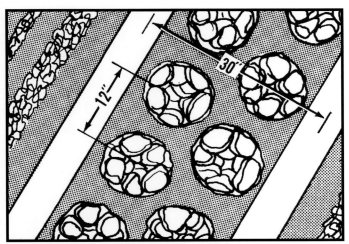

Stagger-plant lettuce down both sides of a 28-30 inch bed. Allow 12 inches between plants for regular head lettuce and slightly less for butterhead and romaine.

Lettuce

Lettuce is a cool weather crop. It does best in an area with a long, moderate spring season. In hot weather the mature plant quickly puts up a seed stalk and bolts to seed. It does great in the fall garden when it can be planted in the heat of midsummer and mature in the fall when the weather is cool. In moderate coastal climates it can be planted in January through August because it is fairly cool, even in summer. In mountain valleys lettuce can be planted in March when the snow is off the ground and the weather has begun to warm a little. It will handle some snow after it is planted, and frost down to 28 degrees F. if the plants are sufficiently hardened before planting (see Hardening). Lettuce can be planted in stale beds prepared in the fall so nothing has to be done to the soil before planting. It can also be planted midsummer for fall.

VARIETIES

There are several general types of lettuce and many individual varieties in each class. It comes in various tones of red and green. The loose-leaf lettuce (40-55 days) is the quickest and easiest to grow, but it does not have the mild flavor of some of the other types. Some excellent **loose-leaf** lettuce varieties are 'Ruby Red', 'Salad Bowl', 'Oak Leaf' and 'Red Sails'. New varieties are coming out every year, so check the seed catalogs. When these heads are cut, if a few leaves are left at the bottom, the plant will produce a new head. This is also true of most butterhead and romaine varieties.

The **butterhead** type of lettuce (55-65 days) forms a small, loose head and has excellent eating qualities. Recommended varieties include 'Buttercrunch' (an improved Bibb-type lettuce which is ideal for home gardens) and 'Red Derby'. Recommended varieties of **romaine** lettuce (60-75 days) are 'Green Towers', 'Marshall' and 'Cimmaron' and 'Paris Island Cos'.

The most commonly used is the **head** lettuce (80-90 days) which is also sometimes called "Iceberg" lettuce. The older 'Iceberg' variety has generally been replaced by newer improved varieties such as 'Great Lakes', 'Ithaca' and 'Mighty Joe'. Iceberg types of lettuce are the lowest in nutrition of any vegetable.

PLANTING

In many climates lettuce is one of those crops which need to be started inside in peat pellets and transplanted into the garden. It doesn't come up very well in the cold wet soil of the spring garden and it has a **hot weather dormancy** which prevents it from coming up for the fall garden when planted in the heat of summer if the soil temperature is above 85 degrees F. Therefore, for the fall garden it needs to be started inside and moved out as transplants. It comes up in 3-4 days in the house at 72 degrees F. Lettuce transplants do well in either the cold weather or heat of summer as long as they are kept wet. (See Growing Your Own Transplant section on pages **57-60** for starting plants inside without them getting tall and spindly and etiolating.)

The loose-leaf, butterhead and romaine lettuce which mature more quickly are recommended for planting in the spring garden because they will be ready to eat before the warm weather of summer. The iceberg (head lettuce) takes 80-90 days to mature so if planted in the spring garden in most areas, it will come on during the hot weather and will not head but go right to seed. For the fall garden the butterhead, romaine and ice berg are best. They mature in the cool weather and even the iceberg types form a good head and do not bolt to seed.

The most common problem which people have when growing lettuce in the home garden is failing to thin it enough. Thin to no more than two plants in peat pellets. If standard head lettuce is planted too thick, it will not head or amount to anything. The small loose-heading Buttercrunch and the Romaine also require room to head properly, and even loose-leaf types do better if given some elbow room. For regular head lettuce, the plants need to be at least 12 inches apart, each way. They are best stagger-planted down each side of a 28-30 inch row. See illustration.)

The loose-leaf, butterhead and romaine lettuce should be thinned to at least eight inches apart. Because most people hate thinning ("I just can't bear to pull up those beautiful plants"), it is easier to plant the seeds inside in peat pellets and thin them sitting at the table with tiny pointed fingernail scissors. Then thin them to one plant in each place when they are established in the garden. It is also easy to space them properly when you start with transplants grown from seed indoors. (See page **59** for proper methods of hardening your own transplants.)

Lettuce is both beautiful and delicious.

FERTILIZING

As with other crops, fertilize lettuce as described in Application of Commercial Fertilizer on pages **21-22.** It should first be tilled into the soil before planting. A second application of Nitrogen can be made but is really not helpful except for iceberg types.

WATERING

Lettuce is a moisture-loving crop so in hot, dry weather, particular attention must be given to keep it from getting too dry. Generally it needs to be watered twice a week but needs to be watered daily when transplants are moved into the garden in the heat of summer.

HARVESTING

Leaf lettuce can be harvested by cutting off most of the outer leaves and leaving the small center leaves intact. This way the plant will continue producing leaves through two or three cuttings. The other three types (butterhead, romaine and standard head lettuce) can be cut off at the base with a sharp knife when properly headed or cut a little higher and allowed to form another head. If they mature in the fall when the weather is cool, they will stand in the field for several weeks (or even longer if the weather is colder). They will handle some frost and not be damaged as long as the weather stays above approximately 28 degrees F. In the spring garden when the weather turns hot and you notice the center of the head begin to protrude upward, it is beginning to put up a seed stalk and almost overnight the plant becomes tough and strong tasting. Then it is only good for compost.

Melons

Melons thrive in hot weather. They can be grown in cooler climates, but require special help to overcome the lack of intense heat. The use of black plastic which absorbs the sun's rays and gets much hotter than the natural soil temperature is one method of increasing the heat on the vine. (See pages **80-82** in the KEEPING THEM HEALTHY section for detailed instructions about the value and use of black plastic in the culture of melons.) The delicious quality, of home-grown melons will compensate you for the additional effort required to produce them.

The author has frequently been told by students that the reason their melons were bad was that they crossed with their cucumbers. In the first place, they can't cross with cucumbers. They don't even have the same number of chromosomes. Even if they could, it wouldn't make any difference to this years' crop. A cross only affects the seed, so unless you are eating the seed (as with corn), this generation's cross could not affect the fruit you eat. Cucumbers will also not cross with squash or pumpkins and squash/pumpkins will also not cross with melons.

Large delicious melons are relatively easy to grow if you have warm weather and enough space.

VARIETIES

There are many types of melons, but the ones discussed here are cantaloupe, Crenshaw and watermelon. (Other melons include Persian, casaba, and honeydew.)

Cantaloupe. Recommended varieties are 'Sugar Queen', 'Primo' 'Whopper' and 'Ambrosia'. These are all excellent quality, disease-resistant varieties which will mature in a relatively short season.

Crenshaw. There is one basic variety of this melon, but the strains of seed from different seed companies will be slightly different. A variety called 'Early Hybrid Crenshaw' is available but has a grainy texture and is not recommended. Crenshaw is an exquisite tasting melon and is recommended if you have a long enough growing season (90-100 days)

Watermelon. There are many varieties of watermelon and new ones are being introduced each year. There are many excellent varieties, but the best include 'Sweet Favorite' (72 days), 'Redlicious' (80

days), and 'Sangria' (85 days). For those interested in healthy food, a good variety of watermelon has more lycopene (antioxidant which helps prevent cancer) cup for cup than a good variety of tomato. If your short season requires an early melon, Whopper II (65 days) is the best. Recommended seedless melon is 'Gypsy' (75 days).

PLANTING

Melons should be placed in the warmest, sunniest part of the garden. Melons take a lot of space so in tiny gardens they have to be eliminated. **Cantaloupes** take the least space of the melons but should be planted on at least 5-6 foot beds with the individual plants being 4-6 feet apart. **Crenshaw** should also be planted on 5-6 foot beds with individual plants being 6-8 feet apart. **Watermelons** should be planted on at least 8-10 foot beds with individual plants being 8-10 feet apart. Larger spacing is preferable but you have to adjust to the space you have available. If melons are given more space, they have more fruit and produce over a longer period of time. The size and quality (sugar and flavor) are also enhanced. (See illustration of the author with a bountiful harvest of beautiful watermelons.)

In planting each hill (group of seeds), pull the dirt back with a hand hoe and place four or five seeds in a cluster approximately one inch apart. Cover the seeds approximately 3/4 inch deep. When the seedlings come up (in approximately one week in warm weather) they should be thinned, leaving the two healthiest plants in each hill. Approximately three weeks later when the plants are large enough so that they are not so vulnerable to damage from birds and insects, thin again to one plant in each hill.

In short season areas where cold weather and danger of frost delay planting directly into the soil, it is very helpful to start melons inside in larger containers like the bottom half of a gallon milk carton. This type of container allows the plant to get to the runner stage without getting root bound. Use good quality potting soil from Lowes, Home Depot or a nursery. (See section on Starting Transplants. Also read section on Hardening Transplants.)

Young cantaloupes, Crenshaw, and watermelons on black plastic. Notice that hoses connected to the five drip lines 3 feet apart under the 20 foot wide plastic are attached to rebar at each end to keep the lines straight when it gets hot. The in-line filter and Y's are not shown in this picture.

In short season mountainous areas or along the coast where there isn't enough heat for good melons, using black plastic over the beds is very helpful. It brings them to maturity 2-3 weeks earlier and increases both size and quality of the melons. (See section about using black plastic on pages **80-82**.) You will want to use transplants in these cooler areas which have been started inside and hardened up to be planted out after danger of frost has passed. Put down the drip system (see drip system on pages **69-72**) using several drip lines 2-3 feet apart so you soak the entire area under the plastic. Cover the bed with black plastic, being sure to put down the plastic in late afternoon or evening because the tops of the leaves will burn with the plastic in the heat of the day. Cut a hole and carefully pull the leaves through the plastic so they can spread over it. Put a rock or brick next to the plant so the wind won't whip the plastic over the plant and put enough heavy rocks or bricks around the edges to hold the plastic down.

FERTILIZING

A good complete fertilizer (16-16-8 and Ironite) should be worked into the soil before planting. (See Application of Commercial Fertilizer on pages **21-22** for the exact mixture and amount.) With melons a second application of fertilizer is not only **not helpful** but it will actually reduce the size and quality of your crop.

WATERING

Whether planting seeds or transplants they need to be watered immediately after planting. Seeds should be watered again in 3-4 days and again as they are breaking through the crust and coming up. Transplants need to be soaked thoroughly, first right around the plant when planting and then soaking the whole bed thoroughly with a drip system 3-4 days later after the black plastic is down. The author does not water again for approximately two weeks depending on the weather. More damage is done to melons by watering too often than watering too little.

Cantaloupes and Crenshaw are very susceptible to fungus diseases such as powdery and downy mildew, so it is important to keep the leaves dry. For this reason, sprinkler irrigation should be discontinued when the seedlings come up. After that time, they should be watered with a drip irrigation system or by furrow irrigation. (See pages **64-72** for a discussion of this process.) Basically melons are a hot weather crop and like to be watered deeply but infrequently. This means that they should be soaked thoroughly every 10 days to two weeks.

The author with a bountiful harvest of watermelons. The vines have completely covered the black plastic. If given enough space you will produce 8-15 watermelons per plant over an extended season. Cantaloupes will produce substantially more.

This obviously depends to some extent on the type and quality of your soil (clay requires less frequent watering than sand and soil which is rich in organic material holds water better than other soil), but for good melons don't water too often. With either drip or furrow it is important to water deeply. For example, when using drip lines with two gallon per hour emitters and the lines three feet apart (3 lines on a 10 foot bed) let the water run at least 3-4 hours, depending on your soil.

PEST CONTROL

Melons can be injured by cucumber beetles as well as by squash bugs and other chewing and sucking insects. Dust or spray with Sevin (Carbaryl) to control these insects. When spraying, do it first thing in the morning. The squash bugs are in the crown of the plant and along the vines so get the insecticide into that area.

The author with two 45's and a 50 pound watermelon. Most importantly, they taste great.

HARVESTING

The term "vine-ripe" has great significance with melons. They are best when allowed to ripen on the vine, rather than being picked green for shipping to distant markets. Most varieties of **cantaloupe** turn yellow-tan when ripe. As they begin to turn from green to yellow-tan, the stem becomes looser and can be slipped off the melon without breaking ("full slip"). The melon should be almost fully yellow-tan

(depending on the variety) and slip off the vine easily when picked. The **Crenshaw** melons should be picked when they begin to turn from green to yellow-orange. Some strains of Crenshaw have a blotchy coloring of green, yellow and orange when ripe. They also develop a fragrant aroma and the blossom end softens as they become ripe.

Watermelons are much more difficult to pick at the proper time. Most people use the thump test, but it is sometimes hard to determine if the melon is ripe in that manner. Generally, the watermelon goes from a high ping when thumped green to a deep, low thud when extremely ripe. Another way of determining ripeness is to examine the curly tendril which extends from the stem near the fruit. These often die and turn brown as the melon ripens. The melon also scratches more easily with your fingernail because the epidermis becomes looser when it is ripe. Probably the most reliable method is to check the ground spot on the bottom of the watermelon. When it turns from white to a pale yellow, the melon is ready to pick. Some melons turn a darker yellow on the bottom when ripe. Watermelons also go from a bright growing green color to a dull green color as they ripen. The surface of the melon develops a dull coloring because it accumulates wax.

Onions

Onions are easy to grow and do well under a great variety of climatic conditions. The only limitation is that they require a long season to mature, so in some areas it is necessary to plant them very early in the spring. They grow well in cold weather and are not injured by a moderate frost.

VARIETIES

Onion varieties have been developed for several different purposes, so it is important to pick the one which is well-adapted to your particular use. For example, there are bunching varieties which were developed to be pulled and eaten as green onions, as they do not form a large bulb. These include

'Beltsville Bunching', 'Southport White Bunching' and 'Evergreen Bunching'.

Other varieties may be used as onion sets. This means that they are planted in mid-summer and harvested in the fall when the bulb is the size of a small marble. These bulbs are then planted in the spring for an early harvest of medium-sized bulbs. The varieties usually used for this purpose are 'Stuttgarter' and 'Ebenezer'. Onions from sets usually do not grow very large nor do they have as high a quality as some other onions. They may also go to seed fairly soon after maturity, so it is necessary to watch them carefully, cutting off the seed pods which appear and digging them as soon as they get a medium-sized bulb.

Onions are induced to produce bulbs by **day length.** It is therefore important to get an onion with the right day length for your area. Summer days are very short at the equator and get longer as you approach the North Pole. In some areas of Alaska there are 24 hours of daylight.

The following are **good varieties of onion** with Day length requirements noted:

Long day (15-16 hours)
'Walla Walla'
'Sweet Spanish'
'Ailsa Craig Exhibition'
'Mars Red'
'Red Zeppelin'
Medium day (12-13 hours)
'Red Stockton'
'Candy'
Short day (10-11 hours)
'Texas Grano'
'White Bermuda'
Day neutral -'Super Star'

It is important to get an onion with the right day length. For example, if you live in Idaho and plant a short day 'Texas Grano' onion from a small plant in late March it will begin to grow, but by mid-May it will reach the 10-11 hour day length and be induced to bulb before the tops are large enough to produce a large bulb. If you had planted a 'Walla Walla' long day onion, the tops would have gotten two or three times as large before the plant was induced by long days in late June to start producing a bulb. With the giant tops producing food to store in the bulb, you will get a giant onion by the time the tops begin to die in September.

PLANTING

Onions do well planted on both sides of a 24 inch row. A fast-maturing crop like radishes or beet greens can be planted down the center of the row between the onions and pulled long before the onions begin to enlarge. Onions should be planted approximately 1/2 inch deep and come up well from seed, even in cool weather. They can be planted fairly thick (three or four seeds per inch) and used as green onions when they are about the size of a pencil. They should be thinned in this manner to at least three inches apart before they start to form a bulb.

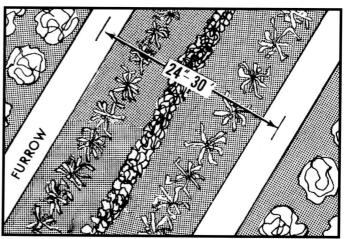

Triple-plant the 24-30 inch onion bed with onions on each side and a short season-crop in the center.

Onions can be started indoors early, planted thick in potting soil in a large container like the bottom half of a gallon milk carton or any other convenient container. Then they should be transplanted into the garden when the base of the stem is approximately 1/4 - 1/2 the thickness of a pencil. At this time they can easily be spaced 2-3 inches apart in the garden. Onion plants can also be purchased at any good nursery for transplanting into the garden in early spring.

FERTILIZING

Although onions will grow in any soil, they respond very well to fertilizer. Mix 16-16-8 and Ironite thoroughly with the top 8-12 inches of soil (see Application of Commercial Fertilizer on pages **21-22** for the amount.) The second application of nitrogen fertilizer should be made a month after planting. This second application gives the onion very large tops before if is induced to bulb, so you get a very large bulb.

WATERING

Onions do well under a regular once-a-week watering schedule. Either drip or furrow irrigation will work well.

HARVESTING

As mentioned above, even bulb-type onions can be harvested when very young as green onions in the process of thinning. The mature bulbs take between 95-120 days to mature depending on the variety, so don't become impatient. When the bulbs are full-sized and the tops turn yellow, dig the onions and let them dry in the sun. They will not store well if they do not dry completely, so let them lay in a dry sunny spot for a couple of weeks if possible. Cut off the tops and brush off the roots for storage and put them in a dry place with good air circulation, preferably hanging in an onion sack.

If fall weather approaches and your onions still have dark green tops and appear to be growing vigorously, stop watering them to help them mature and dry out. Don't bend the tops over as is sometimes recommended because it may cause them to rot and will shorten storage life.

Peanuts

Peanuts are fun for children to grow because of their interesting growth habit of forming pegs which bury themselves in the ground. They also enjoy the end product.

VARIETIES

The two varieties usually planted are 'Jumbo Virginia' and 'Early Spanish'. Peanuts are usually grown commercially in the southeast part of the United States which has long, warm seasons. Even in that area, they take approximately four months to mature. If you live in a colder, shorter season area, you should plant the 'Early Spanish' variety which matures in 100-110 days.

PLANTING

Peanuts prefer a loose, sandy or loam soil. Purchase seeds from a seed catalog rather than from the local grocery store because if the seeds have been roasted, they will not germinate. Shell the nuts and plant them approximately 1 inch deep after the soil has begun to warm and the danger of frost has passed in the late spring. Plant the seeds approximately three or four inches apart and thin them to one plant per foot when they come up.

After the yellow flowers which develop on the plant are pollinated, they form into pegs which bury themselves in the soil under the plant. The peanuts will be formed underground in clusters around the pegs. In order to facilitate this process, the ground around the plant must be kept loose immediately before pegs begin to form. This is usually done by hilling loose dirt up around the plants as you hoe the row of peanuts or putting a grass mulch around and under the plants when the plants are young. (See illustration and text on page **121** for a discussion of this hilling process.)

FERTILIZING AND WATERING

Because peanuts are legumes, it is not necessary to fertilize them as heavily as some other plants, if the proper nitrogen-fixing bacteria is present in the soil. (See legumes on pages **14-15**.) A light application of a complete fertilizer should \be mixed with the soil before planting. Peanuts are basically a warm-weather crop and they should be watered once a week throughout the summer.

PEST CONTROL

Cucumber beetles and several kinds of caterpillars are a problem with peanuts. Dusting with Sevin garden dust is a good way to take care of these pests.

HARVESTING

When the plant begins to die at the end of the season, the soil should be loosened under the plant with a shovel or digging fork and the plant should be gently lifted out of the ground. Carefully knock the dirt off the peanuts and hang them in a warm airy spot to dry. After a few weeks the peanuts should be broken off and stored. Before eating, roast the peanuts at 300 ° for one-half hour.

Peas

Peas require a long period of cool weather in order to produce a large crop and even then they do not yield enough to justify the space which they take in a small garden. On the other hand, there is hardly any garden vegetable which is more delightful eaten fresh out of the garden than peas. A tall variety can be grown on a trellis in a very small garden in order to produce a reasonable crop in a small space. For the most part, however, the bush-type peas are much easier to grow and their quality is outstanding.

VARIETIES

Peas come in several types including the snap peas, which have a tender sweet pod which is eaten along with the peas. Excellent varieties of peas include:

Snow peas –

'Oregon Giant'	(60 days)

Snap peas –

'Sugar Sprint'	(62 days)
'Super Sugar Snap'	(64 days)

Regular peas –

'Laxton Progress'	(55 days)
'Mr. Big'	(60 days)
'Green Arrow'	(70 days)

PLANTING

Peas are planted in both the early spring and fall garden. Because they are a cool weather crop, they should be planted as early as possible in the late winter or spring in order to mature before hot weather comes. They are not injured by a light frost. For fall planting, time the planting so that they will mature after the fall weather replaces the summer heat. Peas should be planted on both sides of a 30-36 inch row, placing seeds approximately two inches apart down each side but thinned to 4-5 inches apart. The seeds should be planted. approximately one inch deep, and watered often enough to keep them moist until they come up.

WATERING AND FERTILIZING

Peas should be watered once per week in cool spring weather, but during any periods of warm weather, twice a week is much better. Peas are very susceptible to mildew, so avoid overhead sprinklers. As with most other vegetables, drip or furrow irrigation is preferable.

A regular application of a good complete fertilizer should be made before roto-tilling so that it will be thoroughly mixed into the root zone. Repeated applications of fertilizer are not necessary because the peas, being legumes, have the capacity to "fix" nitrogen. If you are planting an area which has not grown peas before, inoculate the seeds with nitrogen-fixing bacteria.

HARVESTING

Begin harvesting when the peas have begun to swell in the pods so that they are plump but not old. Not only do the young peas taste much better, but keeping the plants well picked encourages them to continue bearing. Pick **snap peas** when the pod is first beginning to show a bulge and eat the pod and all.

Peppers

Peppers prefer hot weather, but can be grown in most areas of the country. They are divided into two general categories, the sweet bell pepper types and the more pungent hot peppers. In both categories some

You can produce a good crop of peppers, even in short season and cool summer areas, if you choose the right varieties.

varieties turn yellow and various other colors, but most turn from green to red as they mature.

VARIETIES

In the **sweet bell** pepper category, the recommended varieties are 'King Arthur', 'Karma' and 'Revolution'.

In the hot pepper category, pungency is measured in Scovilles which are heat units. **Mild hot** peppers run up to about 2000 Scovilles. **Medium hot** peppers are between 2000 and 10,000 Scovilles with the **very hot** peppers above 10,000 Scovilles. Avoid the **extremely hot** peppers like the Habanero types which run between 200,000 and 400,000 Scovilles, i.e. more than 200 times hotter the 'Anaheim Chili' which is 1000-1500 Scovilles. Don't touch your face after handling the Habanero types.

Three excellent varieties of **mild hot** peppers between 500 and 1500 Scovilles) are 'Anaheim Chili', 'Holy Mole' (mole sauce) and 'Mulato Isleno' (ancho/poblano type for chili rellenos).

PLANTING

Peppers require warm soil and come up very slowly, so they should be started inside and transplanted outdoors when they are approximately

six to eight weeks old. They should be stagger-planted approximately 18 inches apart down both sides of a 36 inch row. They should be planted outside in the late spring after all danger of frost has passed.

FERTILIZING AND WATERING

A good complete fertilizer should be mixed with the soil before planting. The 16-16-8 and Ironite recommended for other crops is ideal. Like other fruit crops, peppers respond to excessive applications of nitrogen fertilizer by remaining in the vegetative growth stage rather than starting to bloom and set on fruit. Water this crop once a week.

PEST CONTROL

Peppers are not damaged by most bugs, but are very susceptible to tobacco mosaic virus. It is therefore very important to wash your hands care-fully after touching any tobacco products to avoid contaminating the plants with this virus. Washing after handling infected plants is also important.

HARVESTING

Most people pick bell peppers when they reach mature size before they turn from green to red. Allowing the fruit to remain on the plant after becoming mature will reduce the number of peppers the plant will produce.

One picking from 6 plants in the author's garden.

Potatoes

Freshly dug "new potatoes" are a great delicacy, so even though potatoes take a relatively large space in the garden, they are worthwhile. They are easy to grow and will store for a period of time in the ground after maturing.

VARIETIES

Recommended varieties are 'Yukon Gold', 'Red Pontiac', 'Gold Rush Russet, 'Butte', 'Ranger Russet' and 'Russet Burbank'.

PLANTING

Potatoes do best in well-drained, sandy soil, but they can be grown successfully in any soil if it has enough organic material mixed in to make it loose and crumbly. If you have particularly heavy clay and have not yet improved it with organic materials, you can still grow potatoes by using the mulching method discussed below. They should be planted in April or May after danger of frost is passed. Potatoes like a slightly acid soil. Organic material makes soil more acid. Sphagnum peat moss has a pH level of 3.0 to 4.0 so it is especially helpful in lowering pH and growing potatoes. Elemental soil sulfur also makes the soil more acid.

"Seed potatoes," available from most seed companies and nurseries, are good quality potatoes which have been certified to be free from serious potato diseases. Potatoes from the grocery store can be used, but they have been treated to prevent sprouting and there is danger of importing soil diseases into your garden. If you use store potatoes, wash them carefully with warm soapy water to remove the chemicals which have been applied to prevent sprouting and then rinse off the soap and store them in a moderately warm place for a couple of weeks. Putting them in a paper sack in a cupboard above an oven is usually effective. In a couple of weeks when you take them out they will probably have sprouts coming out of each eye.

Each average size potato should be cut into 3 or 4 pieces with at least 2 eyes in each piece. After cutting,

if you let them stay in a dry place for a few hours, the cuts will heal over and they will have less chance of rotting after they are planted. Then plant them 3- 4 inches deep and 12 inches apart down the center of a 30 inch row. By making the planting furrow extra deep you will have extra dirt to pull over against the plant after it is up 6-8 inches.

HILLING

When the potato plant is approximately eight to ten inches tall, while weeding with a hoe, widen the furrows and hill the excess dirt up around the potato plant. This soil should raise the ground level around the plant by 4-6 inches providing plenty of loose dirt in which the potatoes will form. The roots will, for the most part, grow in the area below the spot where the potato seed was planted and the potatoes themselves will form on stolen coming off the stem of the plant. An alternative to the hilling process described above is to place 6 inches of mulch (grass, straw or hay) around the plants down the top of the row when the plant is approximately 8-10 inches tall. The tubers will grow in the top 3 or 4 inches of soil as well as in the mulch on top of the ground.

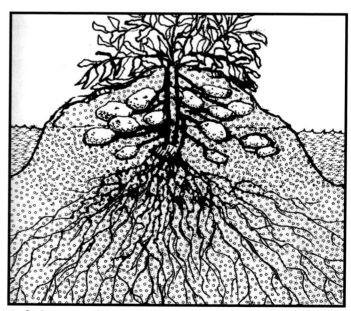

Soft dirt or mulch should be mounded up around the stem where the new potatoes will grow.

WATERING AND FERTILIZING

Potatoes need a relatively even, consistent level of moisture in the soil. This means that they should be watered at least twice a week in warm weather. If the soil is allowed to get extremely dry between waterings, the potatoes will be knobby and rough and sometimes have hollow areas in the center. A good complete fertilizer should be mixed thoroughly into the soil before planting. (See pages **21-22** Application of Commercial Fertilizer for the mix and amount of fertilizer to apply. It also tells how much soil sulfur to apply to make your soil more acid and make the iron, zinc and manganese more available.) Potato plants are also sensitive to zinc deficiencies. If this problem is common in your area, and if you have small, stunted potato plants, you should investigate this possibility and solve it with sulfur and chelated zinc if necessary.

HARVESTING

Dig new potatoes when the flowers form on the plants. For later varieties which are grown for storage, wait until the plant begins to yellow and die before digging. In digging, be careful not to cut or bruise the tubers. Store them unwashed in a cool, dark place.

Pumpkins

(See **SQUASH** and **PUMPKINS**)

Radishes

Radishes are fast and relatively easy to grow, but in order to grow good radishes, you must pay attention to some important details.

VARIETIES

Radishes come in various colors (red, white and black) and shapes (from the carrot-shaped white ones to the round, marble-like red ones). The recommended red varieties are 'Cherry Bell' and 'Champion'. The best white ones are 'Sparkler' and 'White Icicle'. 'French Breakfast' has shades of red and white.

FERTILIZING AND WATERING

You will have mature radishes a month after planting so it is important to have the soil ready and properly fertilized before planting. Work in a substantial quantity of a good complete fertilizer (16-16-8 and Ironite) Radishes should be kept moist by watering twice a week. They need to grow quickly in order to have good quality.

PLANTING

Radishes do exceptionally well in cold weather. They should be planted with the first vegetables which you plant in your garden in late winter or early spring. They can also be planted in the late summer to mature in cool fall weather. Because radishes mature so quickly, they can be planted with other crops rather than wasting space by planting them separately. Some gardeners mix them with other vegetable seed, but it is preferable to plant them between the rows of carrots, beets, onions, etc. in a triple-planted row, so that they can be harvested without disturbing the roots of the vegetable which is left.

PEST CONTROL

Several kinds of insects attack the tops and roots of radishes, particularly if they are planted in warm weather. Dust the ground with a garden dust containing Sevin as they come up and a second time approximately two weeks later.

HARVESTING

Approximately three weeks after planting you can start pulling some of the larger radishes for the table, thereby thinning the row to allow others to grow larger. Radishes must be harvested as soon as the root is mature because they do not store well in the ground. Usually about a week after radishes mature, they get strong tasting and pithy (flesh loses crisp texture and becomes soft with hollow center). Pull all of your radishes when they are ready and store them in the refrigerator.

Raspberries

(See **BERRIES**)

Rhubarb

This hardy perennial is often called "Pie Plant", referring to its major use. It is also used for preserves and sauces.

VARIETIES

Recommended varieties include 'Valentine', 'Flare', 'Canada Red', 'McDonald', 'Cherry' and 'Crimson Red'.

WATERING AND PLANTING

Roto-till a good complete fertilizer into the bed along with lots of organic soil amendment. Rhubarb is usually planted from bare roots, but it is also available in gallon pots from the nursery. Plant the roots or plants from a pot every three feet down the top of a 3 foot bed. If planting a root, it should barely protrude from the surface of the soil. After planting, rhubarb should be fed with nitrogen fertilizer at least once every spring and again in mid-summer.

Rhubarb is deep-rooted, so it only needs to be watered once per week in hot weather. The ground should be soaked thoroughly each time it is watered.

HARVESTING

No rhubarb stalks should be harvested the first year in order to allow the plant to become well established. After the first year, you can harvest all season, as long as you are careful to leave plenty of young inside shoots on the plant each time to keep it healthy. Remember that the food is produced in the leaves, so you must leave plenty of leaves at all times.

It is important to understand that the leaves of rhubarb are poisonous. For that reason, babies should not be allowed to play in the area of rhubarb plants and, when harvesting, the leaves should be cut off and discarded. The stalk from the base of the leaf to the ground is excellent food. The stalks should be harvested by pulling the outside ones downward and twisting sideways until they snap off at the base. This should be done when the outside stalks are 12-18 inches in length and turn a reddish color. Only

remove a few outer stalks from each plant each time, thereby leaving enough young stalks in the center of the plant to continue manufacturing food.

Spinach and Swiss Chard

Although not related, these two vegetables are grown for the same purpose and are conveniently discussed together. They both grow well in cool weather, but Swiss chard will handle hot weather as well. Spinach is a very fast crop and must be cut as soon as it matures before it starts going to seed. Swiss chard, on the other hand, will produce greens over a very long season (a full year in moderate climates). Swiss chard is a near relative of the beet and its leaves have a very mild pleasant flavor.

VARIETIES

The best varieties of Swiss chard iare 'Large White Ribbed', 'Rhubarb Chard', 'Bright Lights' and 'Discovery'.

The best varieties of spinach include 'Melody Hybrid', 'Bloomsdale Long-Standing' and 'America'.

PLANTING

Spinach is like radishes and germinates best in cool soil. Swiss chard also comes up well in early spring weather but a number of plants can be started inside in a gallon pot and transplanted out when the weather is still cool in the spring. The seeds should be planted approximately ½ inch deep and ½ inch apart on both sides of a 24-28 inch row. Spinach can also be planted down the middle of a double-planted row of carrots because the spinach will be harvested in about 45 days and can be removed before the carrots are large enough to cause overcrowding.

WATERING AND FERTILIZING

Being leaf crops, both spinach and Swiss chard respond to regular watering (approximately twice a week in warm weather), but Swiss chard will go longer between waterings without being injured. Water can be applied with either the drip system or furrows. A good complete fertilizer should be roto-tilled into the soil before planting and Swiss chard should receive an application of nitrogen fertilizer midseason.

PEST CONTROL

Spinach is susceptible to aphids and both get leaf miners. These can be controlled by spraying the leaves with Malathion or Sevin. Follow directions on the manufacturer's container. Both spinach and Swiss chard are very attractive to snails and slugs. Because you don't want to sprinkle the poisonous bait directly onto the leaves which you will eventually eat, it is important to keep these pests out by putting a trail of bait around the garden area immediately after planting and on the ground around the plants.

HARVESTING

Swiss chard should be harvested regularly after the plants get to be approximately 10-12 inches tall. Most people try to let the chard get too large before harvesting and it becomes fibrous and loses its mild, tender quality. It can be harvested very much like rhubarb by removing the larger outside leaves, always leaving a clump of small leaves in the center. A much easier way is to cut all of the leaves straight across about two inches above the ground. By cutting only what you need for any particular day, you will gradually move down the row and by the time you get back to a certain plant, a week or two will have gone by and the leaves will be large enough to cut again.

It is very important to harvest spinach when it is mature, before it starts putting up seed stalks and becomes tough and strong tasting. Cut the whole plant straight across about 1/2 inch above the ground. If you start harvesting when the plants are very young and have only five or six leaves, they will grow a new set of leaves for a second crop before going to seed.

Squash and Pumpkins

The distinction between squash and pumpkins is a totally artificial one, based on color and shape. There are three branches of the squash family with so-called "squash" and "pumpkins" in each (cucurbita pepo, cucurbita maxima or cucurbita moschata). Traditionally they are called pumpkins if they have an orange color and a Howden (Jack-O Lantern) shape. In recent years there has been a mixing of these distinctions with 'Dill's Atlantic Giant (over 1200 pounds) looking less like a pumpkin and some squash ('Sunshine') looking more like a pumpkin. All of these types of squash, whatever they are called, will pollinate each other so if you save the seed you never know what you will get in the next generation.

Winter squash have hard skins and provide good eating throughout the winter. Don't pick until the plant begins to die and the stems are tan.

VARIETIES

There are many excellent **varieties of squash** which include: 'Lioness' (yellow straight neck, summer), 'Italiano Largo' (zucchini, summer), 'Spineless Beauty' (zucchini, summer), 'Sunshine' (winter), 'Early Butternut' (winter), 'Butterboy Hybrid' (winter), 'Avalon Butternut' (winter) 'Waltham Butternut' (winter) and 'Pink Banana' (winter). Some of the major varieties of Pumpkins are: 'Small Sugar', 'Howden Biggie', 'Connecticut Field', 'Big Max', 'Prizewinner', and 'Dill's Atlantic Giant'.

Because many pumpkins and winter squash are very long season crops, you need to notice the number of days to maturity in your seed catalog with each variety because it affects when and where you plant. If you live in a short season area, it may be necessary to start a 110 day squash inside for later transplanting.

PLANTING

In planting squash (including pumpkins) you need to know how large the mature plant will be. If you are planting summer squash (zucchini, yellow crook neck or straightneck) they are not a vine but will grow into a fairly large bush so you will plant them at least three feet apart down a three foot bed. On the other hand, the winter squash and pumpkins (except for the bush or semi-bush types like 'Early Butternut') will be 15-25 feet across, so they may need to be eliminated if you only have space for a tiny garden. Standard winter squash and pumpkins need to be planted on 8-10 foot beds with individual plants being 8-10 feet apart down the bed. Even then they will crawl all over each other, larger spacing is preferable and gives you better quality but you have to adjust to the space you have available. The size, number and quality of the fruit is enhanced by larger spacing.

In planting each hill (group of seeds), pull the dirt back with a hand hoe and place four or five seeds in a cluster approximately one inch apart. Cover the seeds approximately ¾ inch deep. When the seedlings come up (in approximately one week in warm weather) they should be thinned, leaving the two healthiest plants in each hill. Approximately three weeks later when the plants are large enough so that they are not so vulnerable to damage from birds and insects, thin again to one plant for each hill.

In short season areas where cold weather and danger of frost delay planting directly into the soil, it is very helpful to start winter squash and pumpkins inside in large containers like the bottom half of a gallon milk carton. This type of container allows the plant to get to the runner stage without getting root bound before planting in the garden. Use good quality potting soil from Lowes, Home Depot or a nursery.

(See section on Starting Transplants. Also read section on Hardening Transplants.)

A mistake often made by beginning home gardeners is to plant too many zucchinis. Two healthy zucchini bushes will adequately supply a family of six. If you plant more, you will find yourself having zucchini bread, zucchini cake, zucchini casserole, zucchini stew and peddling zucchinis all around the neighborhood trying to keep up with them. If you plant even more, you are in big trouble. The same is true to a lesser extent with other summer squash.

FERTILIZING

For both pumpkins and squash, a good complete fertilizer (16-16-8 and Ironite) should be thoroughly mixed with the soil before planting. A second application of fertilizer is normally not helpful. (See Application of Commercial Fertilizer on pages **21-22** for the exact proportions and amount.)

WATERING

It is important to be aware that both squash and pumpkins are extremely susceptible to fungus diseases such as powdery mildew. For this reason, any overhead sprinkling which gets water on the leaves should be terminated when the seedlings come up. Thereafter, squash and pumpkins should be watered by drip irrigation or in furrows. In arid climates, squash can be sprinkle irrigated the first thing in the morning as long as the leaves are completely dry long before evening. If the leaves are wet in the evening and night the mildew spores from the air will stick to the leaves, germinate and grow which will cause the disease to eventually cause the plant to become sick and may cause premature death. Both squash and pumpkins are in that group of plants labeled "seed and fruit" in the watering section and they need to be deeply, but infrequently watered. The summer squash are normally watered once a week and the winter squash and pumpkins every 10 days to 2 weeks. Drip lines with two gallon an hour emitters every foot are an excellent way to water squash. (See Drip Irrigation on pages **69-72**.)

PEST CONTROL

Squash and pumpkins are susceptible to damage from squash bugs and cucumber beetles. These pests can be controlled by dusting or spraying with a garden dust containing Sevin. Squash bugs are usually found along the vines or in the crown of the plant.

HARVESTING

Summer squash should be harvested regularly when the fruit is very young. For example, zucchini is at its prime right after it blooms when the fruit is only about six inches long. Remember that the biggest is not always the best. If left long enough, zucchini will grow almost two feet long but is extremely tough and strong tasting. Other varieties of summer squash should also be picked very young.

The opposite is true of winter squash and pumpkins. They need to be fully mature and you can even wait until the vines die before picking them. During the last few weeks before maturity they develop the hard skin which allows them to keep all winter and also the fine, dry texture and sweet flavor which make them excellent for baking and pies. If stored in a cool, dry place, most winter squash will keep all winter and some will keep until the next June. To avoid rotting at the stem end, cut the stem with a pair of pruning clippers, leaving at least a two inch stub. The stem should be yellow-brown and virtually dead before the winter squash or pumpkin is picked. Now days most pumpkins are grown for Jack-O-Lanterns so it doesn't matter when they are picked as long as they look good.

Tomatoes

Tomatoes are one of the most rewarding vegetables to grow because the home gardener can expect a tremendous yield of delicious food in a very small space. They are very easy to grow if you follow a few simple rules. Although tomatoes often have names reflecting far-away places (where they were taken in early colonial times), they are like so many vegetables and fruits including strawberries, blackberries, potatoes, sweet potatoes (yams), peppers, beans, corn, squash (pumpkins) etc. and are a native American crop.

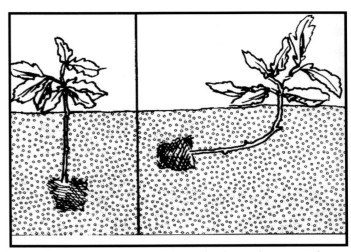

Tomato plants form roots along the buried stem and should be planted deeper than they grew in their original container.

VARIETIES

It is important to choose the right variety of tomato for your climate and personal taste. The size, shape, acidity, sweetness and juiciness change dramatically with the variety. There are many general-purpose tomatoes which can be used fresh on the table as well as for canning, but others are developed to fit particular canning or eating requirements.

The terms "determinate" and "indeterminate" are used to describe the growth habit of tomato plants. **Determinate** plants are bush types with a limited size. The true determinants ripen all their fruit at about the same time and then die. These are the genesis of the commercial tomatoes which are al harvested in one picking for canned sauce, paste, ketchup, etc. The modern home garden tomatoes which are called "determinate" do not ripen all at once but are small bush plants like the true determinates. **Semi-determinate** tomato plants are a medium bush like 'Celebrity'. **Indeterminate** plants grow larger and in some areas do well with stakes, cages or trellises.

Tomatoes come in a broad range of maturity dates from those ripening as soon as 45 days after transplanting into the garden to those taking as long as 90 days. The significance of an early variety is more than just having the crop ripen sooner. The early varieties have the additional ability to set on fruit in cool weather. If the nighttime temperature does not remain above 55 degrees-58 degrees F., the standard mid-season varieties of tomato will set on very little fruit. The plant will bloom but the blossoms will drop. For this reason, home gardeners in northern, mountainous and cool coastal climates should plant early varieties. Cherry and other small-fruited tomatoes have traditionally produced heavy crops under short season and cool summer conditions, but large fruited early varieties have now been developed which produce excellent quality tomatoes under these same conditions.

There are several hundred varieties of tomatoes currently being produced. Many are special purpose commercial varieties but there are over three hundred available to home gardeners. Contrary to popular belief, they are not "all about the same". Of the fifteen varieties listed in the first printing of this book, only one is listed hereafter as still recommended. Generally speaking, the larger, indeterminate varieties of tomato are the best tasting. This is probably because the ratio of leaf surface per ounce of tomato is the greatest. The food being manufactured in the leaves, the amount of sugar and flavor generally would be highest with **more leaf surface** per tomato. Some of the smaller determinate types and some semi-determinates have huge yields of large tomatoes on a very small plant. For that reason it is extremely difficult to get a good tasting paste type tomato.

The following are the **recommended varieties of tomato** listed in order of ripening:

'Sugary' (det-grape)	50 days
'Jetsetter' (ind)	64 days
'Whopper' (ind)	65 days
'Goliath' (ind)	65 days
'Beefy Boy' (ind)	70 days
'Country Taste' (ind)	70 days
'Super Fantastic' (ind)	70 days
'Celebrity' (semi)	70 days
'Super Tasty' (semi)	70 days
'Miroma' (det, paste)	70 days
'Better boy' (ind)	72 days
'Big Beef' (ind)	73 days
'Scarlet Red' (semi)	74 days
'Health Kick' (det, paste)	75 days
'Viva Italia' (det, paste)	75 days
'Brandy Boy' (ind)	78 days
'Porterhouse Beefsteak' (ind)	80 days
'Brandywine' (ind)	85 days

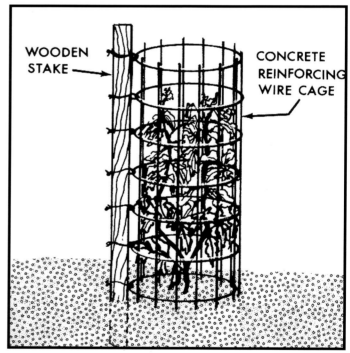

WOODEN STAKE

CONCRETE REINFORCING WIRE CAGE

Training tomatoes in a cage, made from concrete reinforcing wire and tied to a stake, is an excellent method of getting tomatoes off the ground and exposing them to sunlight.

PLANTING

Tomatoes are usually started as transplants rather than direct seeding in the garden. This gives you a head start on the season because the plants are six weeks to two months old when you plant them out in your garden. (See pages **57-60** for a discussion about starting your own transplants from seed indoors.)

Unlike most other transplants, tomato plants should be set deeper when transplanted into the garden than they grew in their original container. The plant will develop new roots along its buried stem and grow much faster than if you planted it at original ground level. If the plant was root-bound in the pot, this situation will be somewhat alleviated by the new root system which will develop along the buried stem.

In picking transplants at the nursery, try to get bushy, dark-green, vigorously healthy-looking plants. Avoid the older, woody-looking plants which are already in bloom, but they can be fairly tall if green and vigorous.

In planting, remove the bottom leaves and branches so that you can place the plant in the ground with only 4-6 inches protruding out of the ground, For semi-determinate bush varieties plant down the center of a 36 inch bed putting the plants three feet apart if they are going to be allowed to spread across plastic and two and ½ feet apart if they are going to be staked up. For the larger indeterminate varieties they can go as close as three feet apart if staked and four feet apart if spreading across plastic. **(See page 60 about using hotcaps to get an earlier crop of tomatoes.)**

STAKING VS BLACK PLASTIC

There are several advantages to putting black plastic over the bed and allowing the tomato plants to spread across it. (See pages **80-82** for illustrations and a discussion of the methods of applying black plastic mulch.) Black plastic prevents weeds, retains moisture, keeps the tomatoes off the ground to avoid spoilage and heats the vines which lie upon it. In areas with short seasons or cool summer weather, this additional heat increases the yield and also brings the crop on two or three weeks earlier. If you have enough room choose indeterminate varieties and let them spread across a 10 foot wide piece of plastic. (Remember that the tomato plants were planted four feet apart under hot caps. After approximately 3-4 weeks when the danger of frost had passed, the caps were removed, the drip lines were put down, the bed was covered by 10

The tomato plants in the foreground were planted four feet apart and allowed to spread across the ten foot wide black plastic mulch until they totally covered the plastic. The three drip lines were three feet apart under the plastic.

foot wide plastic, and each plant was pulled through a hole made in the plastic.)

You will need three drip lines, three feet apart under the plastic to water the entire soil profile. This black plastic method reduces to almost zero the number of cracked or rotten tomatoes. Indeterminate varieties of tomatoes watered and fertilized properly and allowed to spread over 10 foot wide black plastic will produce up to 200 pounds of tomatoes per plant in a season. (For pictures of tomatoes in black plastic, see pages **26 and 36.**) (See illustration on page **146 showing one 267 pound picking from 10 plants on black plastic.**)

Staking is a method of keeping the tomatoes off the ground and exposing the maximum amount of foliage to sunlight. It also promotes good air circulation to avoid fungus diseases. For the tall, indeterminate varieties of tomato, one way to grow them effectively is by devising some method of training them into the air. This can be done either by staking or with a circular cage made from concrete reinforcing wire or some form of trellis. The cage is advantageous because vines do not have to be tied up. They merely need to be poked back into the cage when necessary to encourage them to grow inside of it and they support themselves. Tomatoes are fairly visible and can be

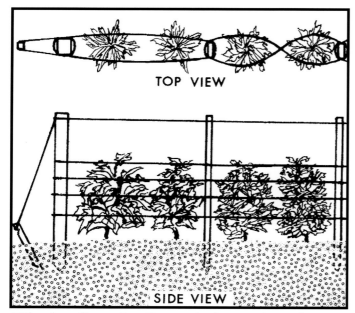

TOP VIEW

SIDE VIEW

Either by a figure-8 or the regular loop pattern, the plants are confined within the strings, the new strings are added a few inches higher each weeks as they grow.

of foliage for purposes of protecting the fruit from sunburn and for manufacturing food for a large crop of excellent tomatoes.

If two plants are placed between a pair of stakes instead of one, a figure 8 configuration of the twine needs to be used going around one side of one plant and around the other side of the next and then around the second pole. In coming back you go around the other side of each plant so that each is fully enclosed in twine. Looking down from the top, the enclosure around the two plants forms a figure 8. (See illustration.) Pull the twine fairly tight between the stakes. Steel fence posts are excellent for this kind of support because they can be driven deep enough into the ground that they don't blow over in the wind when supporting a heavy load of tomatoes.

The other method of staking tomatoes involves the pruning of branches which grow above each leaf along the main stem. When a branch grows an inch or so long, pull the branch out of the socket leaving only the main stem and the leaves and flowers that grow from it. This stem and the leaves that are left grow very large. Thus the plant is left with only one central stem with leaves and fruit growing on it. Be careful in removing the growth bud to avoid cutting off the leaves at the same time. (See illustration.) The leaves are needed to produce the food which is stored in the tomatoes.

picked through the openings. Although it is beneficial to remove the branches up to the first flower cluster, very little pruning is necessary in using this method. Stay away from the small flimsy cages that will tip over or crumple with the weight of a good crop of tomatoes.

There are two traditional methods of staking tomatoes. The first, and the one used by most commercial growers, does not require much pruning. The bottom two or three side shoots (also called "branches" or "suckers") might be pruned off, but all of the rest of the growth is allowed to remain. The tomato plants are placed approximately three feet apart down the center of a 36-42 inch bed. Stakes are placed down the row between every plant or between every second plant. The twine is tied around a stake and then around one side of the tomato plant and then around the next stake and then back around the other side of the tomato plant to the original pole. Approximately once a week as the plants grow you put another strand of twine up about 8-10 inches along the stake and around the plants. The idea is to confine the plants within the strings rather than tying them to the stakes. This forces them to grow up without bruising or injuring the stems or branches. It also encourages growth of the maximum amount

CUT HERE

The second method of staking requires pinching out the growth bud above each leaf, being careful not to remove the leaf below or the flowers above.

In using this second method of staking, the stem of the plant is tied loosely to the stake with plastic ties or twine every 8-10 inches. The plants can be placed much closer together because most of the foliage is removed. It is recommended that they be planted approximately 1 and ½ to 2 feet apart down the center of a 36 inch row. This method gives you a smaller total yield than the other method of staking because there are fewer tomatoes, but each individual tomato is larger and the plants will ripen fruit earlier in areas of cool summer weather than they would without pruning.

This method only works in areas of extremely high relative humidity and/or cool coastal conditions. When this method was tried by the author along the Wasatch front of northern Utah with eight different varieties of tomatoes, almost every tomato cracked to the point that they were totally useless. Even watering them twice a week did not help.

FERTILIZING

A good complete fertilizer should be mixed into the top 8-10 inches of soil before planting. (See pages **21-22** under Application of Commercial Fertilizer for the types and amounts of fertilizer to use.) Tomatoes are one of the crops which are particularly susceptible to zinc deficiencies, so in some areas where the soils have been shown to be low in this element or too alkaline, it is important to add zinc. A very small amount of magnesium sulfate (epson salts) is also helpful for tomatoes

Tomatoes need a substantial amount of phosphorus and potassium for an abundant crop of fruit, but they also need an adequate supply of nitrogen for a vigorous, healthy plant. You must be careful not to over-feed tomatoes with nitrogen. Coupled with a large amount of water, the excessive nitrogen diet will encourage an abundant, vegetative growth, but it keeps the plant from changing from the vegetative stage to the fruiting stage of growth. Careful application of water as discussed below will take care of this problem.

Once the plant is in the fruiting stage and has begun setting on tomatoes, it will usually remain in the fruiting stage throughout the balance of the season.

WATERING

The mistake most commonly made by home gardeners in growing tomatoes is to water them too frequently. With too much nitrogen fertilizer and too much water you will grow a beautiful gigantic tomato plant with no tomatoes. Remember that a healthy tomato plant properly watered will root down 10 feet. If properly watered the plant will be extremely dark green and have a stocky, heavy vine.

As with other seed and fruit crops, tomatoes should be watered deeply, but infrequently. This usually means to soak the root zone thoroughly every ten days to two weeks with large indeterminate varieties of tomatoes. Determinate varieties of tomatoes can be watered as often as once a week.

Water the soil around the plants thoroughly immediately after transplanting and then put on hotcaps for about three weeks until they have grown so much that they are pushing the hotcap from the inside (they frequently push through the hotcap in that amount of time). Then cut across the top of the cap with scissors and open it a couple of inches to acclimate the plant to wind and sun before removing it completely. After removing the hotcaps, the drip lines should be put down. With determinate and semi-determinate tomatoes planted on a 36-42 inch bed, put one drip line on each side of the bed next to the berm (ridge). With indeterminate varieties planted four feet apart put down three drip lines, three feet apart. One goes right down next to the plants and the other two are three feet out on each side. The ten foot wide piece of black plastic then covers the entire bed with a hole or an X cut to carefully pull the plant through the plastic.

The watering time depends to some extent on the weather and the soil involved, but a rule of thumb is 2 hours for the 36-42 inch bed with two drip lines and three hours for the bed with three drip lines three feet apart. These lines have a two gallon per hour emitter every foot and are used with approximately 40 PSI (pounds per square inch of water pressure). (See the section about using Drip Irrigation Systems on pages 69-72 for more details. Also see illustration.) Using

The author with one picking from 10 indeterminate tomato plants grown on 10 foot wide black plastic with three drip lines 3 feet apart under the plastic. The total weight of this picking was 267 pounds which is over 26 pounds per plant. Because you continue picking tomatoes over a long season you can expect to get 150-200 pounds per plant in a season from these kinds of tomatoes if they are well grown. These tomatoes were deeply watered every two weeks.

the above method the plants go from the vegetative growth stage into the fruiting stage and set fruit early in their growth cycle. Watering properly produces huge crops of delicious tomatoes. If you just can't keep yourself from overwatering your tomato plants, stick with the smaller determinate and semi-determinate varieties. They tend to produce a crop in spite of overwatering.

In warmer climates there is less concern about tomato plants staying in the vegetative growth stage because the heat encourages blooming and fruit set. Even there, don't water tomatoes more than once a week and the 10 day to two week cycle is best. (See the watering principles section on pages **25-31** and the watering methods section on pages **64-72** for more details.)

Be careful not to carry the infrequent watering schedule to an extreme. Particularly if your soil is sandy and does not retain moisture well, your tomatoes can get **"blossom-end rot"** which is a black or tan discoloration at the blossom end of the fruit which enlarges, darkens and becomes sunken and leathery as the tomato begins to ripen. This is more apt to

happen with the first few tomatoes from your tomato patch. If it continues, it usually means that you are **not watering deeply enough** or in rare situations it could also mean you were not watering frequently enough. This usually occurs in 'Roma' and other paste type tomatoes. (See illustration.)For this reason it may be necessary to water the small determinate tomatoes once a week instead of every 10 days to two weeks.

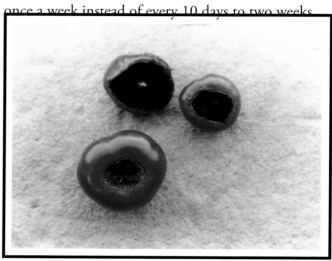

Blossom-end rot is caused by not watering deeply (thoroughly) enough or not watering often enough. It is not often seen except in small determinate types for paste tomatoes like 'Roma'. With this type of tomato, water once a week.

PEST AND DISEASE CONTROL

Tomatoes are susceptible to a number of diseases as well as being vulnerable to certain insect pests. The fusarium and verticillium wilts cause the leaves to yellow and the plant to eventually wither and die. These fungus diseases along with the root knot nematodes are soil-born pests which can be controlled by rotating planting areas (so that you do not plant tomatoes in the same spot two years in a row) and by solarizing the soil. (See pages **83-84**). Avoiding overwatering also helps avoid diseases. A third method is to plant varieties which are resistant to these problems. The letters "VFN", found in the names of some of the newer tomato varieties, mean that they have built-in resistance to verticillium and fusarium wilts and root knot nematodes. A VFFFT variety would also be resistant to three races of fusarium wilt, fungus disease and tobacco mosaic virus.

Tomato plants are particularly vulnerable to certain virus diseases such as tobacco-mosaic virus. This is usually spread by touching tomato plants after contact with tobacco products. After touching tobacco in any form or after handling or removing a diseased plant, wash your hands carefully with soap and water before touching a healthy plant. (See illustration on page 83 for a picture of tobacco mosaic virus.)

Tomato plants can also be easily damaged by tomato horn worms which seem to appear out of nowhere and devour gigantic quantities of the plant almost overnight. They can be killed by dusting with a garden dust containing Sevin, but they usually appear right before and during fruiting season when you don't want to sprinkle any toxic insecticides on your tomato plants. The best way of eliminating tomato worms is to spray with Bt (bacillus thuringiensis) which is non-toxic to people, pets and the environment. It is a bacterium that kills worms (a "worm germ"). It also kills the tomato fruit worm. You can eat the ripe tomatoes the same day as you spray.

HARVESTING

Tomatoes achieve their best quality when allowed to ripen on the vine. They start out very dark green and gradually get lighter colored as they mature, going from whitish-green to stages of pink and red, usually starting at the blossom end. Some tomatoes even have green shoulders and a whitish green core after the rest of the tomato is ripe.

Tomatoes are often picked commercially when they are in their whitish green or pink stages so that they will be firm for proper handling and shipping. They turn red off the vine and look good but don't taste very good. In the fall in climates where frost kills the tomato plants, watch the weather reports and pick off all the tomatoes which are beginning to ripen right before the first killing frost. Store them in a cool dark place at approximately 60° where they will ripen gradually and can be used for several weeks. They will not have the great flavor of vine-ripened fruit, but they will be just as good as the ones purchased at the grocery store.

Turnips and Rutabagas

Rutabagas are a yellow-rooted relative of the turnip. They are larger than turnips and require a longer season to mature, but the other cultural requirements of rutabagas are practically identical to turnips. They both do best in cool weather and should be planted either in the late winter or early spring to be harvested before hot weather or planted in mid-summer for a late fall harvest. The tops of both turnips and rutabagas are extremely high in vitamins A and C and are widely used for greens.

VARIETIES

The recommended varieties of turnip are Purple Top White Globe, Tokyo Cross Hybrid and Just Right Hybrid.

Recommended varieties of rutabaga are Altasweet, Macomber, and Purple Top Yellow.

PLANTING

They should be planted approximately 1/2 inch deep and 1-2 inches apart down both sides of a 30 inch row. When they come up, turnips should be thinned to three or four inches apart and rutabagas to five or six inches apart. They can be thinned by pulling young plants for greens.

FERTILIZING AND WATERING

These crops do best if a good complete fertilizer is mixed thoroughly with the soil before planting.

They are cool weather, water-loving crops, so they should be watered at least twice a week in warm weather. When planted in mid-summer for fall harvest, it is particularly important to keep them moist during July and August while the weather is hot.

PEST CONTROL

Pest problems are more severe in summer planted crops than in those planted in the cool weather of early spring. The root maggots and cabbage loopers can be controlled with Sevin and the aphids with Malathion. Follow the instructions on the manufacturer's label.

HARVESTING

When used for greens, both turnips and rutabagas should be pulled young when the tops are 6-8 inches tall and the bottoms are not yet mature. They get progressively tougher and stronger tasting as they get older.

Both of these crops store well in the ground for many months in mild-winter areas but should be dug before the ground freezes solid in colder climates. Rutabagas also store particularly well in a cool, dark place like a root cellar. In moderately cold areas they can be mulched heavily instead of digging for storage purposes. Pull back the mulch and dig as needed throughout the winter.

Index